THE TEN COMMANDMENTS IN EVOLUTION

Also by Ernst Katz from SteinerBooks

Core Anthroposophy: Teaching Essays of Ernst Katz (2010)

The Ten Commandments in Evolution

A Spiritual-Scientific Study

Ernst Katz

*Edited, rewritten, and translated from the Dutch
by Agnes Schneeberg-de Steur*

SteinerBooks | 2016

STEINERBOOKS
An imprint of Anthroposophic Press, Inc.
610 Main St., Great Barrington, MA 01230
www.steinerbooks.org

Copyright © 2016 by SteinerBooks. All rights reserved. No part of this publication may be reproduced, stored in a retrieval system, or transmitted, in any form or by any means, electronic, mechanical, photocopying, recording, or otherwise, without the prior written permission of the publisher.

Cover image by Marc Chagall:
Moses Receiving the Ten Commandments
(Verve Lithograph, 1956 Bible Series)
Design by Jens Jensen

LIBRARY OF CONGRESS CONTROL NUMBER: 2016940186

ISBN: 978-1-62148-166-9 (paperback)
ISBN: 978-1-62148-167-6 (ebook)

Contents

Foreword by Virginia Sease, PhD vii

Editor's Preface ix

Introduction 1

1. The First Commandment and the Oneness of the Spiritual World . 24

2. The Second Commandment 40

3. Building Blocks of the Third Commandment 60

4. The Fourth Commandment 91

5. Introduction to the Fifth, Sixth, and Seventh Commandments . . 108

6. The Sixth Commandment and the Origin of Death Forces . . 126

7. The Seventh Commandment and the Life Ether 146

8. The Eighth Commandment 166

9. The Ninth Commandment 181

10. The Tenth Commandment 197

11. Concluding Thoughts 217

Notes 237

Bibliography 259

About the Author 263

Foreword

For the many hundreds of people whose lives were enriched by an encounter with Dr. Ernst Katz, this new book, published posthumously through the efforts of Agnes and Herbert Schneeberg, will signify another aspect of Ernst Katz's research. As with many of his smaller publications in brochure form, this book may also acquire a companion status as one turns to it again and again for subject orientation, as well as for the inspiration that such a clear-thinking contemporary offers to us readers.

Ernst Katz was a practical person who focused immediately on the central issue of a question or concern. However, if asked he would gladly share his approach with others. This may seem insignificant, but as his life was dedicated to Anthroposophy first of all but also as a professor, an academician devoted to university life, he exemplified the highest quality of a teacher: What you have discovered, what you have achieved, do not safeguard it merely for yourself for the accolades it will confer upon you, but share it freely with those who demonstrate serious interest in it. His approach to a subject had its source in questions that he could perceive because they lived in the souls of our contemporaries. His small brochure, "Meditation: An Introduction," of merely twenty-two pages became a necessary guide for many people who ever-more frequently after World War II and the three following decades were seeking a wholesome, nonviolent life, which they sensed had something to do with their inner life.

Previously, his smaller publications afforded succinct insights, often in the guise of questions—implicit or explicit—for readers to pose to themselves concerning such themes as "Meditation," "Your Relationship to Rudolf Steiner," and others. They also proved helpful if other people posed questions concerning Anthroposophy, Rudolf Steiner, cultivating the inner life, and other themes to discover the way to find the actual essentials to impart in one's response. His approach was direct: question and answer, such as "What can motivate a person to practice meditation?" "Where to find a teacher?" He then illustrates how Rudolf Steiner offers—through his recommended exercises and meditations contained in his works such as *How to Know Higher Worlds* and *An Outline of Esoteric Science*—a path that any person can follow independently.

For those who have not yet found his book *About Your Relationship to Rudolf Steiner,* which offers important insights into Rudolf Steiner's great task, Ernst Katz's statement is as pertinent today as then (circa 1985): "This booklet is written out of a concern for the spiritual well-being of man in the future, out of a sense of responsibility towards future generations. It is intended as a conversation, reaching out across future times. Contemporaries are welcome to participate."

To conclude this brief foreword, I want to express deep gratitude to Agnes Schneeberg, who edited and translated this work from Dutch into English, because she and her husband Herbert Schneeberg—once they had recovered it from among Ernst Katz's papers after his death—realized that it should become available. Now they have accomplished this significant goal. May it cast new light on a subject that has exerted its influence on civilization for thousands of years!*

Virginia Sease, PhD
Executive Council, emerita
Goetheanum, Switzerland
May 2016

---

*   The booklets mentioned here are all contained in *Core Anthroposophy: Teaching Essays of Ernst Katz* (Great Barrington, MA: SteinerBooks, 2010).

Editor's Preface

This book has been many years in the making. Time and again Ernst Katz returned to the subject of morality in his thoughts and writings. It ran as a red thread through his whole life. Already at age nineteen he wrote in a notebook, "Morality in the old sense no longer has any value in today's world. Inner strength is what is needed—strength to create artistic structure in one's life. But people are always looking for outer guidelines...," and, "It is clear that human nature exists between two polarities: animal and Angel; both are real, and morality is the balance between the two." A year later he put the following question in an essay: "Why is it that the devil, who supposedly is clever, does evil; and that people, who supposedly want to do good, do evil?"

Later still, at age thirty-one, while suffering through the last year of World War II, he wrote an essay on *Justice and Injustice*, trying to establish the relationship between good and evil on the one hand, and justice and injustice on the other. In it he worked out the following: "Whenever, in spite of what our passions may tell us, a new impulse is created through an act of giving, or feelings are purified and transformed through wisdom and love, we enter a domain that transcends the realm of justice and injustice, a domain where the highest values of good and evil reside."

Even in his nineties, Ernst Katz was still putting pen to paper with thoughts about the importance of morality: "There exists a living source of morality of which human beings can learn to avail themselves in order to overcome the widespread uncertainty that prevails in our time regarding questions of good and evil, a living wellspring of morality people should learn to tap into...."

But it was in the most productive middle years of his life that he was working on this book about the moral impulses embodied in the Ten Commandments and the moral evolution of humanity. Ernst Katz wrote most of the original version of this book in the early sixties of the last century. He wrote it in Dutch, his mother tongue. But when he tried to get it published in the Netherlands in the late 1960s, his use of the language was, already then, deemed too old-fashioned. This was the Dutch he had "brought with him" when he immigrated to America in 1947; but in the meantime the language had evolved, both with respect to spelling and everyday usage.

Ernst Katz eventually came to the conclusion, after extensive consultations with the intended publishers, that the manuscript needed to be completely rewritten to bring it up to current conventions; but his busy life precluded any such pursuits for many years. After picking up the typescript again in the late 1980s, he made several rewriting attempts himself; the last one in 1993. (He even prepared English diagrams for an eventual edition in English, updated versions of which are included in this book.) Unfortunately, none of these rewriting attempts encompass more than the first few short chapters; they do, however, provide clues as to how he tried to approach this task.

It was in the mid-1990s that Ernst Katz showed my husband and me the original typescript of this book. He stressed the need for morality in today's world, and told us that he hoped to be able to rewrite and finish the book in such a way that it would respond to this need. But, quite understandably, with only a manual typewriter at his disposal and already advanced in years, Ernst was not able to finish this project himself.

Ernst Katz died in September 2009 after a short illness. He had just turned ninety-six. In the last week of his life he prioritized a number of things that needed to be taken care of; *The Ten Commandments in Evolution* was one of the items on his "wish list." This is where my project began.

The actual job of rewriting went through several stages. I started with the more obvious improvements, such as modernizing the spelling and updating references to books by Rudolf Steiner. Initially I was working exclusively in Dutch; to be more precise, trying to "translate" the original text into the modern Dutch language of today. Before long, however, I found myself working simultaneously on an English translation as well—the final result of which is this book.

The original manuscript included some footnotes, but not nearly enough to provide modern-day readers with adequate background information. And so, to be able to prepare additional footnotes, as well as to thoroughly familiarize myself with the material presented in this study, I had to become (re)acquainted with the Old Testament, or at any rate with the sections that depict the life of Moses, the Israelites' sojourn in the desert, and the receiving of the Ten Commandments at Mount Sinai. I also studied the history of the Hebrew people and of Egypt, as well as a wide range of contemporary scholarly works about the Old Testament, the Ten Commandments, Judaism, and Moses. Most important, I had to return again and again to the basic books of Rudolf Steiner (especially *An Outline of Esoteric Science*), in order to be able to fully appreciate and work with the concepts presented in this study.

I have incorporated the additional information I collected from my research into footnotes and, where necessary, into the main text as well. Some of the footnotes in this book were in the original manuscript, either as footnotes, or as part of the text; I have "reassigned" the latter kind to their new function as footnotes for a variety of reasons—mainly, however, to correct unintended interruptions in the flow of the text.

However, the improvements and adjustments mentioned thus far, were—at least in comparison to what was still to come—relatively minor in nature; for it soon became apparent why Ernst Katz had spoken of "the need to rewrite" the book. Some sections were either unnecessarily drawn out or not wholly relevant to the specific subject under consideration, whereas others had not been worked out in sufficient detail. Consequently, some cutting was called for; but—and this was going to be much more difficult—some augmentation as well! How to know what Ernst's intentions would have been?

Fortunately, by then I had at my disposal his original correspondence with the prospective publishers in the Netherlands, which contained detailed critical suggestions regarding a variety of topics in the manuscript, as well as expressed concern about its length. I also had notes from lectures Ernst Katz had given on the subject over the years (mostly in English and Dutch, some in German), and I had access to letters he had written to friends about his handling of particular themes in the book—some in answer to objections and criticisms.

These indications, in conjunction with Ernst Katz's own rewriting attempts, provided me with defined guidelines for the task ahead. Nevertheless, it has been a long and challenging process, taking me from initially not daring to make even relatively minor changes in the text, to gradually becoming bolder in my approach, for the sake of the overall clarity and quality Ernst Katz would have expected and valued.

The end result, I believe, is a book that presents his fascinating discovery about the connection between the Ten Commandments and humanity's developmental stages clearly and precisely. I have attempted, wherever possible, to convey his original wording and intent, while at the same time acknowledging the changed expectations of twenty-first-century readers. My job has, at times, gone beyond that of an editor and translator; in some respects it has become that of a coauthor as well. But I have consistently attempted to present the material as, I believe, Ernst Katz would have done it himself, given the chance.

Nevertheless, this book should be considered a work in progress. Some sections have not been worked out satisfactorily and would require more detailed research. But as it stands, it provides the reader, at the very least, with an opportunity to become thoroughly acquainted with the Ten Commandments—something most of us, in all honesty, would likely not aspire to on our own! And what is more, the commandments are introduced and explained in the context of—and linked to—the developmental stages of the Earth and human beings, including potential future transformations in the light of Anthroposophy; a unique perspective indeed!

Ernst Katz was, before anything else, a teacher of Anthroposophy to many people. This didactic approach also is evident in the articles, essays, and booklets he wrote over the years (several of which have, after his death, been collected and republished in the aptly named, *Core Anthroposophy: Teaching Essays of Ernst Katz*).[1] This study about the Ten Commandments is, in reality, also a teaching essay, only in a more expanded format. Ernst Katz hoped—this is how he expressed it in his original foreword to this book—to present his thoughts about the Ten Commandments in such a way that it would be helpful not only for people who are just discovering Anthroposophy, but also for those who are already well versed, but would love to renew and deepen their understanding of some of its fundamental concepts, especially in the light of the new context presented here. Consequently, this study provides both an introductory and an in-depth overview of, say, the Earth's planetary stages that may, at first glance, seem a bit repetitive. But the reader will soon recognize that this material is invariably presented within the context of one particular commandment, and therefore from an ever-changing point of view.

With this book Ernst Katz wanted to ignite people's interest in the ever-important questions about morality, both from a historical perspective and within the context of our modern-day lives. This is why he first introduces the archetypal esoteric impulses of each of the Ten Commandments and then explores potential metamorphoses of these impulses, both in the time of Christ and particularly also in our own time. It was his hope that, with the help of the anthroposophic insights worked out in this study, people would be able to discover such transformations themselves and feel inspired to apply these in their daily lives and in their interactions with fellow human beings.

Perhaps this is what Moses, long ago, envisioned as well, when he said, "Set your hearts unto all the words which I testify among you this day..., all the words of this law. For it is not a vain thing for you; *because it is your life*" (Deut. 32:46–47, italics added). If we can indeed discover our own individual way of working with these transformed impulses of the Ten Commandments, we can in truth—and in freedom—become our own inner lawgiver. Then this inner law can really become our *life*!

"Uncertainty about the nature of morality is a widespread characteristic of our modern times," Ernst Katz wrote toward the end of his life, "because people are unable to penetrate the spiritual source from which morality flows as a living force." It was his profound wish that the ideas presented in this book would lead people to this *living source of morality*.

Ernst Katz wanted to light a moral flame in people, to kindle their enthusiasm to work for the good in the world. In this context one cannot but be reminded of the verse Rudolf Steiner wrote about his own mission, shortly before his death, a verse that Ernst frequently referred to in his writings and lectures:

> I want with cosmic spirit
> To enthuse each human being
> That a flame they may become
> And fiery will unfold
> The essence of their being.
>
> The other ones, they strive
> To take from cosmic waters
> What will extinguish flames
> And pour paralysis
> Into all inner being.
>
> O joy, when human being's flame
> Is blazing, even when at rest.
> O bitter pain, when the human thing
> Is put in bonds, when it wants to stir.
>
> *(translation, Ernst Katz)*

Editor's Preface

Editor's Note about Bible References Used

Wherever passages from the Bible appear in the text I have made use of the so-called Updated King James Version, which is not a new translation, but an update of the 1611 King James Version. The KJV is widely considered to be both beautiful in its use of the English language and scholarly in its accuracy of translation—an essential feature in the context of this book's close scrutiny of the exact wording of the Ten Commandments. The Updated King James Version replaces some archaic vocabulary that could easily be misunderstood by modern readers (for example, *assered* becomes *subsided* in Genesis 8:1), and it changes words such as *thou* to *you*, *shalt* to *shall*, *hath* to *has*, while otherwise staying true to the KJV. The UKJV is available online and in the Public Domain.

Agnes Schneeberg-de Steur
London, Ontario, Canada
February 2016

Introduction

The Ten Commandments! This topic invariably elicits a wide range of opinions and reactions—and questions. Is this a subject worth studying? Are these commandments still relevant today? Can something that was once of pivotal importance to one group of people—the ancient Israelites—have any general value in today's world?

The Place of the Ten Commandments in History

These are reasonable questions for contemporary readers to ask. But maybe we should be asking a *different* kind of question: Why have the Ten Commandments had such a lasting impact, right up to our own time? After all, if we study the history of ethics, is it not a profound enigma how these commandments came into being, lasted through many centuries, and have become the primary source for the moral and judicial standards of a large segment of humanity? There are very few impulses to be found in all of history that have had (and still have) such a fundamental influence!

Other nations in the ancient Near East had developed their own laws and guiding principles, such as the Code of Hammurabi, dating back to about 1780 BC, or the Code of Ur-Nammu, from about 2050 BC. But these law codes are only of interest to historians nowadays, and have otherwise faded from memory. Why is it that only the Ten Commandments of the Mosaic Law have endured for more than three thousand years? What is it that makes them so unique?

For one thing, these Ten Commandments were not primarily intended as judicial regulations, but rather as moral principles. We may surmise this, to begin with, from the use of the *second person singular* of the verb in the original Hebrew. In other words, these commandments offer not just dry legal instructions. Instead, every person is addressed individually—also those who were not physically standing at the foot of Mount Sinai, including those who were not yet born when these words resounded. Second, although these instructions were given in an imperative tense, implying a mode of command, there is a hint of a future orientation intrinsic to this particular tense. It does not say, "Do not…," or "Do…," but rather, "You shall not…," or "You shall…," which expresses a moral striving toward something yet to come. Third, the form and style of the formulation of the Ten Commandments differ from those of most other laws in the Old Testament; *for there are no penalties listed for violations.* The Ten Commandments are consistently formulated in the so-called *apodictic* style (simply distinguishing right from wrong), not in the *casuistic* style (prescribing consequences for certain infractions), much more widely used elsewhere in the Bible itself as well as in comparable Near Eastern law codes.[2] In other words, the Ten Commandments essentially state that certain things are wrong, regardless of whether one will be punished or not—again, an indication that these commandments were not in the first place intended as legal rules, but rather as value judgments, as moral guidelines.

Even a cursory reading of the passages in question reveals that the Ten Commandments occupy a very special place within the Bible itself. We note, for instance, that the listing of the Ten Commandments constitutes the *only* case of a longer, (almost) identical passage to be presented *twice* in the Pentateuch (the first five books of the Old Testament).[3] Furthermore, we learn from the Bible book Exodus (31:18) that the two tablets with the commandments were *written with the finger of God*; and from Deuteronomy (10:2 and 31:26) that only these tablets were to be put *in* the Ark of the Covenant,[4] whereas all other laws were to be placed *next* to it. We also read in Exodus (20:1–19) that the Ten Commandments were *spoken by God*, whereas all other laws and regulations were announced by Moses, acting in his designated capacity as interlocutor between God and the Israelite people.

All these indications unquestionably attest to the uniqueness of the Ten Commandments and of that particular time in history. But the true measure of these events can only be understood with the help of Rudolf Steiner's anthroposophic Spiritual Science. In countless lectures and books Rudolf Steiner has brought out in the open, in contemporary, modern concepts, what in earlier times could only be taught in secret in the ancient mystery schools. Spiritual science—one could suitably call it the *new mystery wisdom*—can help elucidate the previously mentioned fields of research, as well as become for us a key with which we can unlock many such links ourselves.

The ideas to be presented in this book are based on and inspired by Anthroposophy.

Moses and the Proclamation at Mount Sinai

It is nearly impossible to overestimate the importance of Moses in the unfolding of the events at Mount Sinai. The more we occupy ourselves with this topic, the more we must come to admire the almost superhuman courage and wisdom of this exceptional human being. The Bible refers to Moses thus: "And there arose not a prophet since in Israel like unto Moses, whom the LORD knew face to face" (Deuteronomy 34:10); and he is acknowledged to be the authorized mediator between God and the Hebrew people (for example in Exodus 20:19). Within the Jewish tradition Moses is "the greatest prophet who ever lived." The framework of our present study does not allow for an elaborate excursion into the life of Moses, but the enduring impact of the Ten Commandments, by and of itself, attests to his cardinal importance.[5] Rudolf Steiner's spiritual research affirms and substantiates that Moses was an advanced initiate who had developed a high degree of insight and wisdom.[6]

Moses stood at a crucial juncture on the path of human history, a crossroads where the last remnants of old clairvoyance were beginning to give way to the emerging faculty of thinking and of the developing "I"-forces in human beings. Moses himself embodied both the old and the new. On the one hand he had the ability to receive the divine revelation out of the mighty forces of nature by means of the old clairvoyance still active in him. But at the same time he was able to translate this divine inspiration into human language with the help of the "I"-forces beginning to stir in him. It is interesting that we can detect an echo of this twofold element in the Mosaic Law itself: in the apparent contradiction, namely, between its contents and the way it was revealed and received. For, whereas these laws were intended for the *inner* human being through religious, moral, and social instructions, the revelation itself could only take place—and be perceived—in the midst of *external* forces of nature, in the midst of "thunders and lightnings, and a thick cloud upon the mount" (Exodus 19:16).

We read in Exodus (20:18–21), "And all the people saw the thunderings, and the lightnings, and the noise of the trumpet, and the mountain smoking...and the people stood far off, and Moses drew near unto the thick darkness where God was." And in this "thick darkness" Moses, the advanced initiate, encountered the divine world. But he needed great courage of spirit to be able to ascend the mountain under these conditions. It was as though everything aspired to invoke fear in his soul: the shaking of the earth, the fire and the singeing heat, the asphyxiating air and the dark clouds, as well as the rumbling thunder announcing the upcoming revelation (also portrayed in the Bible as "the noise of the trumpet"). Only his extraordinary courage and skill gave Moses the strength to withstand this fury of nature. And it is precisely because of the courage he had to summon, that a higher world opened up for him. Through the awe-inspiring elemental forces Moses heard the *word of God* out of the fire and the darkness.

The Bible presents us here with a depiction of outer circumstances that can simultaneously be seen as an image of inner events. Moses ascended not only onto the mountain, but—with a higher state of consciousness—also into the spiritual world. No one else could accompany him on either path. The people, standing at the foot of the mountain, merely had an inkling of the magnitude of this mighty suprasensory event, "And they said unto Moses, speak you with us, and we will hear: but let not God speak with us, lest we die" (Ex 20:19). They sensed that, under normal conditions, no human being could withstand the overwhelming impact of a cosmic inspiration of this magnitude, and live. Only an advanced initiate who had conquered all fear and was able to understand the language of nature could hope to return alive from such a frightful undertaking.

We can try to deepen our understanding of these outer and inner events by repeatedly allowing these images to work on our soul. And if we then, in particular, contemplate the superhuman courage and steadfastness Moses had to summon in order to be able to receive the divine revelation on Mount Sinai, we may well have an important experience. We may well feel as though we were led to a far distant past, to the earliest stage of the Earth—namely, a stage that consisted wholly of warmth; for—so we hear from Rudolf Steiner—this earliest evolutionary phase can likewise only be approached *"with the greatest possible courage and inner firmness,"* and by letting go of all sense impressions, save that of warmth, of fire.[7]

There must be a connection, then, between the archetypal impulse of the Ten Commandments and the profound mysteries of time and evolution, a connection brought to light through the *moral effort of human courage*! Should this conclusion be correct, then the structure of the Ten Commandments must indeed contain an imprint of the whole evolution, from the oldest phases of the Earth, right up to the time of Moses, and possibly beyond. In this study we will investigate the Ten Commandments from this perspective, by learning to read this "imprint" of evolution, contained in them. With this thought image as our starting point we will be able to learn more about the origin of the Ten Commandments, and solve some of the riddles that are embedded in them, long lost to humankind's collective awareness!

Earth Evolution and the Tenfold Human Being

If, as proposed in the previous section, the Ten Commandments do indeed contain an imprint of the whole evolution of humanity and Earth, we must begin our studies about these commandments by considering how evolution has unfolded over the course of time.

Since ancient times all knowledge concerning the evolution of the Earth and of human beings had been guarded by the old mysteries and was only communicated to carefully selected pupils. In our own time Rudolf Steiner has researched this mystery knowledge anew, translated it into modern concepts, and thus made it accessible for everyone. Since these concepts also form the basis of our further line of thought in this study, we must now first provide a brief outline of the four stages our Earth has gone through in the course of evolution. And in doing so, we will have to focus particularly on how the human being, in the course of these developments, gradually became a *tenfold being*. This, to be sure, is not the most common approach among anthroposophic authors, who usually refer to a threefold, a fourfold, and occasionally to a seven- or ninefold human being. But it will become evident, we trust, that the proposed tenfold configuration represents merely an expanded and differentiated view of the more familiar fourfold human being, consisting of physical, etheric, and astral bodies and the "I."

The evolution of the Earth has gone through four great planetary stages: Saturn, Sun, Moon, and the actual Earth phase in which we now live. Rudolf Steiner also frequently referred to these as old Saturn, old Sun, old Moon, and Earth. We must remember, though, that these designations do not have an immediately obvious connection to the planets we know by these names today.[8]

It is incredibly difficult for the spiritual researcher to perceive anything at all about the inner nature of Saturn, the oldest incarnation of the Earth. This, as we pointed out earlier, also requires a great deal of inner courage; courage that then becomes like a sense organ with which one may be able to perceive something of the conditions on

Saturn.[9] It is essentially a world of warmth. For the spiritual researcher this warmth points to the presence of spiritual beings, mighty creating beings who belong to the highest hierarchy of the Angels, namely the *Thrones* and the *Cherubim*.[10] By continually offering something of their own substance to the evolution on Saturn, *warmth* and eventually *time* had emerged, as well as, in its most rudimentary form, the beginning of the whole "physical" world. But this physical world, including the germinal human physical body, existed as yet only as warmth; for there was no other form of "matter," only warmth, on Saturn. Warmth united the whole Saturn phase into one unitary cosmic essence. The human being on Saturn was a unitary entity as well, consisting only of warmth, of "fire."[11]

When this development had reached a certain degree of perfection everything returned to a purely spiritual state of apparent rest. However, evolution continued. Out of this period of rest a second phase arose in human and cosmic evolution—the Sun phase of the Earth, or *old Sun*. The physical world on old Sun revealed a polarity: part of the warmth became *light*. During this process *space* appeared for the first time, and a beginning densification occurred in the form of gases (there were as yet no fluids or solids in this stage of development). And, again, the researcher of the spiritual world can perceive that these events occurring on old Sun were, in fact, manifestations of lofty spiritual beings, in particular the *Spirits of Wisdom* (also called *Kyriotetes*). The human physical body also solidified somewhat more, revealing a first form of differentiation. It now was a structure consisting of warmth (the "fire" element) and gases ("air").[12] Because of this development, human beings on old Sun could now receive an etheric body from the *Spirits of Wisdom* and with it the very first beginning of individual life.[13]

Since these etheric forces on old Sun arose out of the light, they are commonly called *light ether* forces. And so, during the Sun phase, the human being gradually became a threefold being with two physical components, namely the elements *"air"* and *"warmth,"* and one etheric component of *light ether* forces: $2 + 1 = 3$.

When this development had reached a certain degree of perfection everything once again returned to a purely spiritual state of apparent rest.

Out of this period of rest a third phase arose in human and cosmic evolution—the *old Moon*. The process of densification and differentiation continued; and, once again, the spiritual researcher can recognize that lofty spiritual beings were guiding these developments, in particular the *Spirits of Movement* (also called *Dynamis*). The physical world and the human physical body now consisted of *fluids* (the "water" element), *gases* ("air"), and *warmth* ("fire"), and the etheric world of two kinds of etheric forces. The first kind contributes to all life processes and to life in general—these are the aforementioned *light ether* forces. The second kind has a differentiating influence on the life processes. For reasons we will clarify later on, this type of ether is referred to as *sound ether*. And so, the human etheric body on old Moon was made up of light ether and sound ether.

In addition, human beings now received from the *Spirits of Movement* a component of a very different kind, namely the *astral body*.[14] This led to the beginning of an individual soul life, accompanied by—as yet very primitive—inner feelings and, because of the influence of this new astral body, to an already somewhat more specialized level of consciousness. And so, during the Moon phase of the Earth the human being gradually became a sixfold being, consisting of three physical elements, namely *"water," "air,"* and *"fire"*; two etheric forces, namely *light ether* and *sound ether*; and the one new *astral* component: $3 + 2 + 1 = 6$.

All these developments did not, of course, transpire in the simple, uncomplicated way this brief overview may well imply. But for the sake of clarity we will leave specific details—especially those that have a bearing on our investigations into the Ten Commandments—to the appropriate chapters later on.

These developments occurring on old Moon eventually also reached a certain degree of perfection, followed by a period of decline, after which everything, once again, returned to a purely spiritual state of apparent rest.

Finally, after this period of cosmic rest, a fourth planetary phase began—the actual Earth phase. During this development solid matter emerged for the first time and henceforth the whole physical world (including the physical human body) has consisted of four substances: *solid matter* (the "earth" element), *fluids* ("water"), *gases* ("air"), and *warmth* ("fire"). And, once again, the spiritual researcher can observe that exalted spiritual beings were guiding these developments, particularly the *Spirits of Form* (also called *Exusiai*), who in the Old Testament are called *Elohim*.[15]

In addition to these changes in the physical realm, a new kind of ether emerged in the world of the etheric and in all forms of life. This, the most refined, type of ether is able to work on the hardest (and seemingly least alive) substances on Earth—namely the solid materials, to infuse them with life. We can perceive these forces at work, for instance, in the forming of shells and skeletons. These newest etheric forces are referred to as *life ether* forces. These forces made it possible for living beings to have autonomous bodies, thus allowing for a more stable, independent way of life. And so, the human etheric body now comprised three kinds of etheric forces: *light* ether, *sound* ether, and *life* ether.[16]

The human astral body also underwent a further differentiation. What came to pass was a distinction—albeit not sharply defined— between two soul configurations: one more directed toward earthly sentiments and one more aimed at the spiritual. (To appreciate the difference one could think, for example, of a craving for earthly nourishment and a longing for spiritual sustenance.) We may refer to these as lower and higher passions associated with *lower* and *higher* (or coarse and refined) *astral* forces.

And, finally, human beings received, from the *Spirits of Form*, the "I" as a new qualitative principle, during the Earth phase of evolution. With this gift human beings acquired the true inner core of their being, albeit initially only in germinal form. This germinal "I" would, as

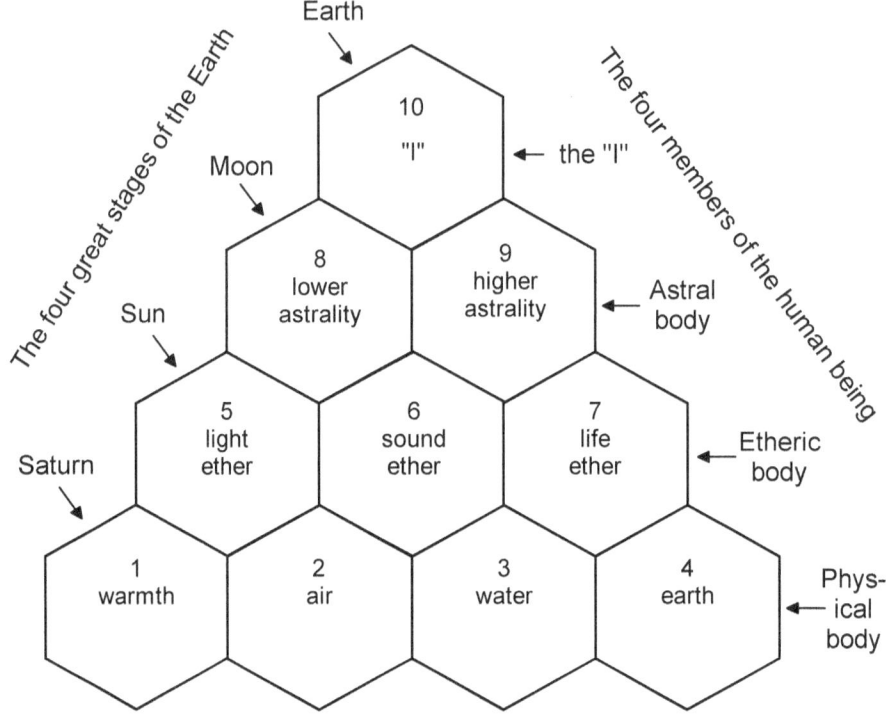

THE TEN PARTS OF THE HUMAN BEING

time progressed, gradually develop into the independent, autonomous human "I."[17]

Our physical body on Earth, then, consists of four elemental components because it has been in existence since Saturn; our etheric body of three kinds of etheric forces because it has experienced three stages of development; and our astral body of coarser and finer astral forces because it has gone through two developmental phases. The "I" is the youngest and most recent gift of the spiritual world and is presently only in its first stage of development. Consequently, the human being now is a *tenfold being* consisting of *four* physical elements, *three* kinds of etheric forces, *two* astral dimensions, and *one* "I": 4 + 3 + 2 + 1 = 10.

As we mentioned at the beginning of this chapter, the old mystery schools had always known about these connections. One can still find an echo of this wisdom in the teachings of the Pythagoreans, who were active around 500 BC. In the famous philosophical school of Pythagoras the number 10 was considered a sacred number, a number furthermore, that was always understood to be the sum of 1, 2, 3, and 4. This is why the Pythagoreans referred to the number 10 as *the Sacred Four* or *Tetractus*.[18]

Preparation and Fulfillment

There is one event that stands out as *the* central event in the history of the world. This is the coming of the Messiah to the Earth; and one nation, in particular, was selected by divine plan to prepare for this event. The whole history of the Israelite people (Abraham, Joseph, Moses, the Exodus out of Egypt, King David, the Babylonian exile, etc.) was guided in such a way that, after many generations, a suitable human body would be ready for the expected incarnation of the Messiah—the Christ: this is the conclusion one can come to through the study of Anthroposophy.[19] We also know that Christ himself had accompanied and guided these developments from the spiritual world since the beginning of time, long before he appeared in a human body on Earth,[20] and that he inspired Moses, who played such a critical role in the unfolding of these events.

Moses was the forerunner and the harbinger of Christ.[21] Rudolf Steiner described this special connection between the work of Moses and the Christ-being thus: "We saw how...the godhead revealed itself from two poles: from the macrocosmic fire of lightning and from the microcosmic fire of the blood. We saw that it was the Christ who proclaimed himself to Moses in the burning bush and in thunder and lightning on Sinai; that it was the Christ and no other power than he, who declared to Moses: I am the I AM. Out of the lightning on Sinai he gave the Ten Commandments as a preparation for his coming. Later he reappeared in microcosmic form in Palestine."[22] But, in the time of Moses, the Hebrew people could not experience the Christ-being directly; they experienced this relationship *indirectly* through their God, Yahweh: "For the Christ-being was indeed living in Yahweh..., but as a reflection of Himself. As the Moon reflects the sunlight, so did Yahweh reflect the Being of Christ. Christ caused his Being to be reflected from Yahweh."[23] And it was Moses who, guided by this Being, acted as the mediator between Yahweh and the Hebrew people.

Seen in this light, the whole history of the Hebrew people reflects the gradual descent of the Christ-being, preparing his incarnation through many generations. Whenever, in the course of this history, the Christ-being actively intervened in the evolution of humanity, we hear God speak, "I AM." These are the words that Moses heard from out of the burning bush, which in the end subdued Pharaoh's obstinacy and inaugurated the revelation of the Ten Commandments at Mount Sinai.[24] We can scarcely imagine today how startling these words must have been for the people living at that time! Before the time of Moses the Israelite people experienced their God not individually, but in the forces of the blood streaming through the generations. This is why God was referred to as "the God of Abraham, Isaac, and Jacob." But the communication of these "I AM" words constituted the beginning of something completely new. The Israelites now had to learn to recognize God as an "I"-being; and they had to do so through their own awakening "I"-forces. After all, these "I AM" words—true signposts on the path of history as it is described in the Old Testament—announced not only the *essence of the godhead*, but also the *awakening "I" in human beings*. This is also the living reality of the proclamation that resounded from the spiritual world at Mount Sinai.

There, accompanied by the tremendous unleashing of the forces of nature, God proclaimed, "I am the LORD your God, which have brought you out of the land of Egypt, out of the house of bondage" (Ex 20:2). The word "bondage" points to a stage of development during which the immature human "I" was still dependent on a higher will—a stage that now had to be left behind. The words "I AM" point to the Christ-being as the true inspiration behind the revelation of the Ten Commandments. This divine proclamation, then, defined the ripening process of the human "I" toward ever-increasing independence, under the guidance of Christ himself.

Starting with the mighty "I AM" words, the Ten Commandments resounded from the spiritual world. But these commandments did not only communicate certain instructions. These words also revealed—if we but learn to uncover the "open secrets" embedded in them—how our astral, etheric, and physical bodies (collectively known as the human sheaths) were formed during cosmic evolution; how these sheaths have been transformed by the Christ-being over the course of eons to eventually make it possible to take up the "I"; and how these sheaths must continue to develop in accordance with their original creative impulses. But, as long as the "I" was not yet strong enough to work on the sheaths in this way, the Ten Commandments were needed, exactly as they were introduced in the time of Moses, to support *every member of the tenfold human being,* by establishing norms for health, justice, and morality.

Many centuries later, when the "I" was "born"—this is how Rudolf Steiner expressed it—with the coming of Christ to the Earth, did this situation change, because the whole human makeup was, by then, a different one as well. Under those new conditions an outer commandment can actually become an inner force because an independent "I" can work out of its own strength on the astral, etheric, and physical bodies. Then it is no longer necessary to prescribe morality in this tenfold way; then the human being no longer needs separate commandments to help keep these sheaths healthy. One single commandment addressing the "I" suffices; this one commandment can then radiate from the "I" into the other human sheaths. This is the new commandment Christ gave when his incarnation on Earth had become a fact and the Mystery of Golgotha was about to be fulfilled: "A new commandment I give unto you, that all of you love one another; as I have loved you, that all of you also love one another" (John 13:34). But this single "commandment" is no longer a commandment in the usual sense of "You shall not...." Although it, naturally, contains the essence of all Ten Commandments, it is not really a commandment any more, but a constructive encouragement to take hold of this new force, and learn to perceive the "I" of the other human being in love. From then on this new awareness can inspire people to develop their own moral judgment, their own inner norm, enabling them to structure their life accordingly.

If we can indeed understand the work of Moses as *preparation* and that of Christ as *fulfillment*, we are looking at a fascinating process. How did this process begin and how will it continue? What form will this fulfillment take throughout the course of history? These questions will determine the course of our explorations in the pages that follow.

The Development of Morality

To be able to gauge the true impact of the Ten Commandments on the moral development of humanity, it is important to know how morality itself has changed over time. Morality is directly linked to "I"-consciousness. Hence, in olden times, morality—or, to be more precise, individual morality—did not really exist yet in the lives of human beings. The human "I" existed only in a dormant state; morality, likewise, was merely a dormant faculty because the "I" could not yet be called upon to acknowledge a sense of individual responsibility. People had a level of consciousness vastly different from ours. Everything that happened in daily life, but also in one's inner life, was determined by the fact that one belonged to a family, tribe, or nation. That sense of belonging transcended any perception of oneself as an individual person. Furthermore—and this is important for the study of the moral development of humanity—every aspect of human life was regulated, ordered, and arranged by the old mysteries.

What are these "old mysteries" of which Rudolf Steiner spoke so frequently? These were mystery schools, initiation centers, where all the wisdom of the past was kept, safeguarded, and taught.[25] But what happened inside the walls of these mystery centers was veiled in secrecy. Rudolf Steiner's spiritual research has helped lift this veil for us. We now know that the pupils of these old mystery schools acquired their knowledge in a manner that was very different from our present-day methods of accumulating knowledge; this wisdom had to be "experienced." We know that only certain pupils were admitted into the mystery schools; that they were specifically chosen and had to go through a very strict schooling that would ultimately "transform their whole being"; and that during their actual initiation they had to be carefully guided (by those who had already been initiated themselves) through an experience that would bring them close to death, an experience of almost dying and then being born anew.[26] The initiation and inner transformation awakened new capacities, enabling the neophyte to receive revelations directly from the spiritual world.

Through their mystery initiation the neophytes developed the required capacities to be able to help support and guide the (inner and outer) development of humanity in the right way; *for this was the task of the old mysteries.* The initiates, who had trained in the mystery schools for that very task, brought all cultural and social impulses that arose in human society from the spiritual world to the Earth. These impulses introduced important life skills such as agriculture and husbandry, spinning and weaving, the construction of dwellings, the making of pottery, the baking of bread, social and ritual customs; but also reading and writing, and knowledge about the stars, laws, mathematics, in short, all the skills and knowledge people needed to give structure to their lives, both as an individual person and as a member of society.

People in those olden times received indispensable guidance through the ordinances of the mysteries, especially also with respect to their moral conduct. Only when the "I" began to develop its own strength—and this stage of human development coincided precisely with the Exodus of the Israelites out of Egypt—could a rudimentary awareness of individual responsibility arise in human beings. The Exodus brought a new independence, not only in an external (political) sense for the Israelite nation as a whole, but also with respect to the inner soul stirring of each individual. (Other nations, naturally, went through similar developments, but the history of the Israelite people can, from a certain point of view, be seen as archetypal and, therefore, as representative of this process.) With the awakening of the "I" it became *possible*, for the first time in history, to feel a sense of personal responsibility and to cultivate a moral lifestyle.

But in this time of transition the immature "I" could be easily swayed. And so, a strong appeal had to be made to the emerging moral cognizance in human beings, an appeal, moreover, that would simultaneously provide support to the not-yet-fully-awakened "I." In response to this need the Ten Commandments were introduced into the evolution of humanity, out of the wisdom of the mysteries and through the mediation of Moses, to help guide the moral conduct of human beings. This *had* to be done in the form of commandments because at this particular stage in history—that is to say, when the "I" was not yet fully capable of determining its own moral conduct—the norms that governed health, justice, and morality *could* only be determined by external powers. But these commandments needed to be formulated and arranged very precisely in order to correspond to the exact inner configuration of the human beings living at that time; for only in that form would these commandments be able to propel the awakening "I"-forces into activity. In the course of this study we will show that the Ten Commandments of Moses did indeed fulfill this requirement and thus constituted a first milestone on the path of moral development of human beings, a first step on the path toward individual responsibility.

The next milestone on this path was reached with Christ's coming to the Earth. As we have intimated, the moral development of human beings is tied to the gradual awakening of the "I." We mentioned earlier that Christ had guided and prepared this development since the beginning of time, long before he incarnated on Earth.[27] But it was his living and dying on Earth that constituted a decisive new phase in the development of the human "I," a phase to which, accordingly, the original objective of the commandments needed to be adapted as well. This is why Christ said—building on the work of Moses—that he had not come to "destroy the laws or the prophets" but to *fulfill* them, or one could say, to fill them with their full potential.[28] At the center of this whole development stands the all-encompassing new commandment of Christ to love one another "as I have loved you" (John 13:34). And so, something new had been placed in the world that, on the one hand, truly was the fulfillment, the culmination of what had been prepared by the Ten Commandments, but, on the other hand, goes well beyond it. It is a powerful new moral impulse that will radiate far into the future!

As mentioned, the old mysteries had played an important role in the moral—and of course the overall—development of humanity up to that time; but these mystery centers gradually began to lose their living connection with the spiritual realities. This situation coincided with human beings becoming less dependent on outer directions. With Christ's coming to the Earth, the guidance of the mysteries was no longer needed to that same extent. As a natural consequence, the culture of the old mysteries came to an end around the beginning of our era.[29]

What happens next with respect to the moral development of humanity? Do the Ten Commandments still play a role in this development today? We cannot deny, of course, that the Ten Commandments of the Mosaic Law have been the pillars of the ethical structure of (a large segment of) human society for more than three thousand years. And they still form, to a certain extent, the basis of moral, judicial, and ethical standards. But in our time moral confusion is rampant. Ours is a time in which old norms, like those represented by the Ten Commandments, no longer meet expectations. And we decidedly do not intend to recommend the Ten Commandments as *the* moral measuring stick for our time; neither to simply dismiss them. The aim of this study is to develop a better *understanding* of the spiritual origin of the Commandments; the reasons for their existence; their meaning and significance; and the various metamorphoses they have undergone since their inception. Such considerations can then, we hope, open a door to the true source of human morality in general. This is of the utmost importance in our time; for all moral values—and this includes the "moral freedom" people frequently crave today—can only be sustained if such values are based on *insight* in the living process through which morality develops in human beings, both in the past and in our own time.

The Structure and Numbering of the Ten Commandments

We have seen that the development of humanity had reached a very special milestone in the time of Moses. The human "I" began to awaken, facilitating the initial stage of a beginning moral awareness. But the "I" was not yet strong enough to develop moral ideals, able to awaken the good in human beings. In the time of Moses this could only be achieved through outer commandments. But such commandments needed to be aimed at the whole human being, in other words, at all the members (the sheaths) of the human being. To express this more precisely, the meticulous wording of each commandment had to conform to the original creative impulse out of which a particular component had been bestowed onto man by the spiritual world. By encouraging people to follow the exact codes of conduct decreed by these commandments, all parts of the human being would then be brought in harmony with these original creative impulses, so as to awaken the good in the whole human being. And since man, as we have put forward earlier, is a *tenfold being*, it took exactly *ten* commandments to achieve this aim.

These Ten Commandments reflect the tenfold evolution of humanity and of the Earth. In the following chapters we will explore in detail how each commandment corresponds to a particular phase of this evolution. To be able to do this, we must now first take a closer look at the structure and the exact wording of the commandments.

As soon as we attempt to do this, however, we run into an unforeseen complication, because the relevant Bible texts do not specify where one commandment ends and the next one begins! In *Exodus*

(20:1–17) the commandments appear as they were given to Moses on Mount Sinai. In *Deuteronomy* (5:6–21) Moses recites the Ten Commandments once again, at the end of his life, as part of his farewell discourses to the Israelite people. These two versions are almost identical, save for some minor differences (for instance in the description of the Sabbath observances). But only in Exodus 34:28, where Moses is about to receive a second set of tablets with the commandments (to replace the ones he had smashed earlier), as well as in Deuteronomy 4:13 and 10:4, where these events are reiterated once more by Moses, do we find a reference to the number *ten*.[30] But these passages do not refer to "ten commandments" but rather to *"ten words"* (in Hebrew, *aseret hadevarim*). This is why the Ten Commandments are often referred to as the *Decalogue*, from "ten words" in Greek (deka logoi). In any case, we know from these circumstantial passages in the Bible that we are dealing with *ten* pronouncements—be they called words, or commandments.

The listing and numbering of these Ten Commandments, however, has fluctuated over the centuries. In Jewish and some Protestant traditions the rejection of other gods constitutes the first commandment; the decree against images is the second commandment. Roman Catholic and Lutheran denominations combine these two commandments (and occasionally leave out the restriction on images altogether). But in that case, if the number *ten* was to be retained, an adjustment had to be made elsewhere. Consequently, within these denominations, the last commandment (about coveting other people's possessions) was split into two categories of ownership, resulting in a ninth and a tenth commandment, both dealing with coveting. This, naturally, had consequences for the numbering of the remaining commandments, which now each must shift down by one number, compared to the traditional way of counting them. However, since there is really no logical reason to divide those objects that must not be coveted into two commandments, most theological scholars prefer to use the traditional numbering. We have opted for this approach as well, because we believe that this way of counting corresponds precisely with the inherent structural order on which the Ten Commandments are based.[31]

To provide the reader with a basic overview of the Ten Commandments, we will lead off with the text as it appears in Exodus 20:1–17, along with the traditional numbering just mentioned:

The Ten Commandments

Exodus 20:1–17:

And God spoke all these words, saying,

1. I am the LORD your God, which have brought you out of the land of Egypt, out of the house of bondage. You shall have no other gods before me.

2. You shall not make unto you any graven image, or any likeness of any thing that is in heaven above, or that is in the earth beneath, or that is in the water under the earth. You shall not bow down yourself to them, nor serve them: for I the LORD your God am a jealous God, visiting the iniquity of the fathers upon the children unto the third and fourth generation of them that hate me; And showing mercy unto thousands of them that love me, and keep my commandments.

3. You shall not take the name of the LORD your God in vain; for the LORD will not hold him guiltless that takes his name in vain.

4. Remember the Sabbath day, to keep it holy. Six days shall you labor, and do all your work: But the seventh day is the Sabbath of the LORD your God: in it you shall not do any work, you, nor your son, nor your daughter, your manservant, nor your maidservant, nor your cattle, nor your stranger that is within your gates: For in six days the LORD made Heaven and Earth, the sea, and all that in them is, and rested the seventh day: wherefore the LORD blessed the Sabbath day, and hallowed it.

5. Honor your father and your mother: that your days may be long upon the land that the LORD your God gives you.

6. You shall not kill.

7. You shall not commit adultery.

8. You shall not steal.

9. You shall not bear false witness against your neighbor.

10. You shall not covet your neighbor's house, you shall not covet your neighbor's wife, nor his manservant, nor his maidservant, nor his ox, nor his ass, nor any thing that is your neighbor's.

There is a structural order in the composition of the Ten Commandments that corresponds to the anthroposophic concept of evolution we have described—that is, the configuration of the Ten Commandments reveals an unmistakable structural division into 4 + 3 + 2 + 1.

The first *four* commandments deal with the relationship between human beings and the divine. The divine manifests in the physical world around us. This world has a fourfold structure, just as the human physical body does. Put differently, the human body is a microcosmic reflection of the macrocosm, or, as it is depicted in the Bible, it is "created in the image of God." The four elements, referred to since antiquity as fire, air, water, and earth (in modern terms, warmth, gases, fluids, and solids) form the structural basis both of the physical world around us and of our physical bodies, because both have gone through four developmental phases, having been in existence since ancient Saturn. This is why there are exactly *four* commandments dealing with the relationship of the physical human being to the divine. There *must* be four of those, because they are directed at the respective components of the physical human body.

The next *three* commandments (5, 6, and 7) regulate the laws of life, death, and the realm of intimate human relationships. There *must* be three of those, because they are directed at the three kinds of etheric forces active in the human etheric body, namely the light, sound, and life ether.

The following *two* commandments (8 and 9) are related to the astral body and are directed at the lower and the higher astral qualities in the human being respectively.

The tenth commandment, the last *one*, stands alone and occupies a unique place amid the commandments. It speaks directly to the "I" of the human being.

With this structural order for our starting point we will, in subsequent chapters, explore the specific relationship that exists between each commandment and the corresponding member of the human being. By developing thoughts and ideas—based on and inspired by anthroposophic Spiritual Science—we will first try to penetrate the esoteric background of the Ten Commandments and their specific relation to the human being. We will consider how each of the Ten Commandments reflects, in its most compact form, the essence of a specific phase of evolution; and how all the planetary stages are, in turn, related to the various components that make up the human being.

Next we will examine in detail how Christ, during his life on Earth, responded to and transformed the nucleus of each commandment. Finally, we will consider whether, and in what form, the commandments can still mean something in our own lives; and where such transformed impulses of the Ten Commandments may be found today.

In the concluding chapter we will try to enter more deeply into the relationship of the Christ-being to the human "I," exploring particularly how he works in the "I" of human beings. It is not possible to refer to this last chapter without mentioning that the all-encompassing significance of Christ far transcends anything that can be described in just a few pages. Nevertheless, the ideas developed in the first ten chapters lead, out of inner necessity, to the attempt, however imperfectly, to give a meaningful form to this subject in the concluding chapter of this book.

Our sincere wish is that these studies about the Ten Commandments will provide the reader with a deeper and more concrete understanding of the connection between the spiritual figure of Moses and the being of Christ, not only from the historical perspectives of the past, but also, and especially, in relation to the needs of today. We hope that the reader will be able to accept the thoughts established in this book as an attempt to offer a small contribution to the great mystery that has been made accessible to us by the spiritual-scientific life work of Rudolf Steiner—the mystery that is contained in the words: *from Moses to Christ.*

I

The First Commandment and the Oneness of the Spiritual World

The first commandment: *"I am the LORD your God, which have brought you out of the land of Egypt, out of the house of bondage. You shall have no other gods before me."* This commandment is commonly regarded as the mainspring of the monotheistic belief system on which the Jewish and Christian religions are based. But, upon closer inspection, it appears that, even after this commandment was introduced, various higher beings continued to occupy a legitimate place both within Jewish and later Christian traditions. The spiritual world was known to be a richly differentiated expanse, inhabited by beings who were not only viewed as mediators between the divine and the human realm, but occasionally also as objects of devotion, in other words, as gods.

In all folk religions up to that time people had worshiped a host of deities—frequently with one upper god ruling a pantheon of lower gods—as a matter of course. We described earlier that the old mysteries mediated between human beings and the spiritual world—also, therefore, between the different peoples and their gods. The initiates, who were working in these mystery centers and were responsible for the guidance of particular nations, "translated" the revelations they received from the spiritual world into suitable images befitting each group's specific stage of development. This is why we can, on the one hand, recognize common characteristics in all ancient folk religions and cultures, but, on the other hand, unique aspects as well, particularly with respect to the contrasting names and functions of the various gods.

For the ancient Israelites the existence of numerous divine beings had been an everyday reality as well; we may conclude this from the wording of the first commandment itself, for it does not *deny* the existence of other gods. Moses himself speaks to God in words that imply the existence of other gods, as for example in, "O LORD God, you have begun to show your servant your greatness, and your mighty hand: for what God is there in Heaven or in Earth that can do according to your works, and according to your might?" (Deut. 3:24). These other gods, then, were not simply eliminated with the introduction of the first commandment. Clearly, the significance of the first commandment cannot be grasped if we *only* understand it as a rejection of polytheism. What, then, is the real impulse of the first commandment?

To find an answer to this question we should, to begin with, try to envision how people perceived themselves and their environment in ancient times, when, as mentioned, all cultural and social impulses were guided and implemented through the mystery centers in accordance with the stars and the laws of the cosmos. Human beings experienced themselves as part of that cosmos. They still had the ability to see spiritual beings clairvoyantly, to perceive these beings outside in nature, but also within themselves, within their own souls. These ancient peoples had no problem with the concept of a divine being working both in the outer world and in the inner being of man. Thus a "God of Wisdom" could simultaneously be known as, say, a "God of Lightning." The spiritual world permeated the earthly consciousness of human beings, overshadowing any awareness of a clear borderline between their own inner being and the outer world.

Abraham's Quest

The conditions we have just described began to change with the gradual awakening of the human "I"; because with it came a change in consciousness that enabled human beings to develop a rudimentary sense of self-awareness. This change in consciousness also affected the way the spiritual world was experienced. It was still possible for most people to get to know the secrets of divine creation by learning to understand the revelations of the cosmic world through thunder, lightning, and through the majesty of Sun, Moon, and stars. But an entirely new way of experiencing the divine world was discovered by Abraham, the patriarch of the Hebrew people, a way that—as we now know—was grounded in the emerging "I," as it was beginning to penetrate the physical body for the first time. Abraham discovered that such experiences could rise up in one's own inner being, quite distinct from the experiences one could have of the divine revealing itself in the outer world. As he became more and more aware of this difference between an inner and an outer world, a burning question now arose in Abraham: "Are there two distinct spiritual worlds, one outside in the macrocosm and one in the inner human being, the microcosm?"[32]

In Abraham's time, only a highly developed initiate could answer this question. Abraham encountered such an initiate in the person of Melchizedek. This encounter is briefly referred to in three short verses in Genesis (14:18–20) as well as in a few other passages, both in the Old and New Testament (Ps. 110; Heb. 5, 6, and 7). These combined passages give only a glimpse, however, of the true importance of Melchizedek.[33] He is given the titles "King of Salem" (peace) and "Priest of the God most High" ("El Elyon" in Hebrew); the latter expression is used only in this context. We also hear that Melchizedek "brought forth" bread and wine—the very substances that would, two thousand years later, be transformed by Christ himself into his body and blood—thus revealing that Melchizedek was, in fact, the harbinger of Christ, the "God most High." Melchizedek was able to guide Abraham as he was pondering the mysteries of the human "I," because this advanced initiate knew that the human "I" is sustained by the "I"-forces of the Christ-being.

Because of his meeting with Melchizedek, Abraham learned that the inner self of a human being indeed constitutes its own spiritual realm, a realm quite distinct from the spiritual realities of the cosmos; but also, that it is the *same* spiritual world that works in both realms, in the microcosm and in the macrocosm. Abraham became aware—though, naturally, on a level befitting the consciousness of his time—that the human "I" itself is a part of that spiritual world and can therefore unite these two realms; that it is, in fact, the *only* force capable of doing so. This kind of rudimentary awareness can only be awakened in a human being whose "I" is beginning to penetrate the physical body. Following this line of thought, one could say that the Israelites' task of preparing the human physical body for the future incarnation of Christ began with Abraham, the progenitor of the Hebrew people.

And so, the encounter with Melchizedek awakened in Abraham the awareness that the human "I" is part of the *oneness* of the spiritual world. This concept of a spiritual unity, attainable through the power of the "I," also forms the basis of the first commandment, which was unveiled at the exact time in history when the "I" was beginning to stir in the Hebrew people as a whole, just as it had earlier in Abraham. The first commandment begins with the mighty words, "I am the LORD your God...," instructing the Israelite people to turn to the *one* God who epitomized that unified, divine world, and as such replaced those divine beings whose active presence only reached into the diverse, manifold etheric and astral realms. With these powerful words the Yahweh–God revealed himself to the Israelite people as their "I AM"-God, as the one God through whom the divine world could be experienced as a unified whole. Yahweh worked out of the "I AM" impulse as the divine unifying principle *both* in the outer world *and* in the innermost human being, leading the Hebrew people for many centuries in that capacity, until the time when Christ himself would incarnate on Earth.

All of this is reflected in the wording of this commandment that, rightfully, claims its place as the first of the Ten Commandments; for it calls out to us: Both the macrocosm and the microcosm point to the oneness of the spiritual, divine world—to the God who speaks "I AM"!

Ancient Saturn and the Meaning of "God's Countenance"

Why doesn't the first commandment simply state, "You shall have no other gods," instead of, "You shall have no other gods *before me*"? When pondering this question, however, it is important to know that the words "before me" in the English translation—just as the words *neben mir* (beside[s] me) in some German translations—do not fully convey the intent of the original Hebrew. In Hebrew the word *panai* is used, which means *face* or *countenance*. Some French and Dutch translations stay closer to the original Hebrew with *devant ma face* and *voor mijn aangezicht* respectively, both meaning *before my Countenance*. So, keeping all this in mind, the question really is: How are we to understand what is meant by *God's Countenance* in the context of the first commandment?

To get some insight into this, we must first turn our attention to the ancient Saturn existence, because, as we pointed out earlier, there is a special connection between old Saturn, the first commandment, and the physical body—to be more precise, to a specific aspect of the physical body that is connected with this oldest planetary embodiment of the Earth. (In our further explorations it will become clear that the second, third, and fourth commandments have a connection to three other aspects of the physical body that have their origins on Sun, Moon, and Earth respectively.)

Trying to envisage the situation on ancient Saturn is not an easy thing to do, because the circumstances were vastly different from our present-day surroundings on Earth. We have to eliminate from our minds almost all the impressions we normally take in with our sense organs. Human senses as such did not yet exist on Saturn, but only a most rudimentary form of what later would become the sense organs. Nor must we imagine the presence of any firm, fluid, or gaseous substances on Saturn. The so-called physical world manifested only as *warmth*.

There was not even anything like space on Saturn. There was only *warmth* and *time*.[34] And it is even more difficult to comprehend that *time* was something very different from what it is today. Time existed on Saturn as a *living activity of spiritual beings*. Saturn development really began with the birth of this living time.[35] And, with the primary creation of warmth and time, the *Thrones* and the *Cherubim*[36] laid the foundation for the physical human body as a warmth body with only a rudimentary indication of the senses. These seminal human beings had a primitive organ of perception that created a certain amount of resistance to the all-pervading warmth currents around them. This organ gave them an indistinct perception of an *inside* and an *outside* that much later—in Abraham's time—would grow into a conscious experience for human beings. But everything on ancient Saturn was still united in the one divine, creative impulse out of which the whole creation arose. In the time of Moses, however, people were beginning to experience both a wealth of inner and of sometimes-conflicting outer impressions, generating the need for a commandment that could point to the one unitary, creative impulse capable of bridging both realms. We can perceive the essence of this unifying power, which brings a *unifying oneness* to the *multiplicity* of the universe, in the words of the first commandment, "You shall have no other gods before my Countenance."

Which part of the present-day physical body reflects something of this "multiple oneness," of this "unity in multiplicity"? In the skin we have an organ that encloses the whole body and thus creates a border between the outside world and us. But it does more than that. It is a complex organ that, by means of diverse, finely tuned processes, not only separates *inside* and *outside*, but also connects us with the world through our senses; many of which are located in the skin. Some of these senses, especially the sense of touch and the sense of warmth, are distributed over the entire body;[37] but other, more specialized senses, such as those of seeing, hearing, smelling, and tasting, are located in the head, and specifically in the countenance. We may well understand the countenance, then, as the embodiment, the focal point of all the senses. Accordingly, when we hear the words "before my Countenance" in the first commandment, we may take this as an indication of the important function these senses have in enabling the human "I" to bring inner experiences and outer impressions together in a higher unity, a higher oneness.

When we stand outside and observe the twinkling stars in the sky, we may well feel a divine cosmic unity within this multitude of stars. Similarly, it is possible to experience the senses, and everything we can perceive with them, as part of the wholeness of the all-encompassing divine impulse. If we then try not to just *think* about the human senses in this way, but to actually *experience* them, we may even become aware that our senses and the observed world not only have a connection to us, but are also part of the divine world, or—as it is expressed in the commandment—of the all-encompassing *Countenance of God*. Once this image becomes alive in us, we may even experience that "before His Countenance" other gods no longer *could* exist because these other gods were active on the level of the astral or the etheric world exclusively, in other words, merely in *part* of the divine cosmos. This is why the first commandment states that one shall have no other gods *before the Countenance* of the God who speaks "I AM."

Having reached this point in our contemplations, the question may well arise: who or what stands before this divine Countenance? First and foremost: the whole creation! But also everything that we as human beings can experience inwardly when we perceive with our sense organs; for, through the gift of our senses, we are able to establish an effective relationship between this outer world and the world of our inner experiences, and thus elevate the isolation of our human existence to *a higher unity with the cosmos*.

But there is more; and we can only approach this aspect cautiously and with a profound feeling of awe. We have already pointed out how each of the Ten Commandments relates to one aspect of the human being, and thus became the norm for the wellbeing of that particular component. With respect to the physical body this norm, this paradigm, is the all-encompassing divine unity, which finds a reflection in the wording of the first commandment. But Rudolf Steiner approached this aspect from yet another perspective when he spoke of the significance of the physical body for the development of humankind and of the cosmos.[38] Human beings think of God when they feel the need to worship a higher entity. Likewise, for the beings in the spiritual world there is something that constitutes the highest religious ideal, worthy of worship, something that gives sense and meaning to all divine activity. This "something" is the archetypal human physical body as it had originally been conceived by the divine powers at the beginning of Saturn existence. It constitutes both the ideal and the goal of all evolution in the spiritual cosmos. We human beings can scarcely contemplate the greatness and the inspired warmth of this archetypal image as it is experienced by the spiritual beings. This lofty image also is the final goal of the spiritual striving of humanity throughout all ages, the image namely, of the physical human body as carrier of—and fully permeated by—the "I." And so, it is ultimately *the ideal human being* who stands before *God's Countenance.*

Once we try to live inwardly with this picture, the first commandment can appear in a new light as well. It then becomes clear that this commandment actually poses the question: Why does the human "I," in order to develop in the right way, have to incarnate in a physical body, equipped with senses that connect it to the outside world? The commandment itself, if rightly understood, also provides the answer: Because only within this physical body, and through the sense organs, can human beings establish a healthy relationship between individual independence and connectedness with the spiritual cosmos—experiences that can then be united in the all-encompassing divine oneness.

Christ and the First Commandment

How did Jesus approach the Ten Commandments? He said that he had not come to "destroy" the law but to "fulfill" it (Matt. 5:17–18). What does this mean? Will this fulfillment add something new to the commandments and to the first commandment in particular? A possible answer to these questions can be found in the episode of the young man who asked Jesus what he should do in order to attain eternal life. Jesus told him that he would have to obey the commandments and specifically referred to the last six commandments (Matt. 19:18–19; Mark 10:19, Luke 18:20). These are the commandments that, according to this book's premise, relate to the etheric body, the astral body, and the human "I" respectively. We may surmise from this answer to the young man that—at least within the framework of this particular question—these six commandments could be "fulfilled" more or less as they had been given, because they could be recommended to him without further elucidation. But Jesus took a different approach with respect to the first four commandments, in other words, to the commandments that have a special relation to the physical body. What does this mean for the first commandment in particular?

The first commandment is only mentioned once. When one of the scribes asked, "Which is the first commandment of all?" Jesus answered, "The first of all the commandments is, Hear, O Israel; The LORD our God is one Lord: And you shall love the LORD your God with all your heart, and with all your soul, and with all your mind, and with all your strength: this is the first commandment" (Mark 12:29–30).

It is noteworthy that this formulation differs from the original form in which the first commandment was introduced in the twentieth chapter of *Exodus* ("I am the LORD your God, which have brought you out of the land of Egypt, out of the house of bondage; you shall have no other gods before me"), although one can certainly recognize the same divine oneness in it. In his answer to the scribe Jesus used the wording of the first commandment as it appears in the sixth chapter of *Deuteronomy*, where Moses, shortly before his death, summarized the divine laws one last time for the Israelite people as a final admonishment, "Hear, O Israel: The LORD our God is one LORD: And you shall love the LORD your God with all of your heart, and with all your soul, and with all your might" (6:4–5).[39]

In comparing these two formulations (in Exodus and Deuteronomy) one can sense that in the meantime—that is, during the forty years that were spent in the desert—this commandment had, as it were, descended from lofty heights to a more human level. There, in the sixth chapter of Deuteronomy—almost as though misplaced amid a miscellany of punishments for wrongdoings, admonishments, and strict demands of obedience—glistens a milder ray of love. This is precisely the passage Jesus referred to in his answer to the scribe. It is as though these words in Deuteronomy, which expressed a momentary hope for the future, were carried on a single light beam from that future and projected by a time mirror to the time of Moses. And so, these precious words about the love of human beings to the divine became the connecting point for Jesus when referring to the first commandment; for, whereas this all-embracing love only existed in seed form in the time of Moses, it could, through Christ, become the center of human life from which all other things can be derived. Christ transformed the way human beings can relate to the divine world through love. Thus he brought about a profound metamorphosis with regard to those commandments that regulate this relationship, that is to say, the first four commandments, and particularly the first one.

Let us now return to the scribe who asked which commandment was the "first of all." One can sense that he was already well advanced on the path of inner development. Having cleansed his soul of individual peculiarities, he could ask this question not only for himself but also as a representative of the Israelite people. This is why we don't hear his personal name mentioned, and why Jesus responded to him, beginning with, "Hear, O Israel." We may well surmise, then, that this scribe was not asking his question simply because he wanted to ask something, anything. This problem truly had become a burning predicament for him, comparable—both in content and intensity—to Abraham's dilemma two thousand years earlier.

The answer to his question helped him become aware that the inner power of love is more important than external rules and regulations. Jesus' answer did not present an abstract solution but offered a living presence, "Hear, O Israel; the LORD our God is one Lord: And you shall love the LORD your God with all your heart, and with all your soul, and with all your mind, and with all your strength." With these words the scribe received a complete and convincing answer to a question that had tormented him as an upholder of the law; for, in that time, the scribes and Pharisees tended to be overly attentive to the formality and implementation of the Mosaic laws, whereas the original impulses of these laws were no longer fully understood. But this particular scribe now was able to say, "Well, Master, you have said the truth: for there is one God; and there is no other but he: And to love him...is more than all whole burnt offerings and sacrifices." Jesus then confirmed this new insight with the words, "You are not far from the kingdom of God." And then this episode ends with the curious comment, "And no man after that durst ask him any question" (Mark 12:32–34).

When we try to envisage the circumstances of this meeting between Jesus and the scribe, at first glance it seems strange that no one *dared* ask any more questions. What was the cause of this anxiety? To understand what actually took place, we have to picture the effect Jesus' words had on those listening to these words. People had been profoundly touched by his response to one of the most burning questions that could be asked, based on the law. They must have sensed that in Jesus' all-encompassing answer an inner soul fire was burning, reminiscent of the outer fires Moses encountered on Mount Sinai when he received the divine law. On that occasion people also called out in fear that they did not want to hear the voice of the LORD anymore "lest they would die" (Deut. 18:16 and 5:25; Ex. 20:19; Heb. 12:19). But there may be another explanation for people's timidity in the face of Christ's answer; for this answer was so far-reaching that it encompassed the whole evolution of humankind, from the beginning of ancient Saturn to a distant future. And we have already heard that this oldest phase of evolution can only be inwardly approached "with the greatest possible courage."[40] People may well have discerned, then, from Jesus' words, that such courage would also be needed to approach a future time, when this sublime love of which Jesus spoke must become a reality. This may well have been the reason people no longer "durst ask him any question."

Upon further examination of Jesus' answer we note, however, a small but significant revision, compared to the original formulation in Deuteronomy. Jesus asked that God be loved "with all your heart, and with all your soul, and with all your mind, and with all your strength." In Deuteronomy the passage reads, "with all of your heart, and with all your soul, and with all your might (strength)." Jesus now spoke of the *mind* as a distinct human quality, equal in importance to a person's heart, soul, and strength. How are we to understand this?

If we look at the circumstances from a historical perspective, we know that humanity had, in the meantime, entered the fourth post-Atlantean cultural era (the so-called Greco–Latin epoch), a time when the development of human thinking and philosophy occupied a place of prominence, particularly in Greece.[41] In other words, the *mind* had become a factor of importance. This truly was the era of the *mind soul* (or intellectual soul), as Anthroposophy calls it.[42] But it is only in our own (fifth) cultural epoch, during which the development of the *consciousness soul* is the central task, that we can become fully aware of how we use our faculty of thinking. Only in our present time are we able to lift our thinking to that spiritual level where the denotation "to love with all your mind" contains no longer any contradictions. This spiritualized thinking is in reality a synthesis of love and wisdom, a thinking in which these two qualities can merge as *wisdom-filled love*. This is the very special—and definitely future-oriented—power of which Christ spoke, referring to the first commandment.

The First Commandment in our Time
and *The Monism of Thinking*

Where can we find a present-day expression of the first commandment in our own time? Ours is the time of modern scientific thinking. It is also the time of Michael.[43] The human "I" has evolved to the point where human beings can think independently. And with our faculty of thinking we can now try to clarify what it means to be human and what our place should be in the stream of evolution. Before the time period of Michael, which started in 1879, it was hardly possible to find clear answers to such questions. Earlier philosophical attempts to explain human thinking can primarily be divided into two categories: the *monistic* and the *dualistic* approach.[44] These philosophical viewpoints were actually still wrestling with the original question of Abraham, albeit in present-day forms: To what degree can the inner human being (that is, the thinking human being) come to understand the outer world, the observed world? And what is the relationship between these two realms, of self and world, subject and object, thought and appearance?

The monistic thinkers responded to this question with the notion that the inner realm is not essentially separate from the outer world; for the monistic thinkers these two realms belonged together, formed a unity. The dualistic thinkers, on the other hand, acknowledged a fundamental difference—and even an unbridgeable chasm—between the inner and the outer world.

The position of the monistic thinkers had gradually become untenable because they could not adequately explain the contrast between the outer and the inner world, which people increasingly experienced. The dualistic thinkers had reached an equally untenable position because they could not satisfactorily explain why and how the apparently autonomous inner and outer aspects of existence interact in the same world. It follows from the objections against, and the arguments for either standpoint, that neither philosophical approach is correct; but also that both contain a kernel of truth. In other words, we are faced with an *epistemological impasse*. This philosophical dilemma is a significant one, not only from the point of view of the historical development of philosophy, but also because of its influence on the way most people—including those who have not been philosophically trained—relate to the world, even today.

A whole new way of thinking was needed to overcome this impasse! Rudolf Steiner realized such a free "thinking deed," one that inaugurated a new phase in the development of human thinking. The fruits of this new way of thinking can be found in his books *Truth and Knowledge* and especially in *Intuitive Thinking as a Spiritual Path* (or *The Philosophy of Freedom*). One might well venture to say that the concepts that are presented in these books are of equal significance for our time as the recognition of the one God, Yahweh, was for the time of Moses!

The Philosophy of Freedom begins, almost by way of an introductory thinking exercise for the reader, by pointing out various failed philosophical attempts. Next, the book develops the key insight that a concept remains *one* concept regardless of how many people think it—it does not become a multiplicity of concepts. The human "I" understands a concept by an act of *intuition*. This forms the basis for the thinking activity of the "I." Through this intuitive cognition the "I" unites itself with the concept. *But the concept itself remains a unity irrespective of how many people connect with it through intuition.*

This absolute oneness of each concept has far-reaching consequences for the epistemological process. The world exists for us as a sum of observations. As we begin to think about what happens when we observe, we experience a chasm between the "I" and the world, between subject and object. But this separation, this chasm, *can* be bridged by the thinking activity of the "I" when we become aware of what happens when we think, in other words, when the "I" observes its own thinking. During this epistemological process, the "I" can lift itself above the separation of subject and object by means of its own thinking activity and can thus unite *subject and object into a higher unity.*

Rudolf Steiner called the epistemological process we just described *the monism of the thinking activity*. Accordingly, the observed world is initially presented as a *dualistic* reality, but can be unified into a *monistic* whole with the help of our thinking process. The monism of the thinking activity is the result of an exact analysis of thinking, which is able to penetrate the source of the thinking process. This analysis is further elaborated in the book *Truth and Knowledge*.[45] There, the reader is led to a particular phase of the soul's existence in which thinking is not yet active, but can be awakened through the forces of the "I." One could call this stage of the soul life the *Saturn phase of thinking*. Only when we are able to reach this stage is it possible to connect the two seemingly contradictory realms of our inner experiences and the outer observed world. Through the thinking activity it then becomes possible to fully unite what—at least initially—manifests as a duality.

By developing this fundamental concept further, Rudolf Steiner reaches a second conclusion. He leads us to an understanding of what, in truth, can be called *reality*. Reality turns out to be the result of a deepening of our observations, to which we then apply concepts through the activity of our thinking. After all, in thinking we grasp the *conceptual* aspect of reality, whereas in observation we have the *perceptual* aspect of reality. Our thinking activity unites these two, and the union thus obtained is *reality*. But the apparent dualism of the outer and inner worlds will remain, as long as the thinking "I" is not yet able to connect the appropriate concepts to the observations through the power of intuitive cognition. As soon as we are able to do this, however, we have grasped a part of reality. Then dualism is transformed into *the monism of the thinking activity*, at least with respect to that part of reality.

Learning to unite concept and percept in this way is a gradual process; it does not happen instantly. At some point we may be able to think concepts about some of our observations that can actually lift us from the level of mere observation to the level of reality, but at the same time we may not yet be able to think appropriate concepts about other observations. The transition of the stage of dualism to the stage of *the monism of the thinking activity* has then only partially been achieved. Whether, or to what extent, someone is able to apply this in daily life depends on that person's individual constitution and circumstances. What is important is that it is now *possible* to exercise our thinking in this way.

So, when we ask whether this new epistemological process, as Rudolf Steiner described it, is monistic or dualistic, the answer is: neither. There is a third possibility. It can become *a living process whereby every phase has a dualistic beginning and a monistic conclusion*. Through our thinking activity we gradually transform a dualistic world, which is torn into an objective and a subjective part, into a world that is one whole, where percepts and concepts unite to give us our knowledge of a full, monistic reality. This transformation can occur because of the previously mentioned fact that a concept spiritually remains a whole, a unity, irrespective of how many people unite themselves with this concept in their thoughts. The spiritual oneness of a concept is one and the same for everybody. *The Philosophy of Freedom* calls out to us: *"You shall recognize only one all-encompassing spiritual reality through the power of intuition in your thinking."* This, one could say, is the present-day form of the first commandment in the epoch of Michael.

2

The Second Commandment

The second commandment begins with the words *"You shall not make unto you any graven image, or any likeness of any thing that is in heaven above, or that is in the earth beneath, or that is in the water under the earth. You shall not bow down yourself to them, nor serve them..."* In short, the making and worshiping of images, in whatever form, is forbidden; at least, that would seem to be the verbatim meaning of this commandment. But, throughout the centuries, this commandment has been subject to a full scale of interpretations, ranging anywhere from a simple warning not to worship idols, to—and this would be the most extreme interpretation—a complete rejection of all art forms.

Regardless, however, of the diversity of explanations about the meaning of the second commandment, one question remains the same: Why forbid this at all? It seems as though a further explanation is forthcoming in the remaining words of the commandment, because this part of the text begins with the word *for*. Unfortunately, this "explanation" does not actually appear to explain anything. It states, *"For I the LORD your God am a jealous God, visiting the iniquity of the fathers upon the children unto the third and fourth generation of them that hate me; and showing mercy unto thousands of them that love me, and keep my commandments"* (Ex. 20:5–6). At first glance these words look more like an ominous warning to obey *all* commandments at all times, a warning that more or less accidentally might have found its way to this part of the text. But, once we enter more deeply into these matters—with the help of anthroposophic indications—it soon becomes clear that this admonition is more than just an accidental insertion. To set the stage for our further investigations, however, we must first take a closer look at the ancient Sun phase of the Earth, as well as at the Atlantean era,[46] and the Egyptian culture in the time of Moses; because all three can shed light on the meaning of the second commandment.

THE SUN PHASE OF THE EARTH

According to the central theme of this book there is a connection between the second commandment and the second planetary incarnation of the Earth, the old Sun. Therefore, in order to be able to understand the esoteric background of the second commandment, we must take a closer look at the Sun phase of the evolution. On old Saturn the human physical body had existed only as warmth; it had as yet no life. But on ancient Sun the germinal human beings received their own etheric bodies from the exalted *Spirits of Wisdom* (the *Kyriotetes*);[47] thus a primitive form of life came into being. But the physical body needed an additional element, less rarefied than the warmth, to be able to assimilate these rudimentary life processes. This was the element "air," which now emerged for the first time. Rudolf Steiner describes how this gaseous structure becomes visible to suprasensory consciousness "through the effect of light that it emits."[48] This is why these earliest etheric forces, which were incorporated into the physical human body during ancient Sun existence, are called *light ether* forces.

These gaseous structures, which in this same context also are referred to as "figures of light" by Rudolf Steiner, now started to reflect images "in resplendent light" back to certain spiritual beings (the *Spirits of Personality*), who then in these reflected images were able to "behold suprasensorially what was taking place on the Sun"; for these beings had already then a highly developed pictorial consciousness—something human beings will only acquire in the next planetary incarnation of the Earth, the so-called Jupiter phase. Accordingly, one could say, by incorporating the light ether forces, the human physical body became like an image, an image of the macrocosm, an *image of God*. The perfect balance of the life processes as seen in the physiognomy of the body can, even today, give us an experience of the wisdom-filled dynamic harmony of the living God. But this is an inner experience, an inner picture that could never be summoned through outer images; for, the concentrated focus required to behold or create sense-perceptible images would, through its very exclusivity, only detract from the *true image of the living God*. We will try to keep this picture alive in us as we continue our contemplations about the second commandment.

It is also important to know that, during each phase of the cosmic evolution, not all beings reach their intended goal. On ancient Sun we already encounter such beings who, during the previous Saturn phase, had not evolved sufficiently to be able to partake directly in the ongoing process of evolution. They had to continue their development elsewhere. This, one could say, is the prototype of a course of action that would be repeated time and again in one form or another. Forces and beings, who could not adapt to the intended course of development, needed to be placed outside the mainstream of evolution, lest they would obstruct and hinder this process.

But meanwhile, the intended "regular" development also continued on old Sun. The physical bodies of our human ancestors now developed chiefly three new qualities. The first quality manifested as a rudimentary form of what, much later, would become human consciousness. This could now occur because the newly incorporated "air" element—already somewhat less rarefied than Saturn's warmth —had a stabilizing effect on the human body. The second quality was an inner mobility that Rudolf Steiner compares to the movements of sap in present-day plants.[49] These moving air streams formed the basis of what later would become our breathing and blood circulation. And the third quality was a primitive, vegetative-like reproduction (almost like present-day cell division)—part of what later would become our glandular system.

A mighty perspective now presents itself. We find here, on old Sun, the earliest beginnings of:

- a rudimentary form of *consciousness*
- the *heart* and other rhythmical processes
- reproductive forces through which humankind is connected with later *generations*

This threefold structure had emerged during the ancient Sun existence as a direct result of the steadily changing circumstances. On Saturn only time had existed. On old Sun, because of the further differentiation of Saturn's warmth into gases and light, *space* had emerged for the first time. Consequently, the germinal human beings were now living not only in time, but also in space. As though echoing this new reality, the human body had developed a germinal form of the nerve–sense system, with which this space could now be *passively* experienced as a kind of mirrored reflection, as well as a germinal form of the metabolic–reproductive system, through which the early human beings now also were able to relate a bit more *actively* to this space. To help keep these two contrasting systems in a living balance, a mediating force had emerged on old Sun in the form of the human rhythmical system in its earliest configuration, with the heart as the main central organ. We will now follow the further development of these three qualities during the Atlantean epoch and the Egyptian culture.

THE ATLANTEAN CULTURE

In almost all early civilizations stories were told about a great water catastrophe that had brought an end to an ancient culture. In the Bible this event is referred to as *the flood* (Gen. 7); Plato describes it as *the fall of Atlantis*—that mysterious continent, situated to the west of Gibraltar in a region now covered by the Atlantic Ocean.[50]

In our own time Rudolf Steiner has given detailed accounts about Atlantis, the Atlantean culture, and the events that led to its demise.[51] From these indications we know that, during the height of the Atlantean epoch, its people lived in a rich culture and in an orderly civilization. But their frame of mind, their consciousness, was very different from ours. Logical, clear thinking was foreign to them, and their perceptions were not as clearly outlined as ours are today. They lived with an instinctive clairvoyance, supported by a remarkable capacity of memory. One could actually call this a clairvoyant *picture consciousness* because it gave the Atlantean people not only visionary impressions, but also a certain awareness of what they experienced in this way. They could, for instance, become aware of the etheric forces, both outside in nature and within living beings.

Not only did people become aware of these forces, they also had a certain power over them. The initiates of the Atlantean mysteries guided people in the correct use and understanding of these forces. But, in later phases of the Atlantean era, its culture began to decline and, eventually, the majority of the Atlantean mysteries fell into decadence as well, which meant that the human ability to use etheric forces was increasingly being abused for selfish pursuits. This misuse of etheric forces, which is also known as *the transgression of the Atlantean forefathers*, finally led to the destruction of the Atlantean continent and its people by a massive water catastrophe—the biblical flood. Only a small segment of the Atlantean population was able to escape this deluge. Manu led one stream of emigrants eastward, the great initiate of the Sun Mysteries, which, of all the Atlantean mysteries, had been least affected by the previously mentioned misuse of etheric forces.[52]

Those who were part of this emigration stream were practical people who, in the words of Rudolf Steiner, were "endowed with the ability to relate to the physical world."[53] They had lost most of their clairvoyant picture consciousness and, as a consequence, also their ability to use the etheric forces in nature. This protected them, at least to a certain degree, from *the transgression of the Atlantean forefathers*. But, in order to help guide the development of this new earthly consciousness—and at the same time further curtail the lingering clairvoyant picture consciousness—certain measures had to be put in place. This is why, already then, Manu taught his pupils—and by extension all of his followers—the concept of one God of whom no images should be made.⁵⁴

With the passing of time, a threefold transformation gradually began to occur, through the new impulses originating from the Atlantean Sun Mysteries, within the human beings whose lives were guided by this great Sun initiate, a transformation that can be summarized thus:

1. The former picture consciousness made way for a new form of *consciousness* that enabled human beings to focus more on the outer world.
2. The *human heart* was being prepared to develop the quality of mercy.
3. Purifying forces were now working through the *descending generations*.

Thus, whereas Atlantis and most of its inhabitants were swept away in the great flood because of human misuse of etheric forces, those who survived the event were forever changed, both with respect to their bodily constitution and level of consciousness. Old forces had made way for new capacities, befitting the further developments yet to come. The descendants (the *children*) of the former Atlantis would now be able to help prepare the way for the next post-Atlantean era when Christ would incarnate on Earth.

In the time of Moses it was known in the mysteries that, in order to prepare humanity—and the Israelite people in particular—for this pivotal event, it was necessary to eliminate all remaining traces of *the transgression of the Atlantean forefathers*, still lingering in the third post-Atlantean epoch. A strong discipline was needed, aimed particularly at the elimination of the old picture consciousness. This meant that:

1. Human *consciousness* should be trained not to give way to the shining glow of the old clairvoyance.
2. The human *heart* needed to be activated to develop moral feelings.
3. Special hereditary forces streaming through the *descending generations* were needed to prepare a suitable human body for the coming incarnation of Christ.

This is the threefold impulse expressed in the second commandment! It forbade the making and worshiping of images in order to stimulate the proper development of human consciousness. It stressed the importance of the heart quality of mercy, and it emphasized that the religious impulses working through the descending generations had to become a significant cultural factor.

The Egyptian Culture in the time of Moses

The Egyptian culture reached its pinnacle during the third post-Atlantean cultural epoch.[55] Most biblical scholars estimate that the Exodus of the Israelite people under Moses took place around the 13th century BC[56]—in other words, in the second half of this third cultural epoch. Jesus lived in the first half of the fourth cultural epoch. Accordingly, everything that happened between the time of Moses and the time of Christ involved human beings who lived in the *third* and *fourth* post-Atlantean cultural epochs. We have to keep this in mind, as it has a bearing on the second commandment in particular; for, after the incarnation of Christ on the Earth, the question of "graven images" took on a whole new meaning, as we will see later on.

In the time of Moses we encounter a situation in Egypt that is comparable—albeit on a reduced scale—to the decadence in Atlantis that eventually led to its destruction. Degenerative magical powers were again being used irresponsibly, especially also within the walls of some Egyptian mystery centers.[57] These activities had infiltrated Pharaoh's court as well. We are told of the Egyptian sorcerers and magicians who used magical powers during the recurring confrontations between Moses and Pharaoh before the Israelites were allowed to leave Egypt (Ex. 7:11–12, 7:22, 8:7, 8:18, and 9:11). And such practices still continued long after Moses' time. We may therefore well say that the children of the third and fourth cultural epochs lived under the spell of the same kind of magic that their Atlantean ancestors had misused to control the etheric forces.

It became crucially important, then, to rescue and safeguard a healthy nucleus from the ailing Egyptian mysteries for the wellbeing of the future development of humanity. This meant that the remaining forces of clairvoyance needed to be completely transformed. These forces had to be turned inward, as it were, in order to prepare new impulses for the heart, with which human beings would be able to develop a sense of morality and feelings of mercy.

In the third post-Atlantean epoch this old kind of clairvoyant consciousness could easily be aroused if people were exposed to certain images. While under the influence of such images, the etheric body became slightly detached from the physical body, bringing about this kind of clairvoyant consciousness, which was detrimental to progress; for, *true* progress meant: the etheric body shall unite wholly with the physical body, to eventually form "the living image of God" in human beings.

We can hardly imagine today what impact such images still had on the Egyptian people, an impact that worked right down into the physical body as well. To some extent, this continued well into the time of the Greek civilization. The Greek sculptors, who made images of the gods for the temples, were well aware of their responsibility in this regard. They created their sculptures not from human models but out of an idealized inner experience. They tried to ascend to the *image of God* within the human being and express this image in their sculptures.

Today all this has changed. We are now able to maintain an inner stability within our human constitution that can no longer, in the same way, be thrown off balance by the impact of images. This has to do with the awakening of the human "I" and the continuing development of the etheric heart. The "I" is now strong enough to transform and stabilize the etheric heart from the inside and thus help maintain an inner balance. The etheric heart today possesses an inner mobility that neutralizes the impact of outer images. But this was different in Egyptian times. A person with an etheric heart in which this inner mobility had not yet been suitably developed—a heart, in other words, that was *hardened*—would not be able to resist the impact of outer images. It is in keeping with this observation, then, that the Bible story about the impending departure of the Israelites out of Egypt, relates how the heart of Pharaoh—the foremost representative of the Egyptian people—repeatedly was hardened.

The old wisdom of the East refers to seven focal points of life forces in the human body, the so-called chakras, represented symbolically by lotus flowers, with each one having its own specific number of petals. The chakra of the heart was represented as a *twelve-petalled* lotus flower.[58] Since a lotus flower can either wither away or come to full bloom, it has long been seen as a symbol of development; we may well understand the *twelve-petalled* lotus flower, then, as a twelvefold conduit for the *development of the etheric heart*.[59] Keeping this in mind, it is fascinating to note that in the Bible story about the hardening of Pharaoh's heart, this hardening actually gets mentioned *twelve* times as though signaling the total stagnation of any potential growth of Pharaoh's heart forces.[60]

And so, we encounter a set of circumstances during the *third and fourth* cultural epochs in which the descendants, the *children* of the people who had lived just before the time of the great flood, found themselves attracted to the same kind of perilous practices as their Atlantean ancestors before them. They were devoted to *the transgression of the forefathers*, caused by the (twelvefold) hardening of the heart. But on the opposite side stood the representatives of the new stream of evolution, that is to say, the Israelite stream. This stream, as bearer of the inspiration of Yahweh, had the task to transform the old clairvoyance in such a way, that new forces of the etheric heart could be developed. As a consequence, those who were devoted to the old Egyptian clairvoyance could not but respond with feelings of intense hatred for the Israelites and their God, Yahweh (..."unto the third and fourth generation of them that hate me").

A remarkable parallel can be discovered between the factors that led to the fall of Atlantis and those that led to the parting of the Israelites from the land of Egypt. In both cases the further development of humankind had to be safeguarded from harmful influences. This parallel reveals many similarities indeed! Again a great initiate appeared (this time in the person of Moses) who led a select group eastward (this time the Israelites). The people who belonged to this group were focused on the outer world, but also tried to experience the body—and the blood in particular—as the *image of God*. This group had the task to transform the old clairvoyance, thereby strengthening the forces that were needed for the ongoing preparation and refinement of the body and the blood for the future incarnation of Christ. The Egyptians who had engaged in *the transgression of the forefathers* viewed this conduct of the Israelites as a threat. They felt impelled to pursue the departing Israelites, driven by hatred toward the new impulse of Yahweh. And whereas the Israelites succeeded in crossing the Red Sea[61] through the receding waters, the pursuing Egyptian army drowned in the returning waves (Exodus 14:28). We have here, on a smaller scale, an exact replica of the destruction of Atlantis!

We are now in a position, with the help of the elements brought together thus far, to appreciate the real meaning of the explanatory passage included in the formulation of the second commandment. In the introduction to the *first* commandment we heard the words "I am the LORD your God, which have brought you out of the land of Egypt." And now, in the *second* commandment, we can actually find the reasons for this inevitable break with Egypt, if we but know how to read it:

> For I am the LORD your God, who must condemn those "children" of the third and fourth cultural epochs who are still committing the transgression of the Atlantean forefathers and who are compelled to hate me, because they want to hold on to their decadent powers. But onto the thousands who will follow my commandments out of

love, I will bestow a new kind of power, a power that supports the development of the etheric heart forces—the power of mercy.[62]

We can expand on this initial reading by taking into account something we have not included in our contemplations so far. It has to do with a particular concept that has long puzzled biblical scholars, the notion, namely, of a jealous God. We must try to understand this word in the context of the time. The Hebrew people were not yet able to grasp the profoundly new quality manifesting in their God. Hence the compelling, descriptive word "jealous" was used in the text of this commandment to persuade the Hebrew people *not* to deviate from this divine quality, a quality that Rudolf Steiner once interpreted in the context of the Ten Commandments as "the divine nature whose influence persists"; it is a quality that lived *within* the Hebrew people as well, as "the eternal divine in you that works into the body and therefore upon future generations."[63] We can now attempt a more comprehensive reading of the second commandment, one that takes into account not only the quality of this divine principle, but also the way it should manifest in human beings in the time of Moses:

> You shall refrain from worshiping those radiant divine images that sustained your former picture consciousness; for I am the eternal divine principle in you that strives to further a new level of consciousness that is compatible with the development of the etheric heart forces. Those among the "children" of the third and fourth cultural epochs, who, like their Atlantean forefathers, want to hold on to their clairvoyant picture consciousness, cannot know me; but those who learn to develop the heart quality of mercy will be able to recognize me as the divine principle in themselves. They will love me for all cultural epochs to come, and follow my commandments out of love.

The development of the heart forces

We have described how the original impulse for the threefold structure of the human being—that is to say, the earliest beginnings of human consciousness, of the heart, and of the realm of reproduction—had emerged during the ancient Sun existence. Next we observed how, during a more recent evolutionary stage, the great Atlantean Sun initiate had guided the further development of these same three qualities in his people; and how, more recently yet, the second commandment had been introduced to strengthen these selfsame qualities, albeit in a form befitting the conditions of the time period of Moses.

But, of these three qualities, it was especially the development of the *heart* forces that became the focal point of the second commandment. Its original impulse was aimed at strengthening the heart forces and at cultivating moral hygiene of the heart. This is the eternal core and aim of the second commandment. In the time of Moses the human heart was in imminent danger of being hardened by the influence of certain images, especially cult images. Moses knew from his own experience how powerful this impact could be; for he encountered it himself as he descended from Mount Sinai with the tablets of the law. Having spent forty days and forty nights without eating or drinking in preparation for what he was about to receive on top of the mountain, he then had to experience that his people were dancing around a golden calf (Ex. 32:1–10). One can hardly imagine a greater disappointment for Moses—having recognized both the magnitude of the new impulse of Yahweh and his own responsible role in these events—than to find at his return that the people were worshiping a golden calf, demonstrating in this way that they had relapsed to a hardening of the heart, that is to say, to an earlier form of picture consciousness that should have been left behind in Egypt. In this episode the Old Testament actually describes an attack on the forces of the heart—exactly those forces that were meant to receive a new impulse through the second commandment.

Following this event, the Israelites wandered through the desert for forty years. Why? The actual journey to the Promised Land could likely have been accomplished in far fewer than forty years. But in those forty years, one could say, the Israelite people *collectively* had to experience what Moses had achieved *individually* during his forty days on top of the mountain. Old forces had to be transformed into new forces.[64] In those forty years all the Israelites who had taken part in the Exodus out of Egypt, save for a few exceptional ones, died;[65] and lingering remnants of the old picture consciousness died with them in the wilderness. The next generation, born in the desert, gradually developed a new kind of consciousness through the emerging forces of the awakening "I," enabling those belonging to this new generation to withstand the temptation to relapse into a former level of consciousness. This, then, was the generation that, forty years later, entered the Promised Land.

Christ and the Second Commandment

We have, again, arrived at that point in our studies where we plan to examine, first, whether this commandment has changed as a result of Christ's life on Earth and, second, where we may find a present-day form of it in our own time. But, before we proceed with such contemplations about the second commandment in particular, it will be helpful to briefly assess where the Ten Commandments—in their original form, that is—still play a role today.

To begin with, it is important to acknowledge that the Ten Commandments still have enough strength and validity to generate a sense of direction, order, and wellbeing for many people, even today. Neither should we lose sight of the fact that the commandments still have a considerable judicial and moral influence in today's societies. The first commandment still plays a role within the monotheistic religions. The third commandment is still accepted as the basis for the (mostly Jewish) tradition of not uttering God's name, and as the rationale for banning the use of profanity in certain jurisdictions. The fourth commandment lives on in the weekly return of a (societal or religious) day of rest. The fifth and the seventh, honoring the parents and marital fidelity, form the basis of family life as we know it. The sixth commandment, prohibiting the willful taking of a human life, is a benchmark in any orderly society; so is the ninth, proscribing false witness. The eighth commandment, prohibiting stealing, forms one of the pillars of the world's judicial systems. The tenth commandment, admonishing people not to "covet" anything that belongs to others, would likely sooner be acknowledged as a soul quality worth pursuing, rather than a command. But in that form it still has value today.

There is one radical exception in this respect, namely the *second commandment*. Our culture no longer frowns on displaying, making, or even "worshiping" images. On the contrary; we are not only exposed to an endless stream of intrusive images in the news, in advertisements, and so on but, fortunately, also have access to a plethora of beautiful paintings, sculptures, and other aesthetic images—especially in religious settings! Churches are filled with paintings, frescoes, icons, sculptures, stained glass windows, and exquisitely illustrated documents. It is true that there was an outbreak of *Iconoclastic Fury* in the sixteenth century, during the time of the Reformation in Europe, but its rate of success can best be compared to that of the sorcerer's apprentice in Goethe's ballad—for each image destroyed, two or more took its place almost immediately![66]

We may well conclude, then, that the actual prohibition of images was meant for a specific time period only, that is to say, for the period that began with Moses and ended with the coming of Christ. It was, to be more precise, meant specifically for the "children of Israel" who lived at that time. The knowledge that the curtailment of images was needed for a specified time period only is actually included as a veiled "open secret" in the explanatory passage for the second commandment: "For I am the LORD your God, who must condemn those among the children of *the third and fourth* cultural epoch... who want to hold on to a past form of picture consciousness."

Can we find evidence of this in the New Testament as well? On several occasions Jesus referred to the commandments in discussions and parables. Only once did he mention a "second commandment," when speaking about the importance of loving one's neighbors.[67] But this is a motif that runs through the whole life of Christ and is not specifically connected with the edict against images. This particular passage provides not so much an explanation of the second commandment as a profound summary of the last six commandments, which govern our relationship to our fellow human beings. But nowhere in the New Testament did Jesus refer to the second commandment as such, that is to say, he never spoke about the prohibition against images. Why not?

We are touching here on something unique, something that only happened *once* in the entire history of human and cosmic evolution. Christ, the true "image of God," as Paul expressed it in two of his Letters (Col. 1:15 and II Cor. 4:4), incarnated in Jesus as a human being of flesh and blood. Because of this deed *image* and *reality* united in *Jesus Christ*. This event had a profound impact on human beings as well. Man had, long ago, been created "in the image of God" (Gen. 1:26); but up to the time in which the second commandment was unveiled, people had only experienced the image of the divine outside themselves, outside in nature, or by worshiping external images of gods. Once the edict against images became a part of their lives, however, people had gradually begun to experience the image of the divine within themselves, within their own developing "I." This, after all, had been the objective of the prohibition against images. But it is only through Christ's deed that we human beings, from that time onward, can unite inwardly with the ideal, *true image of God* that is Christ. This also means that the second commandment was fulfilled with the coming of Christ to the Earth. *Image and reality had become one in the life of Jesus Christ.* This is why Jesus did not need to transform or fulfill the second commandment as he did the other commandments. *Christ himself was the fulfillment of the second commandment!*

We mentioned that Jesus never spoke of the second commandment as such; but there is an account of an event that can shed a bit more light on this whole subject matter. This episode is not mentioned in the Bible, but Rudolf Steiner was able to describe it from his spiritual research.[68] As a young man, so we hear, Jesus was in regular contact with the Essenes. Those who belonged to this esoteric Jewish order lived a simple, pious life, guided by strict observances.[69] Jesus was not a member of this order but was a frequent guest, welcomed in their midst as a revered personage. The Essenes strictly observed the second commandment, so strictly in fact, that they would not let their members pass through the city gates, as these were adorned with sculptures and paintings. Because the Essenes were well-respected in the community, additional gates had been built for them without ornaments. And it was precisely when passing through these unadorned gates, so we hear from Rudolf Steiner, that Jesus experienced the stirring of inner pictures, of inwardly perceptible living images, that would help prepare him to receive the Christ-being during the baptism in the Jordan.

In this account about Jesus and the Essenes we encounter two interrelated aspects of the prohibition of images. On the one hand, because of the Essenes' ordinances against exposure to images, special gates had been built without ornaments; and so, an old clairvoyant faculty, which had constricted and hardened the human heart, could now gradually be eliminated. On the other hand, because he was passing through these unadorned gates, Jesus experienced profound inner images, enabling him to develop the all-encompassing heart forces through which a new spiritual vision could arise in him.

At the very moment that Jesus had these revelations while passing through the unadorned gates, at that moment, one could say, the original impulse out of which the second commandment arose, was fully transformed. The prohibition of images was no longer needed in its original form because of these events. In its place a new capacity can now gradually emerge in every human being, a new faculty, arising out of the forces of the heart, making it possible to experience profound *inner soul images*, independent of the influence of *outer images*.

The Law of Historical Symmetry

There is a cosmic law that, by its very existence and nature, gives us an indication of the true significance of Christ's incarnation for the evolution and history of humanity. The *Mystery of Golgotha*—the expression used by Rudolf Steiner for what took place at Golgotha through the death and resurrection of Christ—is the most important event in the entire evolution of the Earth: this is one of the foremost insights one can come to through the study of Anthroposophy! The Mystery of Golgotha occupies this central position not only with regard to its universal significance, but also with respect to its place in history. It stands as a pivotal point in time, thus creating a special link between events that occurred before and those that happened (or will happen) after it. To be more precise, a historical event of, say, AD 800 reflects something of what happened around the year 800 BC. We can call this law, which mainly applies to the post-Atlantean era, the *Law of Historical Symmetry*.[70] It reflects the historical mirroring of earlier and later events, with Golgotha as a pivotal point right in the middle between these events.

This law will, in a distant future, affect the relationship between the *seventh* and the *first* (ancient Indian) post-Atlantean cultural epochs, as well as that of the *sixth* and the *second* (ancient Persian) epochs.[71] In the same way—and this applies directly to our present investigations—will we be able to recognize that certain characteristics of our own *fifth* cultural epoch have their origins in the *third* cultural epoch. (Note that the *fourth* cultural epoch, in which Christ lived on Earth, stands on its own as the central epoch and does not reflect other cultural epochs.) Knowledge of this law makes it possible to discover how certain elements of the era in which the Ten Commandments were given to humankind are reflected in our own time. Our focus here being the second commandment, it would be helpful to focus particularly on the impact of images on human beings in either cultural era.

Back in the Egyptian–Babylonian era this influence was such that the human soul was in danger of being coaxed away from the Earth by the enticing radiance of images, particularly cult images. In our own time we are confronted with an endless stream of images and pictures that overstimulate the senses and, in the process, tie us ever more to the Earth. One could say that in both cases this kind of overexposure to images had (and has) a negative influence on the development of humanity.

In the third cultural era the influence of images maintained the old clairvoyant abilities artificially, even as these abilities were already diminishing. In our own time, our exposure to a never-ending stream of images poses a threat to a new imaginative faculty that should gradually emerge, the ability namely to perceive spiritual contents—spiritual *images*—in meditative contemplation, while maintaining our normal waking consciousness.

Whereas in the time of Moses a restrictive commandment regulated the exposure to outer images, in our own time we have the freedom to develop the ability and insight to determine how and to what extent we will let today's intrusive flood of images affect our state of mind.

The Second Commandment and the Confrontation with Evil in our Time

We have mentioned that the prohibition of images was not the main objective of the second commandment. The edict was imposed as a means of achieving the commandment's true intent: the healthy development of the human heart. In our own time we have to focus particularly on the *moral* development of the heart forces. This requires a different approach than in the time of Moses; not in the least because the cosmic forces working *against* the healthy development of the heart also work differently today. In the time of Moses the immediate danger was a hardening of the human heart. Today's threat against the forces of the heart comes from a different direction and must be approached differently. In order to understand and recognize this threat to the heart forces, we must come to terms with the problem of evil in the world.

Evil is more than just the abstract counterpart of *Good*. In the anthroposophic worldview evil is seen as a real cosmic force in its own right, caused by the aforementioned fact that certain spiritual beings remained behind in their development, thus becoming spirits of hindrance. This caused an element of resistance to enter into the divine plan. But it is also important to know that these so-called evil beings play a crucial role in the course of evolution; for, without this element of resistance, human beings would not have developed essential new qualities, such as, for instance, freedom. These beings, therefore, occupy a legitimate place in evolution; but they can become evil when they overstep the boundaries of their rightful domain. This kind of evil manifests in two different ways, because one group of these beings had remained behind at an earlier stage of evolution; another group at a later stage. The former are referred to as *ahrimanic,* the latter as *luciferic* beings.[72]

The ahrimanic beings cause hardening, contraction, heaviness, darkness, and materialism. They want to fetter human beings to the Earth. The luciferic beings cause expansion, levity, self-aggrandizement, illusion, and superficiality. They want to entice human beings away from the Earth. We are continually called upon to maintain a dynamic balance between the ahrimanic and luciferic influences. Both are needed for the further development of humankind, but neither one must be allowed to gain the upper hand in the world or in the human soul, if this development is to continue in the right way. The *good,* therefore, is not simply the opposite of *evil,* but rather constitutes a *healthy balance* between *two* extremes. Any type of one-sidedness can become evil. And so, we come to the concept of a *good* central force in between *two adversarial* forces. More than two thousand years ago Aristotle had already formulated a similar definition of the good: "Virtue is human capacity or skill guided by reason and insight, which in relation to the human being holds the mean between the too-much and the too-little."[73]

The heart—the central organ of the rhythmical system—maintains a dynamic balance between our nerve–sense system and our metabolic system. The heart can only exist within us through constant interaction with these two other systems. In the same way, one could say, the *moral good* can only develop within us, within our heart, if we continually weigh and confront the dangers of "the too-much and the too-little." In the past the second commandment provided the norm for the *moral hygiene of the heart*.[74] In our own time we can provide this norm for ourselves through the development of *moral heart forces*. The more we learn to recognize the impact of the adversarial forces, both in the external world and in ourselves, the more we can learn to strengthen *moral goodness* in ourselves as a mediating impulse between these opposing forces. Then moral goodness can flow out into the world—something that is urgently needed today to safeguard the ongoing development of humanity. The human heart is the central organ that makes it possible for us to find and maintain this kind of balance in ourselves; and the true source of our moral heart forces is Christ. Christ represents the balancing force in between Ahriman and Lucifer.[75] Ever since its rudimentary beginnings on old Sun the Christ-being has guided the development of the human heart and will continue to do so well into the future.

3

Building Blocks of the Third Commandment

The third commandment: *"You shall not take the name of the LORD your God in vain; for the LORD will not hold him guiltless that takes his name in vain."* People usually think of profanity when contemplating the meaning of these words. It is true that using coarse language may well contain a last trace, a weak remnant of specific forces active in human speaking, forces that in olden times could actually harm people—we will come back to this later. But careful use of language is only one aspect of the meaning of the third commandment; other concepts are introduced as well.

In the formulation of this commandment we also find a passage that begins with the word *for*, just as we noted with respect to the formulation of the second commandment; and, again, this passage is not intended as a general admonition, but as an explanatory augmentation for this commandment. In this case, however, the explanation is based on the concept of guilt. We must carefully distinguish, then, between *iniquity* (transgression), which is used in the explanatory passage for the second commandment and *guilt*, used in the equivalent section for the third commandment. An initial observation leads us to conclude that iniquity refers—at least within the context of the second commandment—to a deed that destroys the order in the cosmos, whereas guilt refers to something that affects a person's individual karma.[76] We must therefore take a look at the origin and significance of *guilt* (sin), as well.

The third commandment also points to a connection between guilt and a particular way of speaking. To understand this connection we must examine the source of human *speech* as well. Speech in its broadest sense—and this includes any form of expression through sounds or even primitive gestures—can only arise from the soul of a living being. Even the most primitive form of speaking can arise only from a being with an astral body. Accordingly, we must also look into the origin and the nature of the *astral body* itself.

The astral body was given to our human ancestors by lofty hierarchical beings during the third planetary existence of our Earth, the *old Moon*. Speech, guilt, the astral body, and the Moon phase of the Earth evidently all have something to do with the third commandment!

The Law of Recapitulation

Before we take a closer look at the previously mentioned concepts, however, we would like to draw the reader's attention to a special law. This law can help us come to a better understanding of the oldest stages of the Earth, which are exceedingly difficult to grasp with our modern way of thinking. We already discussed the *Law of Historical Symmetry*, which in our time is relevant mainly with respect to the post-Atlantean cultural epochs. The *Law of Recapitulation* is a similar kind of law, but is applicable to every phase of the Earth's evolution. This law is derived from a special principle that forms an inherent part of the whole process of evolution, the principle namely, that each new phase must begin with a short recapitulation of older planetary phases. At the beginning of each new phase of evolution the essence of earlier phases must be repeated once more—at a faster pace, and raised to a higher level, befitting the new conditions. This is a general rule, a law that applies to the entire process of evolution: the *Law of Recapitulation*. And it is because of this law that we can find certain similarities between older and more recent cycles of the Earth.

To begin with, this law makes it possible to recognize similarities between the large planetary stages and the early phases of the Earth's development,[77] that is to say, between:

Ancient Saturn	—	the Polarian age
Ancient Sun	—	the Hyperborean age
Ancient Moon	—	the Lemurian age

What had worked cosmically during Saturn, Sun, and Moon evolution manifests as the forming forces shaping human life in the corresponding earliest phases of the Earth. And, incidentally, because of these three initial recapitulations, the Earth phase came fully into its own only in the Atlantean age—the fourth phase of the Earth.

Likewise, because of the *Law of Recapitulation*, we can discover similarities between the previously mentioned earliest phases of the Earth and the more recent post-Atlantean epochs,[78] that is to say, between the first four stages of the Earth and the first four post-Atlantean cultural epochs:

Polarian	—	the ancient Indian culture
Hyperborean	—	the ancient Persian culture
Lemurian	—	the Chaldean–Egyptian culture
Atlantean	—	the Greco–Roman culture

In the post-Atlantean era we find these cosmic impulses working more within the cultural life of humankind through the guidance of the mysteries. In other words, the forming forces that had shaped the *outer lives* of human beings during the Polarian, Hyperborean, Lemurian, and Atlantean times now affect the *inner lives* of the people living in the corresponding cultural epochs. And, again, one could say that, because of these four initial recapitulations, the post-Atlantean era is only coming fully into its own in our present fifth cultural epoch.

Owing to the *Law of Recapitulation*, we are in a better position to recognize the specific conditions during the various stages of evolution. We can now, for example, contemplate the more recent Egyptian culture, while allowing the older Lemurian age to sound its revelations in the background; and, vice versa, we can get to know the (much) older Moon existence by "listening" to what the more recent Lemurian epoch can tell us. We will keep all this in mind as we now turn our attention to those phases of evolution that have a specific connection to the third commandment.

THE OLD MOON AND THE HUMAN ASTRAL BODY

Our human ancestors received an astral body through the activity of the *Spirits of Movement* (the *Dynamis*) on old Moon. But, before this astral body could be assimilated, their etheric and physical bodies had to be prepared. Accordingly, lofty spiritual beings began working from the astral world on the light ether forces. This activity brought about a differentiation of the light ether; some of it remained *light ether* and some of it was transformed into *sound ether*. This more refined type of ether gave rise to various distinct life forms in the outer world, and to a rudimentary formation of the different organs in human beings. At the same time the whole physical structure of the Moon became denser than it had been on ancient Sun: in addition to warmth and gases, carried over from Saturn and Sun respectively, fluids now emerged.

This densification did, however, decelerate the general pace of development. For some spiritual beings this slower pace was unsuitable. And so, it became necessary that the cosmic planetary body, which at the beginning of this phase had emerged as the reincarnation of the old Sun, be split in two. One part became the reborn, more purified Sun and the other became the actual new planetary body, which we could call the Moon–Earth (because in this stage the Moon was still one with the Earth), or simply *old Moon*. The Sun now consisted of warmth, light, and gases, and became the new sphere of action for those higher beings that were developing more quickly. The lower spiritual beings and our human ancestors remained on the

Moon–Earth. This new planetary body began receiving the influences of the Sun *from the outside* for the first time and the further course of development continued at a slower pace, more suited to the needs of its inhabitants.

We mentioned that our human ancestors received an astral body during the ancient Moon existence. This meant that, for the first time, feelings, passions, and desires became an integral part of the developing human beings. As they became dimly aware of an inner world inside themselves and an external world outside themselves they now began to form mental pictures as well. A rudimentary form of the later *nerve–sense system* now emerged, mainly in the form of—in the words of Rudolf Steiner—an "extension of the senses into the interior of the human body."[79]

The human *rhythmical system* also evolved on old Moon. Certain processes were now taking place in our human ancestors, processes that, on the one hand, can be compared to breathing, but, on the other hand, to metabolism and excretion as well.[80] These "breathing–metabolism" processes could now, because of the newly acquired astral body, give rise to primitive sensations of satisfaction and repulsion; and, for the first time human beings had the possibility of expressing such feelings through sounds, albeit sounds that could not yet be perceived with physical sense organs.

Our ancestors on old Moon began to develop a rudimentary *metabolic–limb system* as well, and were now able to move about. From time to time, they were exposed to the Sun's influences, whereas at other times they turned away from the Sun. This gave rise to two alternating states of human consciousness: one a dull, sleeplike state and the other a slightly more animate one. We may envision the former level of consciousness as existing somewhere between our present-day falling asleep and dying; and the latter one as somewhere between our waking up and being born. Thus the astral body also brought about a very early form of death, albeit very different from death as we know it today. It was more like a kind of self-regeneration, linked to the disposal of those parts that had been rendered useless.[81] Only much later, when the whole body needed to be disposed of, can we really speak of death.

And so, on old Moon our ancestors gradually became *sixfold* beings. They now had a physical body consisting of *three* elements: a warmth structure from the Saturn period, a gaseous structure from the Sun period, and a fluid structure, added during the Moon phase. The etheric body had *two* components: the light ether from old Sun and the new sound ether. The astral body represented the new *single* component human beings had received on the Moon. We should, of course, not envision these six components as spatially separated entities, but rather as interacting, interpenetrating elements.[82]

The picture we have painted thus far can provide an adequate point of departure for our explorations into the origins and the meaning of the third commandment. But, if we want to understand its true significance, we have to take a closer look yet at the cosmic events that occurred on old Moon.

The aforementioned developments on old Moon took place, for the most part, against the backdrop of a well-ordered spiritual universe. But these harmonious circumstances were precipitously disturbed by certain Moon-beings, who had not reached their intended level of development, who had remained behind in evolution. They tried to bring part of the substance of the Moon under their own power in an attempt to create their own world, independent of the Sun. They turned against the influences of the Sun and of the Sun-beings who maintained the cosmic order. This act of rebellion, this *revolt in Heaven*, as it is referred to in Anthroposophy, was a serious cosmic struggle for the governance of the old Moon, which, in the end, was won by the Sun-beings. The result was that the rebellious Moon-beings had to submit to the Sun-beings and, from then on, had to regulate their activities in accordance with the ordinances of these Sun-beings.[83]

Of all the beings living on the Moon at that time, our human ancestors were most impacted by the *war in Heaven*. Even to this day our astral bodies carry traces of this cosmic battle, because it also caused a kind of struggle, an inner discord, one might say, in the human astral body; and this, in turn, affected the etheric and the physical bodies as well. It also gave rise to the onset of the aforementioned regeneration processes, during which parts of the physical body had to be periodically disposed of once these had become imperfect, deficient, and transitory.

We can detect an echo of all this in the third commandment as well. This commandment spoke out against "taking God's name in vain," and the concept *guilt* was linked to such an act. These are concepts that, ultimately, have their origin in the events that occurred during ancient Moon existence, because the *cosmic rebellion* left certain dispositions in our astral bodies, such as a tendency toward isolation, separation, and fragmentation. Our astral bodies inherited these traits, giving us the possibility—and oftentimes the urge—to oppose and resist the divine intentions for cooperation and harmony on Earth. And, just as the Moon-beings became guilty by participating in the cosmic rebellion that destroyed the harmony in the universe, so also can human beings become *guilty* by committing acts that work against cooperative harmony in the world. When human beings find themselves in this kind of discordance with the cosmos, they are no longer in harmony with *God's Name* either. It is this discord with the divine world that was expressed in the third commandment as "taking God's Name in vain."

Three Key Concepts of the Astral World

We have postulated that the third commandment was introduced to support the healthy development of the astral body in human beings. And so, to better understand the third commandment, we must take a closer look at the origin and nature of the astral body. We know that the ancient mysteries were the guardians of an elaborate knowledge concerning the human astral body and the astral world, a knowledge that is intimately connected to the world of sounds and tones. Therefore, in order to learn more, not only about the astral body, but also about the aforementioned innate relationship between the third commandment and human speech, we must get to know this ancient mystery knowledge. It was primarily based on three key concepts:

1. the Music (or Harmony) of the Spheres
2. the True Name of a Being
3. the Unutterable (or Ineffable) Name of God

These concepts refer to certain experiences that mostly fall outside our normal, everyday consciousness. We *can*, however, describe such concepts in words and comprehend them with our faculty of thinking. But to actually become aware of them, we would have to follow a specific inner path of schooling. Rudolf Steiner has frequently referred to this path and to the three higher levels of consciousness that can thus be attained.[84] We may best understand these higher states of consciousness as the continuation of a sequence that starts with *sleep consciousness*, followed by *dream consciousness* and then *waking consciousness*—each representing an increased level of wakefulness. This sequence would then be continued with the previously mentioned higher levels of consciousness, namely, *imagination, inspiration*, and *intuition*. The things we can know with these higher forms of consciousness are always present and active, even though they are hidden from our normal, everyday waking consciousness; just as the things we know with our waking consciousness are normally hidden from our dream and sleep consciousness.

Our normal *waking* consciousness has a special connection to the *first* commandment, which directs our attention to the divine, but also provides the basis for our everyday, physical life on Earth. With *imaginative* consciousness one can become aware of, and develop insight in, the world of the etheric. This first level of a consciousness that is higher than our normal day consciousness has a pictorial character and can thus be seen in relation to the *second* commandment. With *inspirative* consciousness one can become aware of the astral world. It does not manifest in pictures; but with this form of consciousness one can understand the language of the soul world. This is why it has a specific connection to the *third* commandment. The highest level of consciousness is *intuitive* consciousness with which one can penetrate the spiritual essence of another being. There is a subtle connection between this level of consciousness and the *fourth* commandment.

It is also important to know, however, that each of these stages of higher consciousness first appears in our everyday consciousness through soul impressions. These impressions can occur in relation to all three higher forms of consciousness; but, in the context of the third commandment, these soul impressions would be of the *inspirative* kind. In the following pages we will explore the three key concepts of the astral world, while pointing out instances of how one can begin to attain such inspirative impressions, both in the past and today.

The Harmony of the Spheres

To become familiar with the three key concepts of the astral world, it can be helpful to observe them in connection to the kingdoms of nature on Earth. Firstly, with respect to the *Harmony of the Spheres*, we must turn our attention to the mineral kingdom that surrounds us in nature. In doing so, we would do well to pursue an indication contained in the designation *Harmony (or Music) of the Spheres*, by observing particularly how sounds and tones manifest within the mineral kingdom. (Incidentally, the etheric forces that emerged on old Moon, the *sound ether* forces, also point, by way of their very designation, to a world of sounds and tones.)

The sounds of the mineral realm are generated by the forces of the astral world, working through the sound ether of the Earth; this activity itself is not perceptible to our senses. But when the sound ether, in turn, works on the mineral world, this becomes perceptible as audible sound. Because this twofold process is, in reality, perceived as a single one, we can say that the forces of the astral world essentially create the natural sounds of the mineral kingdom. If we listen inwardly to such sounds in nature, we may be able to experience that the mineral kingdom speaks an inner language through these sounds. The ability to understand this inner language exists *potentially* in every human being, and can be further developed through the aforementioned meditative path of self-development. The higher level of consciousness required to hear this inner language, is the inspirative consciousness, as described above.

When continental plates are shifting, when volcanoes erupt with subterranean rumblings, when avalanches come roaring down the mountains, when stony mounts in the desert are crackling at night, we can hear the astral forces of the cosmos mightily at work. Just listen to the crashing of waves coming ashore, the foaming of waterfalls, the gurgling of vortexes in river rapids, the sputtering and bubbling of mud pools and geysers, or the rattling and splattering of hail and rain! The cosmic essence of nature speaks in all these sounds, just as it does in the whistling and howling of the winds and in clapping thunderbolts and lightning flashes.

By listening to the sounds of nature and contemplating how these impressions affect us, we can begin to understand how the astral world works in these sounds. But how is this related to the *Harmony of the Spheres*?

In the sounds of the so-called lifeless mineral nature we can, even today, experience something of the workings of the astral world. However, our impressions today are but dim in comparison to the mighty experiences that our early ancestors still had when they were exposed to the sounds in nature. We read in Genesis (3:8) that Adam had what one might call an inspirative awareness, when he heard "the voice of the LORD God, walking in the garden in the cool of the day." In other words, Adam perceived the voice of God in the elements (in some translations it says "in the breeze of the day," which is closer to the original Hebrew).

There are people who can, even today, under special circumstances, have impressions in nature that may best be described as inwardly audible perceptions. Such impressions are in reality inspirative perceptions. Although these inspirative impressions are not of a character of inspirative consciousness, which can only be acquired through a path of self-development, they nevertheless provide access to the first stage of Inspiration. We can think, for example, of the *audible silence* one might be able to experience in a snowy landscape on a quiet, sunny day in winter. If we are able to let nature work on us in this way through the majestic impressions of the sun, the sea, the mountains, or the stars, we may be able to feel something in our soul that could indeed be described as an inwardly audible perception, an experience that, moreover, frequently elicits a *moral* response within us as well. Even Kant could not escape the awe-inspiring impression the starry expanse of heaven made on him, and searched in vain for concepts capable of interpreting this experience.[85]

The wisdom of the cosmos does not manifest in audible sounds. The secrets of the cosmos are resonating silently, as it were, and are audible only to inspirative consciousness. Pythagoras had a deep insight in the hidden wisdom of the cosmos.[86] He tried to call forth an understanding of inspirative perception in his students, by introducing them to the wondrous world of numbers and the numeric relationships that create harmony both in the universe and in musical sounds.[87] By nurturing an understanding of the inaudible harmonies of such numeric relationships in his students, Pythagoras aimed to build a bridge from the audible musical sounds of the *outer* world to an *inner* inspirative awareness of the secrets of the cosmos, in other words, to the *Harmony of the Spheres*.

What, then, is this inspirative experience of the *Harmony of the Spheres*? To find an answer to this question we should first try to imagine the audible sounds of the outer world on the one hand and the inaudible, inwardly perceptible sounds of the so-called lifeless mineral world on the other hand. This totality of impressions can then point the way toward this all-encompassing, fundamental cosmic principal, which has its origin in the world of the stars. And it is this principle that can evoke both *musical* and *moral* responses in human beings.

Contemplations such as these can open a door to a better understanding of the first key principle of the astral world, the *Harmony of the Spheres*. Since this principle can only be experienced in those kingdoms of nature where the astral forces work exclusively from the outside, we will also briefly turn to the plant kingdom. But there is a slight difference; for, unlike in the mineral kingdom, these external forces working out of the astral world can actually find a delicate point of contact in the plant kingdom—namely, in the flowers. In mineral nature there is no such point of contact; there, the external astral forces work randomly. But in the plant kingdom these forces actually play a delicate role in the forming of the flowers.

Astral forces are, of course, not part of the plant kingdom as such. Its realm is first and foremost the etheric. Plants have an etheric body that follows the order of the sun, through the influence of the seasons and the rhythms of day and night. The *green leaves* of the plants react to the sun through the working of the *light ether*, and—this will be elaborated in a subsequent chapter—the *life ether* forces manifest in the *fruit* and the *seed* of the plants. But it is indeed in the realm of the *flowers*, in their relation to the *sound ether*, that something of the astral world is expressed. When we allow ourselves to intimately observe the wondrous beauty of the fragrant and colorful flowers and let them work on us, we may well sense something of the working of these external astral forces. This is why the world of the flowers, in its infinite variety of shapes and expressions, also can lead us to an inspirative, though inaudible, experience of the *Harmony of the Spheres*.

The True Name of a Being and the Origin of Language

These reflections on the mineral nature and the world of the flowers should have brought us somewhat closer to the first key concept of the astral world, the *Harmony of the Spheres*. As we now continue on this path with similar reflections about the two higher kingdoms of nature, we no longer come to the Harmony of the Spheres, but instead to the other two key concepts of the astral world: the *True name of a Being* and the *Unutterable Name of God*. This is because sentient beings have their own astral bodies; consequently their relationship to the astral world is different from that of minerals and plants, which are only exposed to *external* astral forces.

Acquiring an astral body invariably is accompanied by a degree of distress and pain, because this development can only occur when a being is separated from the universal astral world and thus can no longer fully participate in this world. Separation from the astral world also leads to the first stirrings of inner sensations. As mentioned, our human ancestors received their own astral bodies on old Moon; experienced inner emotions for the first time; and could bring forth sounds, albeit sounds that were not yet physically audible. That became possible only at a much later point in time, namely in the Lemurian era.

In the Lemurian time the early human beings experienced the world in a way we could call clairaudible. This way of "listening" can best be understood as a kind of instinctive, inspirative perceiving of sounds and tones. By hearing and speaking such sounds and tones, similar emotions began to resonate in the listener and in the speaker. This is how our Lemurian ancestors communicated with each other; moreover, they did so in a primeval language that was the same all over the Earth. The Bible refers to a last residue of this universal language: "And the whole Earth was of one language and of one speech" (Gen. 11:1).

Human consciousness in those olden times was focused not so much on impressions from the outer world, but more on the inner soul stirrings of the astral body, such as longing, joy, grief, fear. These emotions could be expressed through sounds and tones that could instantly be grasped by another listening soul. Going even further back in time, we encounter a phase in which human beings did not perceive any outer sounds at all, but instead had the ability to penetrate deeply into the inner sounds of another human soul. Hearing this language was an inspirative, clairaudible way of perceiving, allowing the listener to penetrate deeply into the soul of another sentient being. Our human ancestors thus could experience and perceive a different sound for each living being, a sound that expressed for them the particular soul state of that being. They were, in fact, hearing the *True Name of a Being*.

"And out of the ground the LORD God formed every beast of the field and every fowl of the air; and brought them unto Adam to see what he would call them: and whatsoever Adam called every living creature that was the name thereof." These words in the Bible book Genesis (2:19) give us a compact and precise illustration of what we have just now attempted to describe. Adam, the Lemurian human being, was still so intimately connected with the universal cosmos that he could hear the astral tones of the living beings in front of him and thus was able to give each one its *True Name* in the archetypal language. It is important to note in this context that plants and minerals did *not* receive their names in this way, only beings with their own astral bodies.

We may summarize, then, that meditative contemplations about the mineral kingdom and about the world of flowers can bring us closer to the concept of the *Harmony of the Spheres*; likewise, that meditative reflections about beings with their own astral bodies can open a door to the concept of the *True Name of a Being*. This raises the question: can we find a similar pathway to the third key concept of the astral world, the *Ineffable Name of God*?

The Ineffable Name of God

In olden times human beings experienced God's voice in the sounds of nature. But the divine, all-encompassing oneness that is expressed in the *Ineffable Name of God* transcends even the *Harmony of the Spheres*. It encompasses not only the entire soulless nature but also all the sentient beings. This divine archetype, which exists in every corner of the universe, cannot be communicated by outer sounds of any kind. Its qualitative essence, moreover, also surpasses any inspirative experiences human beings are capable of having. It was only in Lemurian times that our ancestors began to bring forth, and perceive, audible sounds. That could only happen, however, because they now had their own, individualized, inner experiences, and thus were no longer fully united with the divine oneness; they could no longer experience the all-encompassing universe inwardly as before. This meant, in turn, that from then on it was no longer possible to express this divine unity, even in the archetypal language. Consequently, whenever one tries to approach this divine unity, the *Ineffable Name of God*, via the *Harmony of the Spheres*, all *outer* sounds grow silent. And, likewise, whenever one tries to approach it through the inner language of the *True Name of a Being*, all *inner* inspirative sounds grow silent.

We should, of course, not conclude that this *Ineffable Name of God* was too difficult to pronounce. It was something that simply *could* not be uttered; neither in any outer language, nor in the inspirative inner language. The true being of God exists on an even higher spiritual level, essentially beyond the reach of human beings. Any sound used by human beings to designate God can, by its very nature, only be an approximation. (We will explore this topic further in the section "The Name of God").

Human beings may be able to learn something about the universal astral world by experiencing the *Harmony of the Spheres* or about the essential nature of sentient beings by perceiving the *True name of a Being*. But it is only in rare, special moments, when lifted far above these realms, that they might possibly perceive a glimpse of the *Ineffable Name of God*, and of the all-encompassing wisdom and power of the creative source of the astral world.

The Astral Body and Human Speech

We observed earlier that the *cosmic rebellion*, which took place on old Moon, had a far-reaching impact on the continuing evolution of the Earth. Human beings were also affected by this revolt in Heaven, particularly with respect to the development of their astral bodies. As a result, they became more vulnerable to certain temptations. And what is more, human beings were now potentially capable of *opposing* the universal cosmic order through their actions. This could essentially happen in three different ways.

First, human beings could succumb to their desire for power, by snatching objects from their legitimate place in the world order so as to bring these objects under their own dominance, thereby imitating on a much smaller scale the cosmic ambitions of the Moon-beings. The eighth commandment, *You shall not steal*, was intended to protect people against the *astral* dimension of the remnants of the cosmic rebellion.

Second, human beings could turn away from the beneficial influence of the Sun's life-giving forces. This would expose them to excessive death forces. The sixth commandment, *You shall not kill*, was intended to protect people against the *etheric* dimension of the remnants of the cosmic rebellion.

Third, human beings could use the innate magical powers, active in human speech at that time, for selfish ends. This misuse could potentially bring about grand-scale devastation and destruction in the physical world. Even though this was no longer (to that extent) the case in the time of Moses, the third commandment was intended to protect people against the *physical* dimension of these remnants of the cosmic rebellion. This is the aspect we will concentrate on presently.

Again, we can come to a better understanding of the situation on ancient Moon if, in accordance with the *Law of Recapitulation*, we take a closer look at the conditions during the more recent Lemurian era. Just as the early human beings on old Moon had been profoundly affected by the cosmic rebellion of the Moon-beings, our Lemurian ancestors also had an encounter with certain spiritual beings. These were beings that had not reached their intended level of development and now tried to accelerate the pace of human development with the alluring prospect of knowledge and independence. In biblical terminology, this is described as Lucifer, in the form of the serpent who opposed the divine order, tempting Adam and Eve. These circumstances brought about the fall of humankind. As a consequence, human beings were now exposed to illness and death. But, whereas on ancient Moon only *parts* of the human body had to be periodically renewed, in the Lemurian time the *whole body* had to be disposed of during the human death process.

In the beginning of the Lemurian age the hardening impact of these death forces threatened to overwhelm all life on Earth. It was crucial that these forces be removed from the Earth. This is what occurred when the present-day Moon split off the Earth; for, along with the Moon's substance, these hardening forces left the Earth, thereby allowing all life on Earth to be renewed and rejuvenated.[88] From then on, human beings experienced the influences of *two* external planetary bodies—the Sun and the Moon. And, as though echoing this new cosmic polarity, the two human genders emerged for the first time on Earth. Before that time our human ancestors had been hermaphrodite, that is to say, both male and female.[89] Now each human being gradually appeared either male or female, and, for the first time, the participation of both sexes was required for the process of human reproduction.

With the beginning of physical birth and death, human beings now began to experience the recurring process of *reincarnation* as well, resulting in two alternating forms of existence: one within an earthly human body and another one in the spiritual world. As a further consequence of these events, human beings became subject to the laws of *karma*, because they could now become *guilty* on account of their actions—those that then needed to be compensated for in a next life. We note, then, that karma and reincarnation became part of human life during the same time period, and because of the same set of circumstances.

These ongoing Lemurian developments also brought about changes in the way human beings communicated with one another. Whereas on old Moon our human ancestors could perceive a purely inspirative language, the development of the physical body had in the meantime advanced to the point where the Lemurian people were able to bring forth and perceive audible sounds.[90]

This earliest form of speaking was a direct, unrestrained expression of people's inner sensations. Our Lemurian ancestors were, indeed, subject to wild, primitive emotions. Moreover, they could use this speaking to profoundly affect their fellow creatures and their surroundings, because they were able to make use of the innate magical powers active in human speech at that time. We can hardly imagine today how human speech could possibly bring about such effects. But we can still detect a faint residue of this kind of speech magic in the "evoking of spirits" or the "cursing of enemies" in more recent times. Think, for instance, of the biblical story of Balaam (Num. 22–24) who was sent to *curse* the Israelite nation!

In the beginning of the Lemurian time this kind of speaking had, for the most part, a beneficial effect on the recipients. But that began to change when people came to be increasingly influenced by luciferic beings. By using the magical powers in their speaking, some even forged powerful connections with these beings. Such connections could be established based on people's knowledge of the *True Name* of these laggard spiritual beings. By magically calling up their *True Name*, some people were actually able to connect with the astral impulses of these beings and could then use their tremendous powers for selfish ends. One could call this kind of misuse of the magical powers in speech the "taking in vain" of the *Name of a Being*.

When laggard spiritual beings worked on the human astral body in this way, people became as though possessed. They were then able to use the strength of these beings and thus acquire magical powers over sentient beings and over nature. Through their speech they could evoke magical effects, causing destruction and death all around. This caused considerable karmic *guilt* for those souls who succumbed to these practices. Such misuse of speech was rampant in the latter part of the Lemurian age and, in the end, had disastrous consequences for humanity and for the whole Earth. Seen from a spiritual point of view, it was one of the factors that led to the destruction of the Lemurian continent through fire and volcanic eruptions.[91]

In the time of Moses these things were known in the mystery centers. It was known that the same kind of impulses that had been active in Lemurian times—the positive as well as the negative—were once again having an impact in the Egyptian–Chaldean cultural epoch. The positive forces, which in the Lemurian age had guided the *outer* course of events, formed in the Egyptian time the basis for the *inner* lives of human beings, as well as for the knowledge cultivated within the mystery centers. But, at the same time, specific remnants of the destructive speech forces were also still active in Egypt in the time of Moses.[92] The Israelites may indeed well have experienced the fiery glow around Mount Sinai, which accompanied the mighty inspiration of the Ten Commandments, as a cautionary reminder of the fires that brought an end to Lemuria!

The third commandment admonished the Israelites not to abuse their power of speech, for example, by using the Name of the Godhead "in vain." For, although human speech in the time of Moses had lost much of its original magical powers, the danger still existed that people could become *guilty* through misuse of speech. This kind of misuse would have been harmful to them, right down to their physical bodies. The third commandment was introduced to help prevent this from happening.

The Name of God

Up to now we have mainly explored the consequences of wrong use of speech in general. But the third commandment refers in particular to the problem of using *God's Name* in vain. Why was this considered an offense that, elsewhere in the Bible, even called for the death penalty?[93] What is the true meaning of *God's Name*, and why could this Name not be used "in vain" in the time of Moses?[94] Although there are indications that it was also forbidden to speak the names of other gods,[95] it was first and foremost the divine name of Yahweh that had to be approached with the utmost care. This name was known to the High Priest alone and could only be uttered by him once a year in the Holy of Holies of the Jewish Temple—and even then only in the context of prayer—on the Day of Atonement. It is generally assumed that the knowledge of the pronunciation of the divine name was, therefore, forever lost with the destruction of the Temple in Jerusalem in AD 70. The Hebrew language traditionally had only used consonants in written language. Hence, all that was known of the name of God, since the destruction of the Temple, was the letters *YHWH*. This is commonly referred to as the *Tetragrammaton*, which means "four lettered" in Greek. Later attempts to project the vowels of the word "Adonay" onto the four consonants, led to the questionable reconstruction of the name "Jehovah." Most scholars today dispute this conclusion and instead accept "Yahweh" as the most likely approximation of the (essentially inexpressible) divine name.[96]

But why was it considered so detrimental to use this name? Even to this very day, the Tetragrammaton (*YHWH*) in the Torah and other sacred Jewish texts and prayers is never read or spoken as "Yahweh," but as "Adonay" instead. Similarly, following a longstanding tradition, most English Bible translations also avoid using the word "Yahweh," rendering it instead by the more impersonal designation, "LORD." What was it about the name "Yahweh" that gave rise to traditions such as these?

It had long been known in the mysteries that an even higher spiritual being was the true inspiration behind the God who was called "Yahweh," namely the Christ-being—the divine "I AM"-being. In the words of Rudolf Steiner, "For the Christ was indeed living in Yahweh, the Yahweh–God, but as a reflection of himself. As the Moon reflects the sunlight, so did Yahweh reflect the being who then lived as Christ."[97] One can even discover a linguistic connection between the Tetragrammaton and the words that Moses heard out of the burning bush, "Ehjeh asher ehjeh," ("I am The I AM"); both are derivatives of the verb to be.[98] This confirms, even linguistically, that something of the true meaning, something of the essence of the "I AM" lives in the name of God—YHWH. One could even say that this true name *is*, in fact, "*I AM.*"

Speaking the name of spiritual beings invokes something of their essence, their true nature. The divine, macrocosmic essence of the "I AM"-godhead was too powerful for human beings living at that time; it would have overpowered their emerging "I"-forces. God's name, therefore, could not be uttered by the unprepared. Such an experience would have brought an element of disharmony into their inner being, because their own "I"-forces were not yet mature enough to be able to take in the full spiritual weight of the divine "I AM" in a healthy way. The Hebrew people, in particular, first needed to develop their own "I"-consciousness before they would be able to recognize and experience the divine "I" in God. Only the high priest had been sufficiently prepared to invoke the essence of the Yahweh Godhead by speaking the divine name on the Day of Atonement. This is why the name of God initially had to remain "unutterable" for everyone else.

Christ and the Third Commandment

How does Christ relate to the third commandment? This commandment focused on conscientious use of speech. Although Jesus did not mention the third commandment as such, all his words attest to the power of the spoken word. This kind of power, however, was very different from the forces at work in the speech of the Lemurian people; for the Lemurian speech magic had been generated directly from the astral body. In the fourth post-Atlantean epoch both the outer circumstances and the constitution of the human astral body had undergone profound changes. Human speech could no longer bring about such magical effects. But faint echoes of the old speech magic could still be detected at times, for instance in the swearing of oaths. This is why Jesus implored people not to evoke the intervention of higher powers when swearing an oath, "Swear not at all; neither by Heaven...nor by the Earth....But let your communication be, Yea, yea; Nay, nay: for whatsoever is more than these comes of evil" (Matt. 5:34–37). Henceforth, the earnestness of an oath had to be guaranteed by the human being, not by other powers. The power of the word now had to be grounded in the human "I."

The vitality of Jesus' words was qualitatively different from the magical speech forces of the Lemurian era; we can no longer use the word "magic" to describe this new quality. We must instead use words like "authority" or "power," following the example of Matthew (7:29), "For he taught them as one having authority," and Luke (4:32), "For his word was with power." This power in Jesus' words no longer came from the astral body, but now was grounded in the "I AM" and could therefore manifest itself in the forgiving of sins and in the renewal of life forces—this in direct contrast to the often detrimental impact of the magical speech forces of the Lemurian age.

We can find accounts in the New Testament that bear witness to the way Jesus' words affected his surroundings. His words could, for example, have a calming influence on nature, on the wind and the sea.[99] But the authority in his words did not in any way aim to circumvent the laws of nature. Christ's words, rather, had a harmonizing influence on nature because they arose from his all-encompassing knowledge of the *Harmony of the Spheres*. His words could also have an impact on the world of the soul and of the spirit, in other words, on people and even on demons. This was the case when some of his apostles received new names,[100] or when he released unclean demonic spirits from a person.[101] On these occasions Christ's words arose from his intimate knowledge of the *True Name of a Being* (and hence the true names of certain demons as well).

But even under such circumstances Jesus carefully avoided anything that could be construed as speaking the *Ineffable Name of God*. Only on one occasion did Jesus reveal in a few brief words that the meaning of this third key concept of the astral world was known to him. When speaking about his approaching death Jesus said, "Father, glorify Your Name."[102] Instantly, the universe responded with a thunderclap—or rather, that was how most of those present experienced this answer from above. But for some it awakened an inspirative level of consciousness that made them say, "An Angel spoke to him." Only

John the evangelist, who had achieved an advanced level of consciousness, heard a voice from Heaven, "I have both glorified it, and will glorify it again." It is important to note, however, that even on this occasion the *Ineffable Name of God* was not actually revealed.

Such passages in the Gospels appear in a new light when seen in relation to the three key concepts that were taught in the old mystery schools concerning the astral world. It then becomes clear that Christ gave a whole new impulse to the power of the spoken word, an impulse that can now also begin to work in human speech for the good in the world.

But it is not only human *speech* that underwent such a metamorphosis. The whole aspect of human *guilt*—the other concept introduced in the third commandment ("For the LORD will not hold him guiltless...")—also takes on a different form because of Christ's incarnating on Earth.

The *possibility* of becoming guilty is an inescapable consequence of human freedom. Fortunately, we are also granted the opportunity to compensate for the mistakes we make. Because of the laws of karma our missteps can gradually and appropriately be redeemed in subsequent earthly lives. If we understand karma in this way—instead of viewing it as a stern form of predestination—we can sense divine grace at work in it, allowing us to gradually make amends for our inevitable mistakes until, eventually, we may truly live in harmony with the cosmos.

Yet, even after all our efforts to compensate for our karmic sins through many incarnations, something like a residue remains. With each sin we commit, something is generated on Earth and in the cosmos that cannot be fully redeemed by an individual human being. With the coming of Christ, and the Mystery of Golgotha, the possibility is given that this residue, this objective remnant of human sin, will no longer be a hindrance for future harmony in the cosmos.[103] Rudolf Steiner called Christ the *Lord of Karma*.[104] We will take a more in-depth look at the meaning of this concept in the chapter about the sixth commandment, but in our present context it means that Christ has become the mediator of human karma in our time. Christ himself is now the new balancing force within the realm of human karma, a force that, ultimately, will lead to the true redemption of human sin. This is why he can, already during his life on Earth, forgive or redeem sins (Matt. 9:2); why he is the true recipient of things people do (or neglect to do) to other human beings;[105] and why he can say that all human deeds will, in the end, be accounted for within the totality of cosmic sin.[106]

We have pointed out that, in consequence of certain events occurring during the Lemurian age, human beings became capable of acquiring *knowledge* and developing *freedom*. We also observed that, simultaneously, our ancestors began *uttering sounds* for the first time and that *reincarnation* and *karma* became factors in the lives of human beings. This means that, from then on, human speech has been linked to the possibility of becoming guilty, in other words, that people can now become guilty not only on account of their deeds, but also because of what they say. Words that are spoken "in vain" can have karmic consequences and cause guilt. This is why Jesus demanded utter responsibility for every word we speak, *"But I say unto you, that every idle word that men shall speak, they shall give account thereof in the Day of Judgment. For by your words you shall be justified, and by your words you shall be condemned"* (Matt. 12:36–37). These words truly sum up how Christ has transformed the third commandment!

The Sin against the Holy Spirit

There is one striking aspect of human guilt that is of particular interest in our time. There is a specific sin that cannot be forgiven: "Wherefore I say unto you, all manner of sin and blasphemy shall be forgiven unto men: but the blasphemy against the Holy Spirit shall not be forgiven unto men. And whosoever speaks a word against the Son of man, it shall be forgiven him: but whosoever speaks against the Holy Spirit, it shall not be forgiven him, neither in this world, neither in the world to come" (Matt. 12:31–32; compare also Mark 3:28–29 and Luke 12:10).

This is a frightening notion for many people. We tend to think that, deep down, there is a spark of good in all human beings through which we eventually—even if it takes many incarnations—can overcome evil by compensating for our past sins, *all* our sins. But now it appears that one specific kind of sin can never be redeemed through karma, not even after many incarnations; that, in other words, there is no guarantee that the good will come to full fruition in every person in the end. As modern human beings we must occupy ourselves with this topic, because it has a bearing on our time, and even more so on future times; it also has a particular connection to the third commandment.

What is the "blasphemy against the Holy Spirit," and why can this sin not be forgiven? Most people have only a vague notion of what the Holy Spirit is. This is, in a roundabout way, the result of a decision that was made during the Council of Constantinople[107] in the year AD 869, the consequences of which have cast a long shadow over the spiritual development of modern humanity. At this Council it was decreed that the human being was no longer to be regarded as a threefold being, consisting of body, soul, *and spirit*. In other words, the spirit of the human being was "abolished"—Rudolf Steiner's expression—during this Council.[108] Consequently, from that time onward, the threefold nature of the human being has become ever more difficult to recognize. By losing sight of the spiritual in the human being, the concept of the Holy Spirit gradually became more elusive as well; for the microcosm (the human being) is an earthly reflection of the macrocosm (the divine universe), or put differently, humanity was created "in God's image" (Gen. 1:27). Accordingly, we can sense something of the Father God in our physical body; we can discover a path to the Son God in our soul; but, since the year 869, there is no knowledge-based foundation in ourselves to know the third member of the Trinity, the Holy Spirit; for, the Holy Spirit can only be understood by recognizing that this macrocosmic being is represented microcosmically in the human spirit. And so, the denunciation of the *human* spirit has also obscured our understanding of the *Divine* Spirit.

This is the situation today; but humanity's understanding of the Holy Spirit had actually grown steadily until the aftereffects of the Council of Constantinople began to cloud that understanding. In olden times knowledge of the Holy Spirit existed only within the walls of the mystery centers; everyone else would, at most, have been given glimpses of it in the form of stories and pictures. Even in the Old Testament we do not find any mention of the Holy Spirit. The word "spirit" is used repeatedly, but with a different meaning, as can be affirmed from the appropriate biblical context.[109] In the New Testament, in Paul's letter to the Hebrews, we read that in pre-Christian times the High Priest celebrated a special service once a year in the *Holy of Holies* of the tabernacle, during which he had a particular spiritual experience. What he experienced there could not be revealed to the common people, but it had to do with the Holy Spirit.[110] In those early days, only the High Priest and the initiates had an awareness of the existence of the Holy Spirit.

In a second phase we encounter a wider, but still restricted, circle of people who had an awareness of the concept of the Holy Spirit. The New Testament mentions, in connection with the birth of Jesus, that the Holy Spirit "came upon" Mary (Luke 1:35), "filled" Elizabeth (Luke 1:41) and "was upon" Simeon (Luke 2:25). This encounter with the Holy Spirit sparked in them a new understanding of the coming of Christ, an insight that they then felt compelled to relate to others in exalted words. But this insight remained, for the time being, only with a small number of people.

We can distinguish the beginning of a third phase thirty years later, with the baptism in the Jordan, at which time the Holy Spirit descended like a dove upon Jesus and "abode upon him" (John 1:32–33, Luke 3:21–22). After his baptism Christ began speaking openly about the workings of the Holy Spirit.

Finally, we hear that more and more people were "filled with the Holy Spirit." This happened initially during the Festival of Pentecost—the first one celebrated after Christ's death (Acts 2:1–12). After having been filled with the Holy Spirit, people were suddenly able to understand the apostles as though they were speaking in their own language. This is known as the mystery of the *Glossolalia*, the speaking in tongues. In this speaking the all-encompassing truth of the Holy Spirit, the "Spirit of truth" (John 14:17, 15:26), was revealed publicly for the first time.

This event at Pentecost brought a new, all-connecting, communal impulse, capable of overcoming the divisiveness and isolation that humanity had lived with ever since the proverbial "confusion of tongues" at the tower of Babel. Thus a new sense of human fellowship emerged from the shared experience of the *Spirit of Truth*; for the language of truth can be understood by everybody. This is the impulse of the Holy Spirit.[111]

What, then, is the Sin against the Holy Spirit? This is an inner deed someone would willfully engage in, with the aim of undermining the intended course of development—an act most people today (fortunately) are not yet capable of carrying out. To be able to make such a choice, someone would first have to achieve a very high degree of inner development indeed; because this kind of decision can only be made in full inner freedom and out of a profound understanding of the truth. Such a person would *know* that the aim of the Holy Spirit is the cultivation of a true fellowship of humankind, made up of free, individual human beings. If that person then would proceed to deliberately act against this intended ideal, he would, in reality, oppose the impulse of the Holy Spirit. Instead of working toward developing a free fellowship of humanity, such a person's selfish aim would be one of human divisiveness, isolation, and discord. This is *the Sin against the Holy Spirit*. It is permanent and irreversible because it would not have been committed out of ignorance or heedless passion, but out of a profound insight and knowledge of the consequences of this kind of decision. This is why the sin against the Holy Spirit, in contrast to other sins, is unforgivable.[112]

Most people today have not yet developed the required level of insight, the willingness, or the ability to perpetrate the sin against the Holy Spirit. But once that time comes and someone were to decide to undertake this irrevocable sin, this could then be done by using human speech forces "in vain," that is to say, for selfish ends. In the time of Moses this was not yet possible; hence it sufficed to forbid the vain use of God's name. But in the time of Christ it became necessary to indicate more clearly that this permanent sin, the sin against the Holy Spirit, involves a willful choice that is linked to freedom, to truth, and to the forces of speech.

The *first* commandment pertains to reverence for the all-encompassing creation, for the Father God. The *second* commandment pertains to the development of the heart forces in the stream of time, to the Son God. The *third* commandment prepares people to stay clear of committing the sin against the Holy Spirit in future times.

The Transformation of the Third Commandment in our Time

How can we develop the qualities we just referred to—freedom, truth, and the conscientious use of speech—in the right way, now and in the future? How can we learn to permeate these ideals with spiritual content?

Anthroposophy is the modern science of the spirit, of the spiritual in human beings, of the hierarchical spiritual beings, but first and foremost of the Holy Spirit: this is the conclusion we can come to when we contemplate Rudolf Steiner's indications about this subject. By denouncing the spirit in Constantinople in the year AD 869, an esoteric path of development, of initiation that leads to a true understanding of the spiritual world, was eliminated from our culture. But now, more than a thousand years later, this path of initiation by the Holy Spirit can indeed be newly and appropriately enlivened through Anthroposophy. By recognizing the human *spirit* as an equal member along with *body* and *soul* within *the threefold human being* (one of the key concepts in Anthroposophy), the gateway to the Holy Spirit can also be found again.[113]

Once we have found this entry, we can—this is how Rudolf Steiner expressed it in one of his lectures—gradually be led toward a free fellowship of all humanity through "the Spirit of Truth, the Holy Spirit."[114] There, he defines the sin against the Holy Spirit as the "blasphemy against the spirit of truth and wisdom," which brings isolation and divisiveness. On the other side stands the "wisdom that can connect all people"; this "concrete" wisdom is revealed in "the true Spiritual Science." Rudolf Steiner states here unequivocally that Anthroposophy is intended as an instrument for the working of the Holy Spirit in human beings! In another lecture we hear again about this connection between Anthroposophy and the Holy Spirit. There it is stated that we can penetrate the spiritual worlds with "true, authentic Anthroposophy," a pathway that in that same lecture also is referred to as "the presence of the Holy Spirit in the world." [115] Accordingly, we can come to the insight that, through Anthroposophy, the human spirit is called upon to develop a living understanding of the *truth and wisdom that connect all people*, in other words, to carry the impulse of the Holy Spirit out into the world.

Such thoughts can touch us deeply because they carry impulses for the future! Anthroposophy, then, stands for a wisdom that is permeated with the being and the working of the Holy Spirit, a concrete wisdom that can connect all people. Can this knowledge also give us a better understanding of the central theme of the third commandment: the whole realm of human speech? In our time speech has become more and more an external tool of communication. The spoken word has lost most of its original spiritual content and power. Consequently a *command* against the vain use of speech is actually no longer required in our time. What is needed is an inner *awareness* of the way we use our speech, of how we use the spoken word; this is most important for the future development of humanity and of the Earth.

The wisdom of the Orient knew of a prophecy concerning the future development of the forces of speech. It was known that a time will come when the next Buddha, the so-called Maitreya Buddha, will work on the Earth.[116] He will not bring a new teaching to humanity, but he will be *the bearer of noble speech forces*. He will teach his pupils—and through them all of humanity—to impregnate their words with power in such a way that *goodness* will stream into the souls of the listeners. These spiritual word forces will facilitate the development of *the good* on the Earth. And, although these events are only expected to occur in a distant future time, this knowledge can, already now, give us insight into the forces that are active in our speech.[117] In other words, our speech should increasingly become like an instrument of the Holy Spirit in order to help advance the good impulses for the future.

Through our speech we stand in a special relationship to the hierarchy of the Archangels. Every night we have a meeting with Archangels.[118] But only if we learn to develop idealism in our speech can we receive healing forces through this interactive meeting with the Archangels. In the words of Rudolf Steiner, "When we use our speech in a materialistic sense only, we create a problematic relationship with the world of the Archangels in which we are meant to enter every night between falling asleep and waking up. But when we learn to recognize and maintain idealism in our speech…we can enter into the required relationship with that Archangel-being to whom we belong in the world that exists between falling asleep and waking up."[119] Such forces are necessary for the future of the Earth and of humanity.

The following verse of Rudolf Steiner was, frankly, not composed to portray present-day impulses of the third commandment, but it, nonetheless, expresses beautifully and accurately what is meant here:

> In present times on Earth
> We need renewed spiritual content
> In the words we speak.
> For, of the spoken word,
> Our soul and spirit retain
> —During the time of sleep,
> While outside the body—
> Only what relates to the spirit.

For human beings, while asleep,
Need to reach out
Into the realm of the Archangels
For conversation with them;
These, however, can only receive the spiritual content,
– Never the material content—of the words.
Failing such conversation,
We suffer harm in our entire being.[120]

4

The Fourth Commandment

Remember the Sabbath day, to keep it holy.
Six days shall you labor, and do all your work: But the seventh day is the Sabbath of the LORD your God: In it you shall not do any work,
You, nor your son, nor your daughter, your manservant, nor your maidservant, nor your cattle, nor your stranger that is within your gates:
For in six days the LORD made Heaven and Earth, the sea, and all that in them is, and rested the seventh day: wherefore the LORD blessed the Sabbath day, and hallowed it.

In the structure of this comparatively lengthy formulation we can readily distinguish four parts. The first part refers to the Sabbath as a holy day; it speaks directly to the human capacity of thinking and remembering. The second part places the Sabbath in the stream of time: a period of work must be followed by a day of rest. The third part lists the categories of people and animals who were expected to observe the Sabbath commandment. The fourth part points to the connection between the Sabbath day on Earth and the cosmic day of rest observed by the divine creative powers.[121] The careful wording of this commandment reveals a beautifully rounded structure; it begins and ends with *hallowing* ("keeping holy") the Sabbath day, reminding us of the symbol of the snake biting its own tail.

With this rounded structure the fourth commandment also rounds off the first group of commandments in which the human relationship to the divine world is regulated. In the first commandment this is done by pointing to the divine unity; in the second by prohibiting the making of idols; in the third by prohibiting the vain use of God's Name; and here, in the fourth commandment, through the institution of the Sabbath, the day of God.

The universal divine world *initially* manifests itself in the first four commandments through the Father God. In the first commandment He is the source of the all-encompassing divine unity; in the second He is the everlasting force behind time and evolution; in the third He is the judge of guilt and innocence; and here, in the fourth commandment, He is recognized as the creator of the physical world. The physical world is the realm of the Father God; He is the ground of all existence.

This macrocosmic Father God principle finds a microcosmic reflection in the human physical body, because it is structured in accordance with the same laws that govern the entire physical world. This, in turn, means that the first four commandments have a special connection to the physical body; but, within this group, the fourth commandment occupies a unique place. As we observed, the first commandment is related to that part of the physical body that emerged in germinal form on ancient Saturn, namely the *nerve–sense system*; the second commandment to the part that has its true origin on ancient Sun, namely the heart and the *rhythmical system*; and the third commandment to the part of the physical body that came into its own on ancient Moon, namely the *metabolic–limb system* and the organs for reproduction and also for speech. And, just as these three systems form a unity in the human physical body, so do the first three commandments in a sense belong together. They reflect the development of the physical body as it was successively being permeated by the etheric and then by the astral body over the course of evolution. And, just as these three bodies together provide the vehicle for the "I"-organization, so do the first three commandments form the basis for the fourth commandment.

In the fourth phase of evolution, the actual Earth existence, the physical human body had indeed evolved to the point where the "I," a true self, could be implanted in it by the lofty *Spirits of Form* (the *Exusiai*). The young, immature "I" initially was fully embedded in and protected by the physical, etheric, and astral bodies. But, within these protective sheaths, it formed the new independent spiritual essence, the individual core of the human being. Because the fourth commandment has a connection to this newest human component, it (the commandment) occupies a special place within the group of the first four commandments as well. As mentioned, these four commandments established the relationship between the human being and the divine world. But in the first three commandments this divine principle existed primarily as a distant macrocosmic entity—as the One God, the Image of God, and the Name of God. With the introduction of the Sabbath in the fourth commandment, however, this macrocosmic principle began to approach the human realm on Earth; for the principle of one day of rest per week, to be observed by human beings, can indeed be seen as an earthly expression of the divine seventh day of creation on which God "rested from all his work" (Gen 2:3). Something of this hitherto distant divine principle could now actually be incorporated into the practical, physical lives of human beings on Earth. This is what makes the fourth commandment stand out amidst the first four commandments.

Creating a Space for the "I" in the Physical Body

As we observed above, it was during our present Earth phase that the physical body could become the bearer of the "I." But something had to happen first before this newest member could be assimilated into the physical body. The physical body, in and of itself, could never have united with the spiritual entity that is the "I." A space had to be created for it. Certain elements of its physical nature had to withdraw somewhat—one could also say, *recede* or *yield* somewhat—thereby creating a neutral ground for the developing "I" to mature and become active in the human being. But this *receding* had to occur in such a way that the laws of the physical world not be contradicted or interrupted. This is a process that could only take shape during our present Earth phase, when the physical body had evolved sufficiently. Because the Earth represents the *fourth* planetary stage of evolution—and has incorporated into itself all the fruits of the preceding phases—we can distinguish four different ways in which these withdrawal processes are at work in the human physical body, which is itself the outcome of these four preceding stages.

To understand how these processes have evolved over time, let us, to begin with, take a look at the nerve–sense system that initially came into being during the Saturn existence. What appeared so long ago in embryonic form has gone through many stages of development ever since. Especially the structure of the brain—the center of the nerve–sense system—has achieved a high degree of refinement, specialization, and perfection. Today the brain serves as the physical instrument for thinking and memory;[122] both are spiritual activities of the "I." With the help of our faculties of memory and thinking we are able to grasp how our past and present experiences are linked, and then try to give shape to our lives accordingly.

Up to and during most of the Lemurian age, human beings were not yet able to think or remember. Only toward the end of the Lemurian age—after the "I" had been implanted in human beings—did the development of memory begin, thus providing our human ancestors with a first dim awareness of continuity in their lives. In the Atlantean age the human "I" continued to develop, along with an amazing capacity of memory. During the subsequent cultural eras of our post-Atlantean age this ability rapidly diminished and, with the awakening of the "I," some of these memory forces were transformed into thinking forces. The beginning of true human thinking is intimately connected to the awakening of the "I," but also to the parallel development of the brain—the physical instrument that makes thinking possible.

It is important, however, to have a clear understanding of the function of the brain with respect to the human thinking process. Rudolf Steiner explains this process in his book, *The Philosophy of*

Freedom. There he clarifies that our physical organization plays no part in the essential nature of thinking. He uses the image of footprints in the sand. No one would conclude that such footprints were "driven upward from below by forces in the ground." It is obvious that a living being made those prints. "Similarly, if we observe the essence of thinking without prejudice, we will not attribute any part of this essence to traces in the bodily organism." [123] Furthermore, the sequence of those footprints in the sand was determined by that same living being, not by the sand. Similarly, the direction of our thoughts is not determined by physical processes in the brain, but by the "I," which moves unhindered from thought to thought during the thinking process, while following the logical connections between those thought contents. The traces of this thinking activity remain perceptible in the brain for the thinking "I." Similarly, with everything we perceive, the soul impresses something of the process of perceiving onto the brain, making this perception conscious for the "I," so that at a later time it can be formed into a memory picture. One could say, then, that the physical processes of the brain *recede* somewhat in order to make room for the activity of the thinking "I"; and, as a result, the thoughts become conscious. In the words of Rudolf Steiner: "Our organization suspends its own activity—it makes room—and, in the space that has been made free, thinking appears. The effective essence in thinking has a double function. First, it represses the human organization's own activity and, second, it replaces that activity with itself." Thinking and remembering function in this way because the physical processes of the brain are, as it were, pushed back somewhat, *yielding* to the spiritual activity of the "I."

"*Remember the Sabbath day, to keep it holy.*" It would be difficult to compose a more compact, precise summary of what we have described thus far! The word *remember* points to a combination of memory and thinking. The "Sabbath day" points to the day of rest on which the activities of the physical body had to recede, to yield, in order to make room for the spiritual in the human being. In the words "keep it holy" we can recognize the suprasensory origin of the still immature "I" that, in the time of Moses, needed to be strengthened by observing, by "hallowing" the Sabbath. "Keep it holy" also embodies the secure knowledge that human beings need to be mindful of the spiritual in order to support the developing "I." *The first sentence of the fourth commandment,* then, was aimed at reducing the activities of the physical body by appealing to the human faculty of remembering, thus stressing the importance of the nerve–sense system within the human being. But the physical functioning of this system must give up, in other words, *withdraw* or *yield*, something of its physical nature during the spiritual activity of thinking and remembering, thereby allowing the "I" to gradually imprint itself on the physical body from the spiritual world.

Let us, next, examine how the aforementioned *yielding* processes are at work in the realm of the human rhythmical system, which had its germinal beginnings on ancient Sun. We recall that our human ancestors also received an etheric body on the Sun. This etheric body had gradually permeated the physical body. It worked particularly on the human rhythmical system, in such a way, that blood circulation, heartbeat, and breathing gradually began to reflect the harmonious rhythms of the cycles of the cosmos.[124] The human rhythmical processes, then, are intimately connected with those of the cosmos. Although people no longer are bound to or fully dependent on such cosmic rhythms, it is nonetheless better for this connection not to be severed completely. In other words, for the sake of the overall health of human beings, it is important that certain rhythms be included in their daily lives. One way of incorporating such a rhythm is to step back periodically, to *retreat* from normal, everyday activities, and devote time to rest and inner contemplation, thus establishing a healthy rhythm between breathing out and breathing in, between periods of outer activities and time for inner dedication to the spiritual, the divine. In the time of Moses this meant that the rhythm of the Sabbath should be in conformity, on a microcosmic, human scale, with the rhythm that pervades the creative impulses in the macrocosm.

"Six days shall you labor, and do all your work: But the seventh day is the Sabbath of the LORD your God: in it you shall not do any work." An exact rhythm is offered here, a rhythm of six workdays and one rest day per week. It is important to realize, however, that this particular weekly division of workdays and rest days did not just emerge as a consequence of the economic conditions in the time of Moses. True, these conditions likely were such that people needed to work a minimum of six days per week. But there is a more profound reason for this particular six-to-one arrangement within the seven days of the week; for this rhythm mirrors in the human realm what the *Spirits of Form* (the *Exusiai*) had taken on in the spiritual realm. These are the beings who are called *Elohim* in the Old Testament (Elohim is a plural form in Hebrew, commonly translated as *God* in English).

The seven Elohim worked, according to the indications of Rudolf Steiner, in the realm of the Sun.[125] From the realm of the Sun they had helped guide the development of the Earth and of human beings. But the cosmic circumstances had changed in the course of the Lemurian age. This meant that the Elohim also had to find a different way of working. And so, after the Moon had separated from the Earth, six of the seven Elohim remained connected to the Sun; but the seventh and most exalted of the Elohim—Yahweh—transferred the center of his activity to the Moon. Consequently, the influence of the six Elohim on the Sun streamed, with its light and warmth, to human beings on the Earth, and was therefore working on them from the *outside* during the day. Yahweh worked from the Moon, through the Moon's reflected sunlight, on the *inner* human being during the night. Only this combined activity of the six Elohim on the Sun and the one Eloah (singular form of Elohim) on the Moon, could bring about the precise cosmic conditions required for the proper development of the seminal human "I." And it is this special cooperative way of working of the seven Elohim that—at a much later age—was reflected in the seven-day rhythm of human life on Earth, a rhythm by which people worked six days in their *outer* lives, and on the seventh day turned in *inner* devotion to Yahweh, "*the LORD your God*," as it is expressed in the *second line of the fourth commandment*. [126]

Let us now turn our attention to the human metabolic–limb system, again from the viewpoint of learning how *yielding* processes manifest in it. This third system, which emerged in germinal form on old Moon, allows human beings to move about the Earth and to be active in the outer world. But it is important to realize in this connection that all human work, all human endeavor on Earth, carries the hallmark of the astral body. After all, this astral body was also given to our human ancestors on old Moon, and has progressively penetrated our physical and etheric bodies ever since.

The astral world oftentimes reveals itself in a sevenfold form;[127] and it is particularly in the fourth commandment that we encounter a sevenfold configuration. True, this commandment was aimed at supporting the developing "I" within the human body. But the time of Moses was a time of transition in which this immature "I" was still wrapped in an astral sheath. This is why everything related to the remembering and observing of the weekly Sabbath—that is, the *withdrawal* from normal daily activities to make room for devotion to "the LORD"—had to be presented in a sevenfold form. First of all we meet this structure in the seven days of the week, with six days for work and one day for rest, but especially also with respect to the Sabbath day itself. The day of rest was to be observed by a sevenfold set of beings that belonged to the domain of the master—the "I." This is an expression of the fact that, in the third post-Atlantean epoch, people did not yet experience their "I"-being as fully their own, but rather as belonging to, and dependent on, a group, tribe, or family. In these circumstances it was relatively inconsequential whether the daily work was performed by the master or by subordinates who answered to the will of the master. This is why the human "I" here appeared clothed in a sevenfold astral garment.

All this finds expression in the *third line of the fourth commandment* where we find the ostensibly superfluous passage: "(1) You, (2) nor your son, (3) nor your daughter, (4) your manservant, (5) nor your maidservant, (6) nor your cattle, (7) nor your stranger that is within your gates." This sevenfold summary intended to mark the precise borderline of the domain over which the human "I" in those days could exert its influence, that is to say, right to the edge of its own sphere of judicial and external power, to the city limits. Whatever existed outside this area did not need to be considered in those days because it lay outside the immediate and direct reach of the "I." Thus, this section of the commandment signals that the human "I" needed to become stronger by periodically retreating from all outer activities and dedicating itself to inner spiritual activity instead.

Up to this point in our discussions about the fourth commandment we have contemplated the activity of the "I" with respect to the nerve–sense system, the rhythmical system, and the metabolic–limb system. We have seen how certain processes had to yield, to *recede*, thereby creating a space for the "I" to take root in the physical body. All this could only occur during the Earth evolution. But there is something else that only became possible in the human physical body on the Earth; this has to do with the function of the human blood. The red blood has become the bearer of the "I" in human beings. Along with the whole warmth regulation of the body, the blood forms the physical basis for the "I." This could only happen because of another withdrawal process. The red blood corpuscles, in contrast to almost all other cells in the body, do not have a cell nucleus. To express this more precisely, shortly after the red blood corpuscles are produced in the bone marrow, the cell nucleus dies and dissolves within the cell. Here, then, we encounter what may well be the prototype amid the aforementioned yielding processes. With the dying, the *yielding*, of the cell nucleus a space is created in the human blood, enabling the forces of the "I" to penetrate the human physical body!

But, to come to a comprehensive understanding, we must approach this theme from yet another perspective, from a wider angle. After all, the whole cosmos has played a role in the development of the human "I," of the blood as the organ of this "I," and of the whole physical body. The evolution of the cosmos is closely connected to the evolution of human beings. In other words, human development is in reality a reflection of—and runs parallel to—the evolution of the cosmos. This, ultimately, is the reason that the human physical body on the Earth was able to receive the "I" into itself—the "I" as a microcosmic imprint of the macrocosmic Christ-"I."

To be able to support the healthy development of the "I" in human beings—and this was, as we have postulated, one of the objectives of the Ten Commandments—human life in the time of Moses had to be brought into harmony with the laws of the macrocosmic realm of the World-"I." Only then would the most favorable conditions be created for the further development of the human "I." This potential for harmony between human and cosmic life is reflected in the *last sentence of the fourth commandment,* which is inextricably linked to every word preceding it: *"For in six days the LORD made Heaven and Earth, the sea, and all that in them is, and rested the seventh day: wherefore the LORD blessed the Sabbath day, and hallowed it."*

The Cosmic Archetype of the Fourth Commandment

For each of the first three commandments we were able to find an archetypal image that represents something of the essence of each of the three planetary stages preceding the Earth. If we now, likewise, want to find an archetypal, cosmic image that forms the basis for the fourth commandment, we must look for an image that represents an essential aspect of the *Earth* phase of evolution. Speaking in the pictorial language of Genesis, God rested after the six days of creation. The divine creation as such was finished. But this does not mean that creation itself isn't continuing. With the notion of divine powers that are resting, we have entered a whole new phase of evolution. Creation now has to go forward without the supreme aid and guidance of the divine world. During the developments on Saturn, Sun, and Moon, this was not yet the case. Only during the actual Earth phase of evolution did creation take on this "godforsaken" quality. God gradually withdrew from the creating process in order to allow human beings to become active, and thus *develop their own freedom*. One could call this divine withdrawal, this divine *yielding*, the *cosmic Sabbath* of the whole Earth!

Christ and the Fourth Commandment

The development of human freedom, then, is of the utmost importance for the further development of humankind and the Earth. But this development would not be possible had Christ not incarnated on the Earth. At the baptism in the Jordan we encounter what may well be the archetypal gesture of *withdrawal*. This is where the individuality of Jesus made way for the divine Christ-being, the World-"I," to incarnate and work for three years in this unique physical body. During these three years Christ lived and worked as a human being on the Earth and then consciously went through death. This was the *free choice* of a divine being. Through this divine sacrifice something completely new arose, both for the Earth and for humanity. The Earth received a new enlivening impulse and the *spiritual freedom of the human "I"* was from then on guaranteed for all future times. This means that people can now become co-creators toward the further development of the Earth. This world-encompassing deed of Christ is the *divine metamorphosis* of the *cosmic Sabbath* of the Earth!

But Christ transformed the fourth commandment on a more human scale as well, especially for the people living in the culture of that time. The interpretation of the Sabbath observances had become more and more rigid in the course of the preceding centuries. We can find several accounts in the New Testament of the ensuing conflicts, as in the story of the disciples who were hungry on the Sabbath and proceeded to pluck and eat grain from a field (Mark 2:23–28, Matt. 12:1–8, Luke 6:1–5). The Pharisees reproached them for this act; for, although hungry people were allowed to eat grain according to the Mosaic laws (compare Deut. 23:25, Lev. 19:9–10 and 23:22), the Pharisees objected to the fact that this was happening on the Sabbath. Jesus answered them by referring to David who, "when he had need," ate the consecrated breads in the temple, which were meant for the priests alone. Although the Sabbath as such is not mentioned in the original story about David (which can be found in 1 Sam. 21:1–6), Jesus used this story to point out that, in case of emergencies, other laws should take precedence over the Mosaic laws. This principle, then, should hold with respect to the Sabbath as well; the Sabbath was made for human beings, not human beings for the Sabbath (Mark 2:27, Matt. 12:8, Luke 6:5).

This detailed reply also attests to the fact that Jesus knew the laws. He had grown up with the Mosaic laws and commandments. This is why he could speak knowledgeably about the Ten Commandments, as evidenced for example in his answer to the rich young man that we discussed earlier. Jesus observed the Sabbath himself. We hear that he went to the synagogue on the day of the Sabbath "as his custom was," and even taught there (Luke 4:15–16). Consequently we can be sure that, by allowing his disciples to eat grain or by healing people on the Sabbath, Jesus did not intend to violate the true meaning of the Sabbath. Rather, he wanted to heal the Sabbath itself, in other words, to keep it holy, to hallow the Sabbath again. In all these instances he worked out of the innate healing forces of the Sabbath itself. In doing so, he wanted to draw people's attention to the original impulse of the Sabbath, the impulse namely, to help establish a healthy relationship between the human "I" and the physical world (and hence the physical body). In cases where this relationship was disturbed, it was indeed on the Sabbath that a proper balance could best be restored again for the people in question.

A healthy balance between the "I" and the physical world can already be compromised if the body itself isn't functioning properly, as in the case of people who do not have enough to eat (like the hungry disciples)—a situation that can be remedied by obtaining food, even on the Sabbath. Or this relationship can be thrown off balance when disturbances occur within a particular part of the human body, causing specific illnesses. Such illnesses were cured by Christ on the Sabbath as well.

In the Gospel according to Luke we find several accounts of very specific illnesses that were healed on the Sabbath.[128] When the "I" is not able to work properly, say, in the metabolic–limb system, this can give rise to certain deformities, such as the withering of body parts. Jesus healed a man with a withered hand on the Sabbath (Luke 6:6–11, Matt. 12:9–14, Mark 3:1–6). When the "I" is not able to work properly in the human rhythmic system, the life forces working in the heart and lungs are weakened, causing retention of water in the body. Jesus healed a man with dropsy on the Sabbath (Luke 14:1–6). When the "I" is unable to work properly in the nerve–sense system, this can give rise to disturbances in the spinal cord, resulting in a weakening of the muscles. Jesus healed a woman "which had a spirit of infirmity eighteen years, and was bowed together, and could in no wise lift up herself" (Luke 13:10–17).

It is fascinating to compare these three healing processes. The man with the withered hand was made to stand alone in the middle of the synagogue with the whole community witnessing the event. He then was asked to stretch out his hand, as if reaching out to his fellow human beings. This gesture restored the relationship of his "I" to the outside world—and by extension also to his own body—thereby bringing about healing. The person with dropsy was "taken by Jesus," and—one could imagine, although it is not described in detail—was gently taken by the hand in a close physical encounter, thereby bringing about healing through a re-enlivening of the heart forces. The woman who could not "lift herself up," because she was not able to penetrate her body sufficiently with her "I"-forces, felt the hands of Jesus "laid on her," which caused his strength to stream into her, thereby bringing about healing.

In all three cases the encounter with Christ strengthened and revitalized the human "I," allowing it to work into the physical body in the right way. Luke, the physician, had a particularly well-developed ability to perceive and describe these events in greater detail. All of these healing processes could indeed best take place *especially* on the Sabbath, because the Sabbath had originally been introduced to support a rhythmical balance between the human "I" and the physical body, thus keeping the whole human being healthy. In all these cases Jesus affirmed the metamorphosis of the fourth commandment with the words, "Wherefore it is lawful to do well on the Sabbath days" (Matt. 12:12).[129]

The Fourth Commandment in our Time

The fourth commandment pertains to the human "I." Consequently, this commandment—just like the other ones that have a connection to the "I"—differs in character from the commandments that help support the etheric, astral, or physical body. We note, for instance, that the fourth commandment does not start with a "You shall not" formulation, but with an encouraging "Remember..." instruction.[130] This variation in the wording might already give us a first indication that this commandment likely will not have to undergo as comprehensive a metamorphosis as, say, the second commandment, for it to mean something in our own time.

In pursuance of finding such a modern-day form of the fourth commandment, it is helpful to reflect on the development of human thinking; for it is intimately connected to the development of the "I"—the essence of this commandment. Moses lived in the *third* post-Atlantean cultural epoch, a time in which the "I" began to awaken in human beings, but conceptual thinking had not been developed as yet. True, the Egyptians and Babylonians had gained an expansive knowledge of geometry and astronomy, and Abraham was called "the Father of Mathematics,"[131] but their thinking was very different from our way of thinking today. It was more like a "comparing of memories," more like a *remembering*.

In the *fourth* post-Atlantean cultural epoch, the human "I" came into its own in the physical realm. The earlier *remembering*, which had been contingent on suprasensory, clairvoyant capacities, now gradually became a *thinking* that was more tied to the physical brain. The brain had evolved to the point where it could serve as the instrument for thinking in people's striving for truth and knowledge. In the Greek era philosophical thinking had emerged; but this new way of thinking did not yet have a noticeable impact on the daily lives of human beings. During the subsequent Roman civilization, however, people's thinking became more practical and relevant to their everyday lives. This was also the epoch during which Christ spoke the words, "And all of you shall know the truth, and the truth shall make you free" (John 8:32). These words point to a future time, because true freedom can only be achieved through the thinking "I." But the foundation for it was laid with the beginning of philosophical thinking in the fourth cultural epoch.

We now live in the *fifth* post-Atlantean cultural epoch. Compared to the time of Moses, our faculty of memory has diminished, but our thinking capacity has increased. In accordance with the aforementioned *Law of Historical Symmetry*, we may anticipate that certain elements of the third cultural epoch will reappear in our time, albeit in a new form. But what does this mean, for example with respect to the various elements that are contained in the fourth commandment? How can, say, the activity of *remembering*, with which the formulation in Exodus begins, find an appropriate form in our time? Or, how important is the weekly rhythm in observing something like a Sabbath today? In short, where can we find a modern form of the original impulse of the Sabbath?

We may safely assume that Rudolf Steiner did not write his book *Knowledge of the Higher Worlds* with the explicit intention of creating a modern metamorphosis of the fourth commandment! But if we follow the line of thought established in this book, we can definitely recognize corresponding concepts in it. After all, the path of development described here also leads from *remembering* to the activity of *free thinking*. But then the reader is introduced to another stage in this process, to a whole new form of thinking. This inner thinking activity is *meditation*, a new thinking activity that can, in time, lead us to imaginative consciousness.[132]

Remembering, thinking in freedom, meditation—these concepts form a progressive sequence that concurs with the course of development during the three cultural eras we have referred to, that is to say, the *third, fourth, and fifth* post-Atlantean epochs. If we follow this line of thought further, we will be able to find specific indications in *Knowledge of the Higher Worlds* that, taken together, can be seen as the modern metamorphosis of the fourth commandment because it points to the ongoing development of the "I." Let us try, then, to compare these indications to specific sections of the original text of the fourth commandment. A fascinating picture will arise!

Over against "*Remember the Sabbath day, to keep it holy,*" we now find as a first principle (expressed in our own words): All people can acquire knowledge of higher, suprasensory worlds, once they choose to follow the modern path of meditative training. But the decision to follow this path can only be taken in inner freedom. We can no longer obey a commandment in this respect. It only makes sense to start on such a path if it is done out of love and insight. A meditative path of schooling of this kind can only be based on a deep inner feeling of devotion, an awareness of keeping it holy. It must be based on a feeling of veneration, not for persons, but for truth, wisdom, and insight. After all, true knowledge can only be gained if we first learn to value this very knowledge.[133]

Over against the second part, "*Six days shall you labor, and do all your work; but the seventh day is the Sabbath of the LORD your God,*" we now find as a specific exercise: Provide for yourself moments of inner tranquility, and learn in these moments to distinguish the essential from the nonessential. During such moments we would do well to let pass before the eye of our soul the multifaceted experiences we go through and the deeds we accomplish in life, and then try to look at them as though "from a higher standpoint."[134] This daily, quiet, meditative review is the modern form of observing the Sabbath. One could say that in this way the prototype of the *weekly* Sabbath rhythm can be transformed into a *daily* meditation rhythm. In observing these practices we can, writes Rudolf Steiner, eventually awaken "the higher human being" within ourselves.[135]

The third section of the fourth commandment describes the domain over which we in our daily lives often try to exert our authority (..."*your son, your daughter,*..."). Our actions within this sphere of life can be transformed once we learn to let go by observing the situation, as it were, from the outside. We should try to rise above the circumstances of our daily life to which we are emotionally attached. This can happen with the help of a specific exercise, a daily meditative exercise in which we inwardly contemplate events of general human concern, even though we ourselves live in entirely different circumstances. "In this way something begins to live within us that transcends the personal,"[136] allowing us to gradually turn our attention to the higher worlds.

Through such meditative exercises, which in this context could only be described in a most compact and schematic form, we gradually begin to develop new concepts about reality, about the true value of things, and about life itself.[137] "Whoever rises through meditation to the point where nature is united with the spirit," says Rudolf Steiner "begins to kindle to life what is eternal in a person, what is not confined within the boundaries of birth and death."[138] Then we come to understand that both the pleasant and the not-so-pleasant aspects of our individual lives need to be experienced within the framework of a larger, spiritual, divine alliance to which we as human beings belong.

It is this spiritual alliance, this universal order that issues from the most distant past, when "God created the Heaven and the Earth," leads via the Mystery of Golgotha as the center point in the stream of evolution, and onward toward a time in the future, when people, out of inner freedom, will truly be able to be part of the spiritual cosmos again. All of this was already foreshadowed in the last sentence of the fourth commandment: "*wherefore the LORD blessed the Sabbath day, and hallowed it.*"

5

Introduction to the Fifth, Sixth, and Seventh Commandments

The fifth commandment: *"Honor your father and your mother: that your days may be long upon the land that the LORD your God gives you.* The sixth commandment: *You shall not kill*; and the seventh commandment: *You shall not commit adultery."*

We have described how the Ten Commandments can be subdivided into four groups, with the first group consisting of the first four commandments. These four commandments have a connection to the human physical body, which has gone through all four planetary stages of the Earth. The second group includes three commandments, namely the fifth, sixth, and seventh; these are connected to the etheric body that has gone through three planetary stages. The third group is comprised of the eighth and ninth commandments; these relate to the astral body that has gone through two planetary phases. And finally, the fourth "group" consists of the tenth commandment;[139] it has a connection to the "I," the youngest member of the human being.

With the fifth commandment, then, we are entering the realm of the etheric. At this point the question may well arise: What exactly is this etheric body to which, according to the above, the next group of commandments has a special connection?

We know that all living beings have an etheric body.[140] The forms in which these living beings appear on Earth are determined by and dependent on natural inherent conditions. These conditions determine how a species develops. Whereas an organism's substances are continually renewed during its lifetime, the species remains constant and its specific features are passed on through subsequent generations. The unique form of each living entity is an outward expression of this species-determining force. Although we cannot perceive this force with our physical senses, we can observe how it manifests in the myriad forms and shapes of living beings. This species-determining force is the *etheric body*. One could also call it the *life body* or even the *time body*, because all life processes occur in time.[141] All living organisms have a specific form and life cycle, each a testament to the wise, meaningful, formative order of the etheric world.

What then, we may well ask, is the difference between etheric forces and an etheric body? Wherever etheric forces are working collectively within a living being, as in the case of most (higher) plants, animals, and also of human beings, we speak of an etheric body. Wherever the working of these etheric forces is less specific, as for example in the formation of dunes or coral reefs, we speak of etheric forces. But, since it is also perfectly justified to call these etheric forces collectively *the etheric body of the earth*, we may well state that it is not at all easy to establish a sharp border line between etheric forces and an etheric body.

Within the domain of the etheric forces—and therefore also of the etheric body—we can distinguish four different types of ether at work: warmth ether, light ether, sound ether, and life ether.[142] If we principally were to study the specific functions of these etheric forces, it would be important to clearly distinguish *four* types of ether. If, on the other hand, we focus our attention on the etheric forces in relation to the planetary evolution of the Earth—as is the case in this book—it is justified to base such explorations on *three* kinds of etheric forces. After all, the earliest onset of warmth ether must be sought on ancient Saturn, where etheric forces as such did not actually exist yet. Warmth on Saturn existed in a form *so* rarefied, that it simultaneously had elementary and etheric qualities. Consequently it is almost impossible to distinguish between this most rarefied matter and this earliest etheric force. They still formed a unity. Life, in its earliest form, only emerged on ancient Sun, where the light ether began to work as an etheric force for the first time. Consequently, in this study we take for our starting point the *four* elements known since antiquity as "warmth," "air," "water," and "earth," and *three* kinds of etheric forces, namely the light ether, the sound ether, and the life ether, which came into being on old Sun, old Moon, and the Earth respectively.[143]

Taking all this into consideration, the question may well arise: How are these etheric forces different from each other? How can we recognize the distinctive aspects of these etheric forces?

Light ether creates *boundaries* and bestows a certain degree of *stability* on what we perceive as living processes. Light ether frequently is active in those processes that take place *in between* two opposite impulses, like formation and disintegration, growth and decay. This then gives rise to *three* qualities, namely those of the two polarities and a third quality, emerging as a result of the interaction between the two opposite impulses. Thus we can experience a plant as living *between* the sunlight and earthly substance in the yearly rhythm. Or we can perceive human life *between* birth and death in the rhythm of continuing incarnations; or the human rhythmical system *between* the nerve–sense system and the metabolic–limb system.

Sound ether differentiates, diversifies, and *creates order*, thus giving rise to a sequence of features with independent characteristics. Within this realm one can often find a series of *seven* distinct qualities, as, for example, in the seven colors of the rainbow, with each color having its own characteristic quality. In such cases we speak of a "spectrum of qualities." Within such a spectrum each quality reveals a distinctive, individual character. One might possibly assume that further differentiation within such a spectrum would point toward yet another kind of ether; this is not the case. Any further differentiation and specialization takes place within the realm of the sound ether.

The working of *life ether* is revealed wherever *no further formations are possible*; wherever something is rounded off, has reached its completion; wherever *a new higher unity* is formed within a particular spectrum of distinct qualities. We also encounter life ether at work wherever a life cycle returns to its starting point; wherever a circle is closed, a circle, moreover, that is frequently composed of *twelve* elements, as for example in the twelve semi-tones of an octave. Life ether also manifests in the shaping of a living being's life as a whole. And, because life ether "closes the circle," we have herewith reached the end of this classification of the various types of etheric forces as well.

The etheric forces working in the cosmos and in human beings have long been part of the stream of evolution. Ancient Saturn had consisted only of warmth. On ancient Sun—through the mediation of high spiritual beings—two new substances were added; one was denser, the other more rarefied than warmth. The former can be qualified as the element "air," the latter as the etheric *light*. And so, the physical human body, which now consisted of "warmth" and "air," was given a first form of life on old Sun. This newly acquired etheric body was a structure comprised mostly of *light ether* that had a stabilizing influence on the air and warmth streaming through the human body. This first form of life also encompassed a seminal form of reproduction. New life now flowed through succeeding generations following the cosmic rhythm of the old Sun, a rhythm that moved from a light phase to a dark phase, from growth activity to stabilization. This process may be compared to a seasonal rhythm of spring and summer, of growth and unfolding, followed by another spring and summer; but as yet no fall or winter, no decaying and dying.

We can find remnants of all this in human existence on Earth, namely wherever *light ether* is active. The rhythm of human life flowing through the generations has its origin in these events on old Sun. The *fifth commandment* was aimed at supporting the light ether forces in the human being. This is why it mentions a "long and stable life," and points to the stream of life through the generations, which human beings should be honoring as a gift of high spiritual beings.

The Sun phase was followed by the Moon phase of the Earth. Both the physical world and the physical human body now consisted of warmth ("fire"), gases ("air"), and fluids ("water"). In order to assimilate the latter into the life processes, the light ether had to be further differentiated. Accordingly, some of the light ether was transformed into a new kind of ether: *sound ether*. (Note that, during each subsequent planetary incarnation, the newly formed *element* is denser, whereas the accompanying newly emerging *etheric force* is more rarefied than the one[s] already in existence.)

Consequently, both the etheric world and the human etheric body consisted of two components on ancient Moon, namely the light ether, which had a stabilizing function on life in general, and the sound ether, which had a differentiating and regulating influence on life. To get to this stage, part of the light ether—that is to say, some of the universal life forces that are an inherent part of the light ether—had been offered up and then transformed into sound ether. All this was a direct result of the fact that human beings received an astral body on old Moon that made it possible to develop the very first beginnings of individual consciousness. Life at this stage took place mostly between two kinds of forces—forces of growth and of decay. The Sun gave life; the Moon brought specialization and differentiation—qualities that tend to restrict and confine life as such. In the end this had led to a cosmic battle on old Moon, because these restrictive forces needed to be subdued.

Again, we can find remnants of all this in human existence on Earth, namely wherever *sound ether* is at work. Wherever differentiation and specialization are emphasized exclusively, the possibility for friction arises, because the *better* tends to become the enemy of the *good*. Hence it was important to prevent the confining, restrictive aspects of the sound ether from having too great an impact on life in general. The *sixth commandment*, which was introduced to help support the proper development of the sound ether in human beings, prohibited the willful taking of a human life, thus signaling that human beings should not sever their vital link to the life-giving forces of the light ether. The negative aspects of the sound ether needed to be curtailed in favor of the light ether; people had to learn to cherish and respect *life*—human life as well as any form of life.

Introduction to the Fifth, Sixth, and Seventh Commandments

The Moon phase then was followed by the actual Earth phase. Again, a further metamorphosis occurred; human beings now received the "I." The physical world and the physical human body began to form solid substances (the element "earth"). In order to facilitate the assimilation of this denser matter into the life processes, the most refined of all etheric forces now emerged, namely the *life ether*. These forces are active wherever a new life cycle arises out of an earlier one. This is why the *seventh commandment,* by forbidding adultery, indirectly addressed this very special aspect of the life ether in human beings as well.

Through the influence of the *light ether* the biological processes emerged on Earth, and life was streaming through the generations. The great polarities, which had manifested on ancient Sun as forces of activation and stabilization and on ancient Moon as processes of growth and decay, now appeared as *birth* and *death* during the Earth evolution.

Through the influence of the *sound ether* the different organs were formed, each with increasingly *specialized* functions; but the impact of the sound ether during the Earth phase also caused human beings gradually to become mortal beings. *Death processes* began to play a role within the organism.

Through the influence of the *life ether* during the Earth evolution the human body could now maintain the *autonomy of the whole organism*, giving people the possibility to develop and use their spiritual independence in a more conscious way.

The fifth, sixth, and seventh commandments are connected to these three types of etheric forces, as they manifest in human life. The *fifth* commandment referred to the life stream through the generations and the possibility for a long life. The *sixth* commandment aimed to curtail excessive death forces. The *seventh* commandment was intended to support those etheric forces that are active in generating a new life cycle.

Keeping all this in mind, we are now ready to take a more detailed look at these three commandments.

The Fifth Commandment

The fifth commandment: *"Honor your father and your mother: that your days may be long upon the land that the LORD your God gives you."* It is important to take equal notice of the second half of this formulation along with the more familiar "honoring of the parents," mentioned in the first part. After all, the wording of this commandment refers to a causal connection between a particular code of conduct, namely the honoring of the parents, and the prospect of a longer life. (We will consider the very last part, referring to "the land that God gives us," later on in this chapter about the fifth commandment.)

In the theological literature the "honoring of the parents" is usually seen as consistent with the universal respect the ancient Israelites displayed as a matter of course toward all older people. It followed, then, that adult children were expected to assume social and financial obligations toward their aging parents, once they were no longer capable of contributing to society themselves.[144] This certainly is a valid point of view because the Ten Commandments, among other things, were also meant to cultivate social hygiene in the lives of the Israelite people. But there are other aspects to be considered as well. After all, feelings of reverence (for people, that is) generally emerge in the early years of life. We may well conclude, then, that with this particular wording, the fifth commandment also points to the importance of recognizing the inherent causal connection that exists between childhood and old age.

Human life runs its course between the two poles of birth and death. At the one pole we experience growth and differentiation; at the other one ripening and spiritualization. But these contrasting qualities actually play a role in the whole course of human life, not only at its beginning and end. It is exactly in the interplay between these two impulses that we can recognize the working of the etheric body, and in particular of the *light ether*, to which the fifth commandment has a special connection. Therefore, in order to discover the meaning of this commandment (and of the working of the light ether), we have to investigate where and how this kind of interaction occurs in human life.

People have always known that a causal connection exists between the beginning and the end of life. Think, for instance, of an old saying like, "What is learned in the cradle lasts to the grave"! We know that particular incidents in childhood can have aftereffects in later life; and it is the etheric body, also called the time body, that creates this link. The etheric body retains, well into later stages of life, the impact of events that happened early on in life. Harmful influences in the child's early surroundings, especially those that have a weakening effect on the etheric body, can therefore cause infirmities in old age.[145]

This is why the fifth commandment refers to certain actions that can be undertaken early on in life, in order to generate favorable conditions for later life, so "that your days may be long." What is needed for the etheric body of the growing child to stay healthy and retain its vitality? To be able to answer this question we must first, very briefly, take a look at the three developmental phases in the life of the child (from birth to adulthood), limiting ourselves to those aspects that can contribute toward a better comprehension of the fifth commandment.[146]

The *second* of these three phases, each of which takes approximately seven years, is of direct interest to us in connection to the fifth commandment; but, in order to understand how it is related to the other two phases, we will first outline the characteristic gestures of the *first* and *third* phase.

During the *first* phase of approximately seven years (from birth to the change of teeth) everything is focused on growth. All forces are directed toward the growth of the body and the processes that gradually transform the body's inherited physical matter into the child's own physical substance. The growing child at this stage is highly dependent on and affected by its surroundings. All these impressions work directly and deeply into the physical body. The child imitates everything it perceives. This capacity for imitating—in it we can sense something of the molding and sculpting activity that is typical of the etheric body—belongs to this stage of life. Ideally, then, the child's environment should be such that it is worthy of imitation!

The *third* developmental stage of approximately seven years (from puberty to adulthood) shows an entirely different picture; it forms a counter-pole to the first seven years of life. The focus now is on finding one's place in the world, no longer on growth and imitation. The adolescent experiences sexual feelings welling up from inside the body, but simultaneously discovers the light-filled power of thinking that helps create order, as well as a basis for knowledge, insight, and judgment.

In the *first* seven years we can observe how *unconscious* impulses of the will are at work in the depths of the organism; in the *third* seven-year phase how *conscious* ideas and thoughts are formed. Although different qualities are expressed in these respective gestures, we can recognize the activity of the etheric forces in both processes. In the *first* stage the etheric body works mostly in growth and metabolism; in the *third* stage more in the thinking activity.

Let us now take a look at the *second* phase of development (from the change of teeth to puberty). At the beginning of this phase, around the seventh year of life, we can observe how the etheric forces gradually are released from the unconscious domain of the will and become available toward the development of the child's increasing mental capacities. One could also say that, with the change of teeth, the child's etheric body becomes less connected to and dependent on the hereditary stream, in other words, that it now really becomes the child's own etheric body. In Anthroposophy this is oftentimes referred to as the birth of the etheric body. (In the same way we can speak of the birth of the astral body at puberty and the birth of the "I" around age twenty-one.)

It is exactly in this middle phase of childhood that respect and *reverence*—the focal point of the fifth commandment—can develop quite naturally. This is why, as mentioned above, this phase is of particular importance for our studies about the honoring of the parents.

In this middle phase we can observe how the feeling life of the child blossoms. Naturally, smaller children and teenagers also feel emotions; but in this second phase of the child's development the feeling life actually creates a bridge for the child, a connecting link between it and the world. This is the time when children develop deep feelings of affection or contempt, of justice or injustice, but especially of *reverence*. At this age the child looks up to the adult as a living example of what a human being should be, triggering spontaneous feelings of esteem. (It goes without saying that the adults need to conduct themselves in such a way that the child can indeed develop feelings of respect and not, say, of fear.)

Reverence, esteem, respect are the basic elements of the richly differentiated feeling life of the child in this middle phase of development. Being able to nurture such feelings in childhood creates a basis for the healthy development of one's etheric forces in adulthood. Moreover, early feelings of admiration for an esteemed personality can, later on in life, become reverence for *truth* and *wisdom*, respect for other cultural values, and above all for the *freedom* of every human being.

In the time of Moses all this could be summarized in a commandment to "honor one's parents." Such feelings of reverence shaped people's lives, both outwardly and inwardly. Since these feelings were directed toward human beings—the parents—the focus here was on forces that are active primarily in the earlier years of life. But we have to remember that, in the time of Moses, the process of maturing into adulthood did not follow quite the same laws as it does today. Thinking and critical judgment did not have the same meaning or importance in human society. The desire to honor one's parents was a sentiment that would have welled up quite naturally in people until a much later age than would be the case today. Accordingly, this commandment could also be directed at adult children in this way.

What was really meant, though, with the decree to *honor* the parents was that the Hebrew people needed to take the etheric body of the parents as the model for their own etheric body. The commandment really instructed them, "You shall try to grow according to the divine growth laws in the parents." This could not be accomplished through a conscious effort, but only as the result of complete devotion.

The Fifth Commandment in Relation to the Second Commandment

We have postulated that the *fifth* and the *second* commandment each have a connection to the etheric body of human beings. The *second commandment* prohibited the worshiping and making of outer images. This meant that the etheric body, which has an inherent affinity for sculpting, shaping, and creating, needed to receive nurturing, health-giving forces from elsewhere. The *fifth commandment* offered this possibility by encouraging people to develop feelings of reverence, in other words, precisely those feelings that nourish and strengthen the etheric body. In the time of Moses this honoring had to be directed at the parents; not because this was traditionally expected, but because the parents represented the natural point of connection. The individual "I" was not fully awakened, was not yet born in human beings. The blood ties were still working powerfully in the soul, much more so than is the case today. People lived their lives first and foremost within the stream of the generations; they intuitively perceived the parents as the living embodiment of an ideal, an ideal that needed to be honored on the level of the consciousness of that time.

We may well conclude, then, that the fifth commandment was not in the first place introduced to satisfy any parental needs or wishes. The fact that parents would have been pleased with this commandment was merely an agreeable side effect. The primary aim of this commandment, rather, was to support and strengthen the etheric forces in the members of the next generation, and thus create the proper conditions for their sustained health well into old age. After all, the inspiration for this commandment had its origin in the knowledge that *feelings of reverence, developed early on in life, will gradually be transformed into vital life forces for the latter part of life*. This is exactly what is expressed in the causal formulation of the fifth commandment, "Honor your father and your mother: that your days may be long..."

It was important in the time of Moses that people should be exposed to the right kind of impressions, that is to say, to impressions that nurture the etheric body and keep it healthy. In our contemplations about the *second* commandment we observed that people were not permitted to receive such impressions through outer images, because these would have impeded the development of "the image of the living God" that was meant to gradually become a reality in every human being. But, since the human etheric body, one way or the other, needed to experience the ideal example of this *image of the living God*, the *fifth* commandment raised the *parents* to the level of the living representatives of that image, an image people could look up to. And so, the honoring of the parents became the forming impulse for the health of the etheric body through the generations. Accordingly, the positive qualities of the parents could be accentuated in the lives of the children, whereas the negative qualities, in other words, those qualities that were not in accordance with *the image of the living God*, would gradually be eliminated through the subsequent generations. And so, through the combined impulses of the second and fifth commandments, the healthy development of the human etheric body could be supported.[147]

These purified etheric forces eventually became an essential factor in the preparation of a suitable human body in which Christ would, many generations later, be able to incarnate on the Earth. Once that event had become a reality on Earth, a new impulse became active in human beings as well; an impulse that henceforth imbues the human etheric body with stabilizing forces through the power of the "I."

Christ and the Fifth Commandment

The fifth commandment in its original form needed to conform to the forces of heredity and of the blood ties because these forces were still active in the time of Moses. But, at the beginning of the Christian era, the human physical and etheric body had meanwhile evolved to the point where hereditary forces no longer contributed anything essential to the further development of the bodily constitution of human beings. This is why Christ could incarnate in a human physical body at this turning point in time. And, with Christ's coming to the Earth, the "I" in its purest form—the cosmic World-"I"—appeared on Earth for all humanity. This meant that, henceforth, human beings had the possibility to be freed of the limitations of the old blood ties, and imprint their own individual coloring onto the etheric body through the strength of their own "I"-forces. It also meant that relationships needed no longer be based only on the blood ties. People were now capable of forming relationships, both to other human beings and to the divine, out of the forces of the "I." It should not surprise us, then, that this particular commandment underwent a radical transformation through Christ. The Gospels refer to this transformation in several passages of which we will quote a few:

Matthew 10:37, "He that loves father or mother more than me is not worthy of me: and he that loves son or daughter more than me is not worthy of me" (see also Mark 10:29–30).

Matthew 12:48–50, "But he answered and said unto him that told him, who is my mother? And who are my brethren? And he stretched forth his hand toward his disciples, and said, behold my mother and my brethren! For whosoever shall do the will of my Father who is in Heaven, the same is my brother, and sister, and mother" (see also Mark 3:33–35 en Luke 8:21).

Matthew 23:9, "And call no man your father upon the Earth: for one is your Father, which is in Heaven."[148]

It goes without saying that Jesus did not advocate to sever ties with one's family members as a matter of course. The essential point expressed in all these passages is that, henceforth, feelings of veneration need no longer, of necessity, be linked to the human blood ties. Jesus encouraged people to establish ties of reverence to the divine world instead; or, put differently, "Free yourself from the blood ties— follow the "I AM"-principle." This was now possible for the first time in history because the "I" had been born in human beings. (For, just as the individual "I" matures around the age of twenty-one in the young adult of today, so humanity as a whole had reached the stage where the "I" was born in human beings through the deed of Christ, the World-"I.") This meant that the human "I" was now capable of sustaining the etheric body inwardly with the same kind of nurturing forces that in earlier times could only have been generated outwardly, namely, through the "honoring of the parents." The etheric body had been prepared for this transformation throughout long ages, first through the hereditary stream, and subsequently through the deed of Christ.

The Fifth Commandment in our Time

In what form can the fifth commandment still have significance in our time? Before we explore this topic, it is important to realize that there is one stage in human life in which the original impulse of the fifth commandment still plays a role today, namely in the second phase of childhood (from the change of teeth to the beginning of puberty). As we pointed out earlier, feelings of reverence for parents and teachers can emerge quite naturally in the growing child of that age. For this age group the focal point of the fifth commandment—reverence—is a natural part of life.

With the beginning of adolescence, however, feelings of reverence for parents and other adults are no longer a naturally occurring phenomenon in our present-day culture. Likewise, when children become adults, they relate, for the most part, very differently to their parents than was the case in earlier times. But the impulses that were working in the past do not just disappear. This has to do with the *Law of Historical Symmetry* we discussed earlier. Such impulses remain active in our time, but they work differently, transformed, as it were, to serve contemporary conditions. To discover where these transformed impulses of the fifth commandment are active today we will try to answer four specific questions.

The first question focuses on reverence. In what form can reverence still mean something today? Developing feelings of reverence and devotion continues to be essential for the health of the etheric body. But it is necessary that we find a suitable form for such sentiments, a form that matches the inner requirements of our times. A commandment forcing us to honor parents, or political leaders, or other figures of importance will be of no help whatsoever in this regard. On the contrary, the catastrophic consequences of the dictatorships of the last century, and of our own time, clearly demonstrate that feelings of reverence, which in childhood quite naturally are centered on human beings, actually can be harmful if they well up—or are induced—in adults in that form. Such feelings must instead be inwardly transformed into reverence for everything that is *true, beautiful, and good*. But this constitutes an individual course of action that can only be embarked upon in full inner freedom.

In Rudolf Steiner's book *Knowledge of the Higher Worlds* we are made aware of a suitable vehicle for feelings of reverence in our time. There we read that it is necessary to first find a "fundamental attitude of the soul" if one wants to achieve even the slightest progress on the path toward higher knowledge. This basic mood is there referred to as "the path of veneration, of devotion to truth and knowledge."[149] The description of this path then continues, "There are children who look up with reverent awe to certain venerated persons...But it must not be thought that this will lead to submissiveness and servility. What was once childlike veneration for persons becomes, later on, veneration for *truth* and *knowledge*. Experience teaches that those of free bearing are those who have learned to venerate where veneration is due." And, "Failing such preparation, we will encounter difficulties at the very first step, unless we undertake by rigorous self-education to engender within ourselves this attitude of devotion." A little further on, "It must be emphasized that in the domain of higher knowledge it is *not* a matter of venerating persons, but of venerating knowledge and truth." "Veneration, respect, devotion are nourishing foods that make the soul healthy and vigorous, especially in the activity of cognition."

Thus we may now formulate a first metamorphosis of the fifth commandment for our time: *Imbue yourself with feelings of reverence and devotion toward those things that are truly worthy of respect—truth and wisdom in particular—so that forces of health may be generated in you.*

The second question focuses on the relationship between adults and their parents in today's world. How can an ongoing, meaningful relation between parents and their adult children be established? Such a relationship can no longer be based on devotion and reverence; these are sentiments that, by rights, belong in an earlier phase of life. Parents and adult children ideally should aspire to notice and acknowledge the *true human being* in each other—the individual "I" that is worthy of each other's recognition and respect. Only on this basis can a relationship be established between the generations, a relationship that is based on mutual respect and trust.

Thus, we may now formulate a second metamorphosis of the fifth commandment for our time: *Recognize and honor the "I" in one another.*

The third question has to do with the socioeconomic aspects of "honoring the parents." How can we create a suitable environment for older people in our society? In the time of Moses it was assumed that (adult) children would support their aging parents once they no longer played a productive role in society. In our own time things are different. Because it is no longer a foregone conclusion that the fate of older people is dependent on family ties, we need to develop new social forms of financial and other support to comply with today's meaning of the words "that your days may be long." This now has to become everyone's responsibility. Advances have already been made in this field. In many places there is excellent support for older people, be it financially, medically, socially, and in many other ways. Rudolf Steiner's ideas about the *threefold social order* also have contributed much in this respect. In the context of our present study, however, it would take us too far afield to follow up on these groundbreaking ideas.[150] Only from a general point of view we may infer that, increasingly, the welfare of older people will depend less on family ties and more on the social sense of responsibility of society as a whole.

And so, we may now formulate a third metamorphosis of the fifth commandment for our time: *Recognize that, today, the wellbeing of older people depends on society's collective sense of responsibility and social awareness.*

The fourth question arises from the last few words of the original text, the section we have not yet considered in our discussions about the fifth commandment. What is meant with "the land that the LORD your God gives you"? This will have to be looked at from a wider perspective. At first glance we might think—and this is of course justified from a certain point of view—that this land is the Promised Land that the Israelite people hoped to find after forty years of wandering through the desert. But is there possibly a deeper meaning connected to "the land that the LORD your God gives you"? Where is this land in which people can truly feel at home?

Most of us may well, at some point in our lives, have suffered from homesickness. Such a feeling is actually like an echo, a reverberation of a deeper longing that lives in every human soul—namely a yearning for a suprasensory land not of this Earth, a realm where Angels and other spiritual beings live, in short, the only place where human beings truly are at home. This, ultimately, is the land that God gives to people when they have seriously prepared themselves for it.

In olden times people knew of this land. In the mystery centers of Tibet people spoke of a faraway mystical land, called *Shambhala*. Rudolf Steiner mentions that the initiates have always been able to withdraw to Shambhala, in order to acquire what is needed for humanity, but that this land has disappeared from the view of most other people. It will, however, become a reality again "when beginning forces of clairvoyance will become stronger and more widespread and people recognize that these are good forces, which originate in the spiritual realm of the Sun...that is when Shambhala will return."[151] Today's initiates can and must even now go to this land from time to time, according to Rudolf Steiner, to draw new forces from it. With the passing of time, more people will be able to enter this land where they will see "its radiant light, as Paul saw above him the light that streamed from Christ."[152] But it is also mentioned there that people can already now enter this land—while retaining their waking consciousness—when they develop themselves through a suitable path of inner development, *filled with reverence for truth, wisdom, and insight.*

And so, we may now formulate a fourth metamorphosis of the fifth commandment for our time: *Only via "the path of reverence" may people be able to find entry into the "land of the spirit."*

This is the realm, the land in which the soul can truly feel at home and where we hope that "our days may be long upon." Rudolf Steiner once wrote a beautiful verse in which he communicated how the human soul belongs to this realm and how the path to it can be found:[153]

> The sphere of the Spirit is the soul's true home,
> And we will surely reach it
> By walking the path of honest thought,
> By choosing as our guide the fount of love
> Implanted in our heart,
> By opening the eye of our soul
> To nature's script
> Spread out before us through all the universe,
> Telling the story of the Spirit
> In all that lives and thrives,
> And in the silent spaciousness of lifeless things,
> And in the stream of time—the process of becoming.

6

The Sixth Commandment and the Origin of Death Forces

The sixth commandment: *"You shall not kill."* Before we consider the deeper meaning of this commandment, we should first briefly explore the meaning of "You shall not kill" in the context of the Old Testament. In that context some forms of killing were acceptable and, therefore, not directly governed by the sixth commandment. The Israelites frequently were encouraged (even by God) to "slay the enemy" in wars with neighboring peoples. Moreover, within the framework of the Mosaic laws, specific infractions called for the death penalty. But the Hebrew word for *killing*, as it appears in the formulation of the sixth commandment (*tirtsah,* from the stem *ratsach*), is used far less frequently in the Old Testament than other words used for killing, be it in connection with wars or in reference to the death penalty. *Ratsach* has a specific meaning. For this reason the sixth commandment is usually translated as "You shall not murder," to clarify that this type of killing implies an intentional act, an act with evil motive, a killing out of hatred and malice.[154]

Seen from the wider perspective we have embraced in these studies about the Ten Commandments, however, the core message of the sixth commandment focuses on the ultimate, profound meaning of death itself, as well as its implications for human beings. We will explore some of these aspects and implications in the pages that follow.

The Sixth Commandment and the Origin of Death Forces

Throughout the entire history of humankind, human beings have killed one another in overwhelming numbers, for a wide variety of reasons. Even in the Bible, right after the story of creation, we are confronted with Cain who killed his brother Abel.[155] And Moses himself killed an Egyptian in a moment of unguarded rage and indignation.[156] The victims of Herod's infanticide, of the Inquisition, of the Holocaust, of political persecution, and of many other injustices all cry out to Heaven in anguish. And it seems as though the dark human instincts behind all these events are just as powerfully present in our time as they were in the past, maybe even more so.

Of all the commandments, the sixth commandment may well be the most fundamental one, as the preservation of human life *must* precede any other regulations regarding the conduct of human beings living on Earth.[157] The sixth commandment, therefore, occupies a central position both with respect to its significance and to its place within the compositional structure of the Ten Commandments (as can be seen, for example, from the diagram on page 219). The sixth commandment stands in the middle. But, despite the fundamental quality of this commandment, it has—as evidenced by history—had limited success over the course of time in deterring human beings from killing each other. Why is it that we seem to be endowed with such dark instincts? If we want to find more than a superficial answer to this question, we must take a closer look at the origin and the characteristic features of the *sound ether* because, as we have postulated, these particular etheric forces have a special connection with the sixth commandment.

The name *sound ether* is only one of several designations commonly used to describe this type of ether; other names that can be used with equal justification are *number ether*, *chemical ether*, or even *astral ether*, thus indicating the complexity of these etheric forces. However, for the sake of clarity we will here use the term *sound ether* exclusively. Sound ether has a differentiating, diversifying, and ordering influence, often creating a series (a spectrum) of distinct characteristics. These forces were not yet active during ancient Sun existence, which was governed mainly by great polarities, such as light and darkness, progress and rest. But on ancient Moon we can, for the first time, perceive the differentiating influence of the sound ether at work. It was, for example, on the old Moon that a rudimentary spectrum of the different organs first emerged in human beings; we have, in a previous chapter, described this aspect from the point of view of the astral forces. This time our starting point will be taken from the realm of the sound ether, even as the distinction is a subtle one. These forces are, after all, closely linked to the astral forces (as mentioned above, this type of ether can even be called *astral ether*).

Everything that happened on ancient Moon had certain consequences for the development of the sound ether, especially the complications resulting from the *conflict in Heaven*, outlined in earlier chapters. The reader will recall that, during this cosmic struggle, the rebellious Moon-beings attempted to bring about a separate course of development for all the beings living on the Moon (including human beings)—a development independent of and disconnected from the Sun's influences. Put another way, they wanted this development to take place in isolation, without the beneficial influences of the light ether radiating from the Sun. This cosmic struggle has affected the human astral body ever since. But,—and this is important for our further explorations into the sixth commandment—it has also had a bearing on the sound ether forces; for it is mainly through the influence of the sound ether (in conjunction with the astral forces to which, as mentioned above, these etheric forces are closely related) that the physical bodies of all living beings have become imperfect, temporal, and subject to death forces.

Death forces form an integral part of the etheric bodies of living beings, which are now subject not only to processes of growth, but also to various forms of decay. All living beings—and this is particularly the case for human beings—must be able to maintain within their organism a natural equilibrium between these death forces and the life forces that renew and support life. On the other hand, death forces actually play an important role in the development of

The Sixth Commandment and the Origin of Death Forces

human consciousness. In that sense, death forces belong to and are necessary for our development. But, if the working of these forces on human consciousness becomes too strong—and this danger is ever-present—the inherent inner balance would be disturbed, potentially even leading to a desire to kill. The *struggle in Heaven*, ultimately, was fought by the Sun-beings to help curb the inharmonious impact of these forces.

And so, we can indeed find the origin of death forces, which later were to become the focus of the sixth commandment, on old Moon—albeit only in germinal form. It is necessary, then, that we try to understand the conditions on old Moon, difficult as this may be within the framework of our present-day concepts and language. But the attempt must be made; for it will lead to a better understanding of the sixth commandment. To be able to describe the character of the ancient Moon existence, Rudolf Steiner often made use of rather peculiar sounding double concepts.[158] He refers to mineral–plants, to plant–animals, to animal–humans, and to a process of nutrition in our human ancestors that should be envisioned as transpiring "somewhere between nutrition and breathing." The planet's surface is described as consisting of "a semi-living substance" and the environment as "an element that was neither water nor air."[159] Rudolf Steiner did not use these double concepts as a result of inexact observations; he used these concepts because it is the only way to express the unique, essential character of old Moon in human language. It is interesting to note, then, that the continuing development on old Moon also reveals a kind of *double image*; for, on the one hand we encounter a harmonious, varied progression, and on the other hand the emergence of forces of death and disintegration.

And yet, *death* did not actually occur on old Moon, at least not in the present-day sense. It was a process that, in the words of Rudolf Steiner, must be envisioned as taking place somewhere between "falling asleep and dying." The part of the human body that had been hardened by the Moon influences had to be shed from time to time; the other part lived on—the part, namely, that bore a germ for the future in it because it had absorbed the influences of the Sun. This particular process would then be followed by another process that must be envisioned as "somewhere between present-day waking up and being born." During this process a new human being would be formed out of the previously mentioned germ, "as if from the grave of the old bodily nature." This was a kind of self-regeneration, a process that incorporated elements of both reproduction and reincarnation, and must be understood as a forerunner of either. The new type of consciousness accompanying these developments is described as "very close to reproduction."[160] We are here right in the midst of a whole series of these unconventional double concepts used to describe the situation on ancient Moon!

In summary, we may say that the archetypal picture arising from these events invariably shows a double image: *development through differentiation* and exposure to the *impact of death forces*. Because of these developments three new qualities emerged in our human ancestors on old Moon:

1. a primitive form of consciousness
2. a precursor of death
3. an early form of reproduction

An inevitable consequence of all this was the fact that human beings would, from then on, also be capable of killing; but this tendency had to be curtailed from the outset. And so, the lofty Sun-beings called out, as it were, a warning to the inhabitants of the old Moon that, conveyed in present-day language, would have sounded like, "You shall not kill." These words were heard again, at a much later time in evolution, in the sixth commandment—words that echo the original warning of the Sun-beings, if we render them in keeping with our present line of thought, "You shall not allow the Moon-forces to gain mastery over you in your astral ether." Or, put another way, "You shall not follow the death impulses of the astral body beyond their legitimate sphere; you shall recognize the holiness of the life principle in every human being."

We observed that, in accordance with the *Law of Recapitulation*, certain aspects of the Moon phase had to be repeated once more at the beginning of the Lemurian time. This meant that the circumstances during this third phase of our actual Earth existence eventually became just as unsettled as those on old Moon had been. The impact of death forces had increased over time to the point where the actual survival of Lemurian humanity was threatened.[161] During this critical time, a section of the Earth had to be split off the rest of the Earth—the section namely, that had absorbed too much of the aforementioned death forces. This part became the external planetary body that still rotates around the Earth as our Moon today. With the removal of these death forces the future development of Earth and humankind was secured.

As our Lemurian ancestors continued their development, several changes were taking place. Human consciousness became more focused on earthly matters and on knowledge. This, in turn, meant that human beings became capable of making mistakes and errors. Life on Earth was no longer experienced as a seamless continuation of cosmic existence before birth. Human beings now had to go through a real death process and hence also became susceptible to the earliest forms of illness. The strong impact of these earthly forces also caused a change in human reproduction. In the earlier phases of Lemuria our human ancestors had been both male and female. Now one sex gradually became the more dominant one, and eventually our human ancestors began to appear exclusively male or female.

In summary, we may say that all these developments, which had their very first beginnings on old Moon, continued in the Lemurian time, bringing about a further specialization of the three rudimentary qualities that had initially been developed on old Moon:

1. In human consciousness—knowledge and the possibility of error
2. In human life on Earth—illness and death
3. In human reproduction—the separation of the sexes and procreation through birth.

Now that death had become part of human life in Lemuria, our ancestors were, for the first time, capable of killing. And indeed, a lot of human blood was spilled during the latter stages of the Lemurian era. In order to safeguard the future of humanity, the impact of these excessive death forces needed to be curtailed. A colossal fire catastrophe finally wiped out most of human life and brought an end to the Lemurian age.[162] A new beginning had to be made by a small group of survivors who would find a new home in the serene and bountiful valleys of Atlantis, an area unaffected by the catastrophe. This would herald the beginning of the Atlantean era, an era in which human beings would be more capable of keeping all these impulsive, tempestuous forces in balance. During that new Atlantean age it would also become possible for an even more rarefied kind of ether—the life ether—to be integrated into the earth. And what is more, through the inspiration coming from the Atlantean mystery centers, human beings would, for the first time, be guided by the words "You shall not kill."

Biblical Images of Lemurian Events

We can find a fairly accurate portrayal of these cosmic events in the beginning of the Old Testament as well, told in the form of a biblical story.[163] Here we meet Adam who lived in Paradise, a place where neither birth nor death yet existed. We are told of the unmistakable connection between knowledge and death in the words, "But of the tree of the knowledge of good and evil, you shall not eat of it: for in the day that you eat thereof you shall surely die" (Gen. 2:17). Adam, the human being, first existed as a single being; Genesis (1:27) mentions that God created him "male and female," thus pointing to a time period when human beings were hermaphrodite, both male and female.

This, then, is followed by a cosmic pause in which life almost ceased to exist—a deep sleep fell upon Adam, almost like death. Next, we encounter the image of a rib being taken from Adam, resulting in the appearance of Eve, a female human being next to Adam as a male human being. This paradisiacal state then is followed by "the fall into sin." In its description we can recognize the three human qualities that had developed in Lemuria through the influence of the astral body and of the sound ether, that is to say, the beginning of:

1. conscious knowledge
2. death
3. sexual reproduction and physical birth

The possibility of acquiring *knowledge* finds a biblical image in the tree with the forbidden fruit, "a tree to be desired to make one wise" (Gen. 3:6). *Death* is pictured as the consequence of the eating of the fruit, "till you return unto the ground; for out of it were you taken: for dust you are, and unto dust shall you return" (3:19). The beginning of physical *reproduction* is reflected in the words, "in sorrow you shall bring forth children" (3:16).[164]

According to the Bible, Cain was the first human being born out of two parents. Although this new physical birth gave him the beginning of a certain inner independence, it also caused a sense of isolation and separation from the spiritual world. Also, because birth is inextricably linked to death, Cain was the first human being exposed to the death aspects of the sound ether and of the astral body. In him lived not only the new forces of birth, but he was also subject to the powerful influence of death forces that he was not yet able to resist, causing him to kill his brother, Abel. The immediate consequence of this act was a further separation of the human being (Cain) from the spiritual world (the LORD). And yet, God did not punish Cain with death. He made him a fugitive in the "land of Nod, on the East of Eden" (Gen. 4:16). God also granted Cain a sevenfold protection lest he should be killed (we recall that the number seven is derived from the astral world), "And the LORD said unto him, Therefore whosoever slays Cain, vengeance shall be taken on him sevenfold. And the LORD set a mark upon Cain, lest any finding him should kill him" (Gen. 4:15).

Ever since the fall and the murder of Abel it has proved exceedingly difficult for humanity to resist the impact of these negative aspects of the sound ether and of the astral forces working through it. In Genesis (4:23–24) we read that Cain's descendants were even more prone to such passions than Cain himself. We hear of Lamech, Cain's great-great-great-grandson, who would not have hesitated to take revenge "seven and seventy fold." Such unbridled passions eventually needed to be subdued and transformed, if the further development of humanity was to be safeguarded.

We can find an indication of this kind of transformation actually beginning to take place at the end of the Bible story about Lamech. At this point there is a hiatus in the account. To be able to read old chronicles like this Bible story in a meaningful way, it can be helpful to take note of such interruptions in the flow of the storytelling. These can tell us of a profound turning point occurring in the course of events. It is as though an opening were created to let a light beam of ancient mystery wisdom pass through. In this case its light illuminated the blind alley that had been reached as a result of Lamech's excessive, selfish willfulness. Then the story ends and we are led back to Adam and Eve who have another son, Seth,[165] followed by a listing of Adam's descendants in which no further mention is made of Cain and Abel, but only of Seth's bloodline.

This mysterious break in the story also gives us a veiled indication that, with it, we have reached the end of the Lemurian age. With the fiery catastrophe that brought an end to Lemuria, Cain's descendants, who had lived with the full force of the dangerous aspects of the sound ether, had been wiped off the Earth. A new era had started with Seth. The Bible presents an uninterrupted lineage between Seth and Noah,[166] in other words, from the beginning of the Atlantean epoch right up to its destruction in the flood.

One could say that Abel was the representative of those who still lived mostly within the realm of the *light ether*, close to nature and to God. He then was displaced by Cain, the representative of those whose lives were guided mainly by the forces of the *sound ether*. His descendants were strong; they mastered the "brass and iron" trades,[167] but also the gentler trades of husbandry and music,[168] manifesting even here the double nature of the sound ether. But, in the end, Cain's descendants were wiped out by a powerful force of nature. Finally Seth was born, the representative of those who lived more in the realm of the *life ether*. His lineage continued all through the ages, culminating in Jesus.[169] And, with the coming of Christ to the Earth, the powerful death forces can be transformed into resurrection forces, thus shining a new light on the commandment "You shall not kill."

CHRIST AND THE SIXTH COMMANDMENT

The sanctity of human life obviously is of such fundamental significance that Jesus was able to use it as the basis for all his teachings. It would, for instance, be difficult to reconcile his words regarding "loving one's neighbor" with the killing of another human being. But did Christ also transform the core of the sixth commandment, in other words, human death as such?

There are several aspects to this question. We have seen that, ever since the Fall in Lemurian times, human beings have been exposed to the steadily increasing influence of death forces. Christ was able, through his living and working on the Earth, to bring these forces into a renewed balance for human beings. He also manifested his sovereignty over these death forces by healing the sick and raising the dead.

But the determining and pivotal deed took place on Golgotha. On Golgotha Christ *overcame* death; this has had the most far-reaching consequences for humanity and for the Earth. We cannot emphasize strongly enough that this event constitutes not just the experience of one human being, or even of one divine being. It is an event that fundamentally changed the conditions of existence for all human beings living on the Earth, for all times to come. ("And, lo, I am with you always, even unto the end of the world," Matt. 28:20.) To grasp the full significance of this event, however, we must first develop a more comprehensive picture of the meaning of human death, for it is above all the human experience of dying that underwent a significant change through the event on Golgotha.[170]

From a day-to-day point of view, death is the end of life. But in reality it is so much more than that. Seen from a spiritual point of view, *nothing on earth is more spiritually real than death.*[171] What does this mean?

In olden times death was experienced as a return to the harmony of the spiritual world, to the true source of creation. But in more recent times, that is to say, in the centuries leading up to the time of Christ, human beings increasingly began to experience a sense of loneliness, of isolation during the dying process. They had to go through the actual death experience alone. One could also say that, at the very moment of death, human beings attained their most individual, most independent state of being.

After death they gradually became part of the spiritual world again. While there, human beings perceived that they bore valuable experiences within themselves because of the very fact that they had to live on the Earth, and therefore had to go through the human process of dying. And so, human beings increasingly carried an inner quality through the gate of death, a strength that would eventually become the true essence of their existence.

But human beings were not able to communicate these experiences to the other beings in the spiritual cosmos. Although the beings of the higher hierarchies were aware that human beings carried a mystery in their essential nature, they did not know, *could not know*, the experience of death on Earth. It was inaccessible to them; it was something that could not be communicated. This was a specific dimension belonging only to human beings. We know that, under certain circumstances, some spiritual beings were able to permeate a human soul and live within a human body for brief periods, but they invariably had to withdraw before death occurred. These beings were not able to experience the final process of dying. Only human beings went through death. *Only human beings carried the mystery of death in their inner being.*

With the passing of time, this human mystery grew into an ever-increasing dilemma for the beings in the spiritual world, who were involved in guiding the destiny of evolution. They knew that it contained a spirit seed, from which the next planetary phase, the so-called Jupiter phase, was destined to be formed in the future. But the higher beings could not penetrate this secret. It was essential, then, that the mystery of death—and the human isolation from the spiritual world that is intimately linked with it—should be reintegrated into that spiritual world.

Christ took it upon himself to fulfill this deed. He entered a human body, lived in it as a human being and stayed with it right through the experience of death. What made this particular death so exceptional is the fact that Christ went through this experience both *as a human being* and *as a spiritual being.* This was a unique event in the entire history of the cosmos and of the Earth. With this deed a new link has been established between two realms that were in danger of being separated, between the spiritual and the physical realm, between the hierarchical universe and the human world.

The death on the cross was of fundamental significance for both worlds. On the one hand it was indeed an "affair of the gods." In that sense, one could say, humankind was only a spectator and, by having prepared the body of Jesus of Nazareth, an instrument toward this goal. But, on the other hand, humanity became deeply affected by this event.

A special aspect of the Mystery of Golgotha was the fact that Christ accepted death *in full inner freedom.* Because of this deed, *human* freedom was also raised to a higher spiritual level than had been possible before. The earliest seed of human freedom, we recall, had been planted in the Lemurian time through the actions of laggard spiritual beings; but at the same time, and intimately linked to these events, human beings had become exposed to death forces, with potentially tragic consequences, as evidenced in the story of Cain and Abel. But now, because of Christ's deed on Golgotha, human freedom could be lifted out of this domain and into the realm of the Sun-forces of Christ.

Moreover, by dying on the cross in full inner freedom, Christ also created a spiritual counterbalance for Cain's murder of Abel. Additionally, this deed inaugurated a new phase in the evolution of the *sound ether*, particularly in regard to the more problematic aspect of these forces, that is to say, the death aspect. It is almost impossible to express the full significance of this deed in human concepts, but it belongs to the essence of earthly existence.

THE HUMAN DEATH EXPERIENCE TRANSFORMED— DYING IN CHRIST

The death on Golgotha also transformed the way human beings can now experience death. Had this event not taken place, the aforementioned feelings of loneliness and isolation, which presently always accompany death, would have become *the* all-consuming experience, eventually shriveling the human spirit. But Christ's deed on Golgotha created something new in this respect; for, although feelings of isolation will continue to accompany the process of dying, we have now been given the assurance that we also *belong* to the spiritual world, are part of it. Finding an inner balance between these simultaneously occurring feelings of isolation and of belonging will in the future increasingly become a new source of strength for all human beings. And with the deed of Christ on Golgotha it is now *possible* to experience death in this new way. This is the reason we have now been given a new guiding principle in addition to the original commandment. We are now encouraged to *die in Christ*.[172] What does this mean?

To find an answer to this question, we will first consider the Bible. All four Gospels give accounts of two other men being crucified together with Jesus Christ. In the various translations of the Bible they are called thieves, malefactors, robbers, murderers, or simply "two others."[173] We have reason, then, to assume that these malefactors had stolen, robbed, and killed in the pursuit of their crimes. In a way, one could say, they were carriers of the Cain-destiny of humanity.

The Sixth Commandment and the Origin of Death Forces

Many have met Jesus during their lifetime, but only these "two others" had the *privilege* of going with him through death. A very special fate indeed! And yet, although these two died the same death outwardly, they went through entirely different experiences inwardly. We mentioned earlier that the human death experience has two aspects: on the one hand an awareness of being connected with the cosmos and on the other hand a sense of isolation and loneliness. This is exactly the twofold aspect we encounter in the double image of these two malefactors dying on either side of Christ on the cross! The one murderer's death experience could be integrated into the cosmos in a fruitful way, because, through awareness of his guilt, he was able to feel a connection to the rest of humanity. But the other murderer's death forces were linked with ridicule and malice—sentiments that harden and isolate the soul. The great painters of the past have at times attempted to express the deeper truths of this scene by portraying one murderer in the light and the other in the dark.

Luke, the physician, was able to describe this episode in its purest form: "And one of the malefactors that were hanged railed on him, saying, if you be Christ, save yourself and us. But the other answering rebuked him, saying, do not you fear God, seeing you are in the same condemnation? And we indeed justly; for we receive the due reward of our deeds: but this man has done nothing amiss. And he said unto Jesus, Lord, remember me when you come into your kingdom. And Jesus said unto him, Verily I say unto you, Today shall you be with me in paradise" (Luke 23:39–43).

This is a very moving scene indeed, because all those present realized that they were witnessing the awesome reality of death. Here was no longer any room for the web of earthly illusions. What was spoken here came from the innermost being of these two men and already pointed to the path they would have to take, a short while later, after having passed through the gate of death. The one malefactor was aware of his karmic guilt, turned to Christ, and was released from his sins. For him Christ could spiritually transform the impact of the Fall, thus guiding him to the cosmic *Harmony of the Spheres*.

His death experience was graced by the Sun-forces working in Christ. The other one died alone, shut off within himself, lost and wandering through the spiritual cosmos. His death experience, one could say, was clouded by the lingering influence of the laggard Moon-beings.

The Lord of Karma

The Bible story about the two malefactors dying on the cross on Golgotha also presents us with the earliest indication of what is meant by "Christ becoming *the Lord of Karma*"—a very early, specific, unique case indeed. As we mentioned briefly in the chapter about the third commandment, Christ will increasingly take on this new task of *karmic judge*, beginning in the twentieth century. But, as with all new developments, there will always be early manifestations of what is to come. Such was the case on Golgotha in the interchange between Christ and the two malefactors.

Christ has now become the Lord of Karma! This is an event of such order of magnitude that it will forever change not only how karma works in our lives, but also how we as human beings undergo the process of dying. The experience of death will gradually take on a new form, particularly in our own time. What does this mean? We know that, during the first three days following our death, we will perceive a grand etheric panorama of our entire life. After experiencing this etheric memory tableau, but before continuing on our path after death, we will then meet a judge-like figure who will appraise the moral value of our life; he will evaluate our life in relation to our own personal karma. For most people this spiritual figure will appear in the form of Moses, the bringer of the first moral laws of humankind.[174] He presents the person who has just died with an objective, but irrevocable karmic judgment of his or her life.

This role of karmic judge will, according to Rudolf Steiner, now gradually be taken over by Christ, beginning in the twentieth century. More and more people will now meet Christ as their karmic judge. And, although the moral value of their lives will still be evaluated individually, it will now also be weighed against the needs of the time and of humanity as a whole, in other words, against *the karma of humanity*. This value judgment by Christ goes far beyond the context of a person's individual karma because it will now be linked with Christ's. This also means that, although the karma of that person's next life will still be individually formed, it will now be shaped in such a way that he or she will be able to work and contribute toward the healing of humanity, for the good of all humankind.

Once we become familiar with this picture, the question may well arise: Which souls will meet Moses as their judge, and which souls Christ will judge? What are the determining factors? We live, with respect to these questions, in a time of transition. Do not believe for a moment, though, that this would in any way depend on one's religion or ancestry.

Most people who live a moral life by following a set of ethical values—and in our culture this would probably include some version of the values expressed in the Ten Commandments—will likely meet Moses as their karmic judge after death. This is, according to Rudolf Steiner's spiritual-scientific observations, still the case at the present time for most people. At the same time, however, there will now also be those who meet Christ as the judge of their moral values and actions. A particular quality is needed for this to happen. But this quality, this impulse, can only be acquired *during life on Earth*. Nowhere in the spiritual world, after we have died, can we find the strength that would lead us to Christ as our karmic judge unless we already bring it with us as the fruit of our life on Earth. This particular strength, this quality, has to do with what we usually call *conscience*.

Ever since human conscience began to manifest itself for the first time in ancient Greece, a few centuries before Christ, this new soul quality, this inner voice has led human beings on the personal path of morality. Before that time, in cases of wrongdoing, people would have felt as though being pursued by an external force of condemnation— such as the avenging furies we encounter in Greek tragedies that were written *prior* to that time—rather than by the inner voice of reckoning we now know as our conscience. Today we stand at the dawn of an era in which some people will begin to develop a *new* form of conscience, one that extends beyond one's personal perspective of right or wrong. We could call this new inner sensitivity a *higher conscience*. Gradually, more and more people will acquire this new faculty. They will develop a subtle awareness, that everything they do—or fail to do—has an impact on the world and on the development of humanity, for which they themselves will feel accountable before Christ. With the passing of time this kind of awareness will develop naturally in more and more people, but we can also, already now, consciously activate a new sense of responsibility in ourselves—something that can only be done during our life on Earth.

Developing this sense of responsibility toward Christ, toward the whole Earth, and toward our fellow human beings will also change the way we experience our own death process. If we learn to develop this higher awareness, something can arise within the human soul that can be likened to a light. It is this inner soul light shining out into our etheric surroundings that makes visible for us the etheric form of Christ as our karmic judge after death.[175] Developing this kind of *higher conscience* during our life on Earth, then, is an essential precondition for what we have called the new experience of dying, that is to say, *dying in Christ*.

Those who die the *old* death meet with death forces that belong to the realm of the Father God. Those who die the *new* death are carried by forces that radiate from the Christ-being. They die in Christ. Their spiritual path after death will take on a different quality as well. New life forces are kindled in them through the Holy Spirit, forces that will carry fruits for later incarnations, well into the future. This can then become a source of strength through which they will be able to accept suffering for the sake of humanity and the cosmos.

It would be difficult to overstate the comprehensive significance of the Mystery of Golgotha for the Earth and for humanity; but it is particularly also with regards to the development of the *sound ether forces*, that the deed on Golgotha was of crucial importance. Because of this deed, the sound ether—and especially everything related to the death aspect of these forces—could be reintegrated into the spiritual universe. The original commandment "You shall not kill" was aimed at the potentially dangerous aspects of these forces that people were exposed to in pre-Christian times. Christ, by bestowing his own spiritual substance onto this commandment, has brought a new kind of death experience to the Earth for human beings, a death experience that points to the future.

The Sixth Commandment in our Time

Many people today are struggling with the problem of death—the essence of the sixth commandment—or, in particular, with their responsibility toward the timing of someone's death, for example in cases of euthanasia, abortion, medical intervention, and so on. But in most instances the ensuing discussions tend to focus primarily on ethical and/or moral implications of human intervention in the timing of death, rather than on the karmic consequences for the soul, both after death or in a next life. Anthroposophy can help us gain insight in the things human beings experience during and after death.[176] This does not make the dilemma any less complex, but it makes possible for us to include the spiritual realities in our thoughts about the circumstances surrounding death.

It will also become more and more important, in regards to all ethical and moral questions we face in life (and in death), that we examine the value of our thoughts and conclusions in light of the aforementioned *higher conscience*, in other words, in light of the fact that we will have to account for them before Christ as the *Lord of Karma* after we have died.

The only way to do this is by seeking a conscious connection to Christ. Such a connection cannot be established after death, however, but *must* be formed during life on Earth. This is the crucial point.[177] But many people pass through the gate of death at the present time without, for a variety of reasons, having been able to develop such a conscious connection in their souls. They will not be able to take up the revelations of the Christ-being after death; for this requires a particular quality of consciousness that cannot be developed after death. The dead cannot do this on the other side of the threshold. But we, who are living on the Earth, *can* develop this quality of consciousness. This means that we can help those who have died. We can help them through our meditative work. Special meditations, dedicated to the dead, can have a "consciousness-widening" effect on these souls.[178]

Today, many souls are subsisting in a state of spiritual deprivation after death—comparable only to physical starvation while alive—which has endured for such a long time that their ability to take up spiritual nourishment has withered. This ability must first be enlivened again in these souls on the other side. Meditations, specially dedicated to these souls, can provide life-giving nourishment and thus be truly therapeutic for these souls after death.

One could begin such meditations for the dead, for instance, by thinking intently about the meaning of Christ's life on Earth and its significance for all humankind in general; this initial meditation could then become more defined by trying to envision a particular episode in the life of Christ in greater detail, or by carefully contemplating one of his sayings. Through meditations such as these we can actually help the dead find a connection to the Christ-being, something they were not able to establish on Earth. This is a gift we can give to the souls of the dead out of our own free will. In this way the true impulse of the sixth commandment can live on and be transformed for our time.

It goes without saying that an external commandment against killing still holds a valid place in society today because of its fundamental premise. But it can now also assume an entirely new form when people decide in full inner freedom to help the souls of the dead, in the way we just described.

We all carry a destructive impulse in our innermost being. This has been the case ever since the actions of the rebellious Moon beings and of Cain and his descendents. More murders will be committed and more wars will be fought. We should not foster any illusions in this regard. But, because of the Mystery of Golgotha, a new force is now available to all humankind, the only force that, over time, can truly redeem these destructive impulses. This force can also give rise to the present-day metamorphosis of the sixth commandment, one we can aspire to in our time, and can be put into the following words: *If you so wish, you may help empower and invigorate the souls of the dead with the force radiating from the Christ-being.*

7

The Seventh Commandment and the Life Ether

The seventh commandment: *"You shall not commit adultery."* This directive is usually seen as one of the fundamental principles of marriage. We can, of course, without further ado take this guideline as a meaningful and reliable starting point; but, along with it, we may want to look for a deeper, more spiritual meaning, both of this commandment and of marriage as such. To be able to do this it will be helpful to take a closer look at the working of the *life ether*, because the seventh commandment has a special connection with this, the most refined type of ether.

It is even more difficult to penetrate the life ether with our everyday concepts than the light ether or the sound ether, which had their origins on old Sun and old Moon respectively. The life ether emerged relatively late in the course of evolution, namely during our present Earth phase.

In our contemplations about the sound ether we noted both the complexity of this type of ether and the limitations imposed by a singular designation, by a label that can name only one of its characteristics. The reader will recall that, along with *sound ether*, several other designations are used to indicate various other aspects of this type of ether, such as *chemical ether* or *number ether*. In the case of the life ether the restrictions imposed by a singular definition are even greater. If we again want to bring out the various aspects of this type of ether we may also refer to it as *word ether, thought ether,* or *"I"-ether.* And there are other names that could be used to describe additional characteristics of these etheric forces. However, to simplify things we will here use the term *life ether* exclusively.

As mentioned, the life ether only emerged during our present Earth phase of evolution. In the earliest stages of the Earth phase (Polaris, Hyperborea, and the first half of Lemuria) these etheric forces worked mostly inwardly, invisibly, within our human ancestors. But, starting in the second half of the Lemurian and then continuing in the fourth, the Atlantean era, the life ether began to work externally as well, that is to say, in the cosmos, in the earthly surroundings, and also in human beings. This is the stage during which solid matter was formed on Earth. And, even though these solid materials may appear to be lifeless, it is exactly in this seemingly dead matter that the life ether is most active. One could say that *solid matter relates to the life ether as the shadow to the light.* Wherever solid matter is formed, life ether is at work. This applies to the formation of the human skeleton as well; yet, we also know that it is exactly in the inner core of these apparently dead bones, namely in the bone marrow, that our blood is formed—our blood that, through its living warmth, is the bearer of the human "I." It is important to keep this aspect in mind as well, when studying the life ether. And so, if we want to understand what distinguishes the life ether from the other etheric forces, we would do well to study those forming processes through which the various life forms bring structure to and make use of solid matter.

To begin with, we could look at the Earth as a whole. We could then examine how the different continents have gradually been formed throughout long geological periods; and how the formation of the local mountain ranges tends to display more of a north–south alignment on some continents and an east–west alignment on others. We could then study what impact either of these mountain range alignments has on the local weather conditions and by extension on all life forms in these regions.[179]

We could also observe the finely structured soil around us. Its granular structure makes the soil eminently suitable to nurture plant life on Earth because of specific chemical processes that can only occur on the surfaces of solid matter, such as crystallization and disintegration. Or we could observe on a cold winter day how the layers of snow, covering the landscape, contain multitudes of tiny sparkling crystals, and how each snowflake is uniquely shaped. Or we could think about the gems and minerals in the earth; how the diamonds, sapphires, and quartz crystals function as the Earth's senses, as it were, through which the Earth is able to perceive and absorb cosmic influences from the stars and the zodiac.

To be able to comprehend the activity of the life ether in any of the processes just described, we would first need to develop a sense for the Earth as one entity, as one living organism. This can be done, but it is a difficult concept for most people today. An easier way to get to know the life ether may be found by concentrating on the different realms of nature because these are more accessible to our modern way of thinking.

The plant kingdom, naturally, is eminently suited for observations of, and research into, etheric forces—*all* the different etheric forces. But if we particularly want to understand how the *life ether* works, a good start can be made by observing how the various growth stages of a plant form a totality, a *life cycle*, revealing an integral picture of that plant. Then we can look at how this image of the plant is expressed in its yearly cycle from seed to leaf, flower and fruit, and then again returning to the seed; and how the plant's life cycle is integrated in the cycle of the year during which the Sun moves through the whole zodiac. Learning to see the life cycle of a particular plant as an ever-changing metamorphosis of the essential *being* of that plant, can give us a sense of how the life ether works.

The activity of the life ether can also be detected in one specific growth phase of the plant. For, just as the light ether plays a role in the formation of the green leaves and the sound ether in the forming of the flowers, the *life ether* works wherever life forces seem to be *least active*, that is to say, in the hardest parts of the plants, in wood and bark, in thorns, pits, and nutshells, and so on. One could also say that the life ether works wherever the life forces of the plant are most condensed, as in the fruit and especially in the seed. It is in the seed that the whole life cycle of the plant returns to its starting point. In the seed we are actually confronted with something akin to death. How new life emerges from the seemingly lifeless seed: this is the profound secret of the life ether; *for these forces always lead through death to resurrection.*

Summarizing what the plants can reveal to us about the influence of the different etheric forces, we may say that in the green leaves the *universal life processes* become manifest through the working of the *light ether*; that in the flowers the *distinguishing features* of the species come to the fore through the influence of the *sound ether*; and that in the seed and the fruit we can get to know the *true essence* of each plant species through the specific influence of the *life ether*.[180]

In the animal kingdom it is more difficult to detect the working of the life ether, because it is primarily through the influence of the astral world (along with the sound ether) that the characteristic features of the different animals emerge. But with the help of a phenomenological way of thinking we may be able to recognize where and how the life ether works in the animal kingdom as well. We can do this by reflecting on how the life cycle of a particular animal runs its course, with each phase expressing something of that life cycle as a whole; or how body shape, eating habits, and behavior are related to that animal's characteristic way of life. Or we can examine how an animal uses solid matter, earthly materials, for shelter or for nest building; because this is where the life ether forces are especially at work.

We can also recognize the activity of the life ether in the animal itself, in its bodily structure, in the forming of the skeletal system and of teeth and tusks, as well as in the animal skin, especially in the various forms of hardened modifications, as in hair, hoofs, horns, claws, nails, quills, shells, scales, fins, feathers, or beaks. Or we can think about the organs that serve specific aspects of the lifestyle of the animal, and about the senses through which they relate to their physical surroundings.

In this way we can find points of contact, both in the realm of the animals and that of the plants, which can help us understand how the life ether works. We have pointed out earlier that life ether forces are working wherever we encounter a twelvefold cycle or configuration in nature.[181] This is why we can detect these forces at work in the yearly life cycles of the plants, which oftentimes reveal a twelvefold process,[182] as well as in the lifestyles of the different animals that come about through the influence of the Sun, the stars, and the twelvefold zodiac.[183]

Now we come to the human realm. How are the life ether forces working in human beings? Just as we observed with respect to the other realms of nature, we may picture these forces at work in the formation of the hardest parts of the human body, as well as in the structure of life as a whole. But, in order to develop useful concepts about the influence of the life ether in human beings specifically, we would also do well to reflect on the inherent connection between life ether and the human "I" (we mentioned in the beginning of this chapter that *life ether* can also be called "*I*"-*ether*). A fruitful starting point may be found in the fact that we can walk upright, speak, and think; for these are three very special skills that can only be developed in human beings, precisely because we have an "I," which was bestowed on our ancestors during the actual Earth phase of evolution.

The ability to *walk* and *stand upright* emerged in rudimentary form in the Lemurian time, when the germinal "I" first began to work on the human body. In order to be able to stand and walk in an upright position the skeletal system has to be strong enough to provide the necessary support and firmness to the whole body. The formation of the bone structure develops through the influence of the life ether. As mentioned above, life ether forces often manifest in a twelvefold order. It is interesting to note, then, that we can indeed find a twelvefold structure in certain parts of the human skeleton.[184]

The ability to *speak* emerged in rudimentary form at the beginning of the Atlantean time, when the young "I" had permeated the human body somewhat more. Human speaking is essentially different from the sounds produced by animals. We use consonants and vowels. Animals primarily generate sounds that could be described as something akin to vowels. When animals produce sounds that could be perceived as consonants, these usually consist of but a single consonant, such as *sss* or *rrr*. Our speaking, in contrast, displays a systematic articulation through the use of multiple consonants, something animals are incapable of doing. We make use of a refined sense of touch within the speech organs. This sense of touch—as it is present in the lips, teeth, tongue, and palate—is actually a specialized form of our general sense of touch, located in the skin all over the body. What makes all this possible is the working of the life ether forces.[185]

The ability to *think* emerged in rudimentary form in the later Atlantean phase, when the young "I" had permeated the physical body even further. Our thinking is also dependent on the activity of the life ether, which again manifests in a twelvefold way. Our brain allows us to think; there are twelve pairs of cranial nerves in the brain. The activity of thinking is stimulated by our twelve senses.[186] Furthermore, there are twelve possible worldviews or ways of thinking accessible to our faculty of thinking, each of which has a special connection to one region of the zodiac.[187]

In summary we may say that, wherever life ether is working, we frequently encounter processes that, eventually, would lead to something akin to dying; but that these processes, by completing a twelvefold cycle, can then be brought to a new and higher form of life.[188]

Now that we have gained a better understanding of the life ether, we can turn our attention to the seventh commandment itself.

The Spiritual Background of the Seventh Commandment

We have tried to determine the esoteric origin of each of the commandments discussed so far. Can we, in the same way, also find the spiritual roots of the seventh commandment "You shall not commit adultery"? Or, put another way, can we discover the deeper meaning behind the existence of marriage and marital fidelity?

The fundamental premise of this commandment is such that one could simply accept it at face value, as an indispensable basis for life in a well-ordered social community. One could, for example, point out that this fundamental principle helps create family stability, by providing a protective setting for the children to grow up in. One could further point out that a logical connection may be surmised between the fifth and the seventh commandment, because children can honor their parents only if the family stability is not undermined by the fallout of infidelity. Also, if the Mosaic laws (as has often been done) are interpreted as essentially a set of rules governing people's physical and social health, then the seventh commandment could be viewed as primarily a measure to prevent the spread of sexual diseases. And there are various other practical and appropriate ways to approach the meaning of this commandment. These viewpoints unquestionably represent important aspects, but do not touch on the spiritual core of the seventh commandment. Moreover, we are repeatedly confronted with the indisputable fact that such considerations do not carry sufficient weight to legislate marital fidelity in today's society.

In the Dutch language the word *marrying* (*trouwen*) is closely related to the word *fidelity* (*trouw*) and, incidentally, to the word *trust* (*vertrouwen*). This linguistic assertion, naturally, does not guarantee that any two married people are going to stay together for life. And yet, the basic premise of marital faithfulness has long been accepted and respected as a moral ideal in large parts of the world. In order to discover the roots of this basic premise, we must again return in our thoughts to an earlier evolutionary phase, in this case to the Lemurian era, where the separation of the sexes first occurred.

Our Lemurian ancestors had not yet developed the capacity of remembering. Their actions were motivated mainly by momentary impulses, welling up instinctively in their souls. Such instinctive impulses also dictated how children were brought up. A connection existed between the parents for the duration of child rearing, while the children needed their help and protection, but this parental bonding would dissolve soon after. Only in the Atlantean age did people start to develop their faculty of memory. They gradually became aware of continuity in their lives, of a link between the past and the present, making it *possible* for the first time that two people could establish a *marital bond for life*. From then on we encounter the institution of marriage—and the expectation of lifelong fidelity—all over the Earth. We have to assume that this particular lifestyle must have been instituted by the Atlantean mysteries; for, as we observed earlier, all important ordinances governing human life in those ancient times had their origins in the mysteries. The question may well arise, then: Why did the Atlantean mysteries organize human society in this way?

During the Lemurian time high spiritual beings had implanted the germinal "I" into our human ancestors. This meant that human life had to be structured in such a way that it would accommodate the further development of this new seed. But only in the Atlantean time, when both the germinal "I" and the faculty of memory had become stronger, do we encounter what may be called a human lifestyle; for only when human life is grounded in the emerging forces of the "I" can it be shaped as a meaningful totality from birth to death. Life ether forces play an important role in shaping a human life. In order to support these etheric forces (and hence strengthen the "I") the Atlantean initiates introduced certain lifelong, enduring elements into the outer ordinances of human life. They knew that the emerging "I" would develop best within the boundaries generated by such guidelines.

These developments set the stage for a significant process to occur: *the human soul united with the emerging individual "I."* This uniting was a suprasensory event, a process that can also be understood as an archetypal image. It was the final outcome of a lengthy course of development that had been prepared for eons.[189] By introducing the principle of faithfulness into the institution of marriage, the Atlantean initiates affirmed that this unity needed to be protected, both in society and within the individual lives of human beings. They knew that, by structuring human life in this way, the developing "I" would be able to grow and prosper.

In the middle of the Lemurian time, through the influence of the *sound ether*, the separation of the sexes had occurred. In the Atlantean time, through the influence of the *life ether*, this separation could be brought to a *higher unity* by introducing the principle of fidelity (which also embraces loyalty, trust, faithfulness) into the lives of the Atlantean people. This principle needed to be linked specifically to the institution of marriage because this whole realm is closely connected to the life ether forces. True, the life ether works in the forming of the human life cycle as a whole, from birth to death, but it is particularly in marriage, in the uniting of two people, that these forces are most active. In fact, within the human realm, *marriage* is the true representative of the life ether forces; just as, within the realm of the plants, *fruit* and *seed* form the focal point of these forces.

Preparing the Foundation for Spiritual Love

It was not just in olden times that people incorporated the notion of marital fidelity into their lives. Many people still recognize the enduring value of faithfulness and trust between marriage partners—even today. Cultivating this kind of loyalty is intimately connected to the development of the "I" and is therefore only possible if it is based on the unique qualities of the "I." These qualities can be strengthened when two life partners ever anew try to see each other as unique human beings; for the human "I" actually prospers when it learns to recognize and value the unique qualities of the other "I." This may seem to be a paradox, but is, in reality, one of the special characteristics of the spiritual world in which the "I" is rooted, and that, ultimately, is based on spiritual love.

True spiritual love, to be sure, is something that for most people is not yet attainable at present. The "I" is not developed enough. But there are three human soul forces, three qualities that can help lead us toward this lofty goal on our life's path. These three qualities are *courage*, *tactfulness*, and *loyalty*. In the Dutch language these three concepts are linked together in the commonly used everyday expression, "moed, beleid en trouw."[190] This threefold linguistic jewel in its own way affirms that courage, tact, and loyalty do indeed belong together and mutually support each other. For, in the world of the *spirit* we live through *courage*; in the world of the *soul* we must balance conflicting passions and impulses through *tactfulness*; and in the physical world (the world of the physical *body*) we live through *loyalty* and trust.[191]

Because the human "I" has evolved and matured over the course of time, most people can expect to find an adequate inner basis for the *courage* needed in their daily lives. We also carry in our souls hidden spiritual fruits from earlier incarnations that provide most of us with a reasonably stable basis for the *tactfulness* required in managing life's obstacles. But, of the previously mentioned qualities, *trust* is least developed. This particular weakness is actually a remnant of the *conflict in Heaven* that happened on old Moon, and is something that needs to be strengthened during our life on Earth as a preparation for a higher form of love, that is to say, for spiritual love. This is why the Atlantean mysteries embedded in the lives of human beings the principle of trust, of faithfulness, as the basis for love; and why, at a much later time in history, this same concept was incorporated in the commandment, "You shall not commit adultery."

In olden times human society was regulated by the mysteries in such a way that it reflected the universal cosmic order. This safeguarded people from harmful external influences. When, in later times, the authority of the mysteries began to wane, people's lives also became more susceptible to meaningless coincidence.

The age of Moses was a transitional time when, on the one hand, the old cosmic order no longer had a determining influence in human society, but on the other hand, the human "I" was not yet strong enough to handle the coincidences of life in the right way. People needed an external commandment, a commandment that governed marital faithfulness (and therefore also the realm of human procreation), in other words, the domain of the life ether forces. To strengthen these etheric forces it was necessary in the time of Moses to forbid people to succumb to the kind of infidelity to which the coincidences of life could well entice them. All this is reflected in the words of the seventh commandment, "You shall not commit adultery."

In the Atlantean age the life ether forces had to be strengthened in human beings in order to facilitate the assimilation of the "I." To help guide this process along, people's way of life—and in particular the whole realm of human sexuality—needed to be regulated and structured through marriage and marital fidelity. The Atlantean mysteries were able to develop the required form for this because they understood the inherent connection between the forces of sexual attraction and the forces of love that lay slumbering in the developing human "I." They knew that sexual love had to be structured through marital faithfulness; for this was the only way to create a stable foundation, a preparatory stage, for the true spiritual love that people will only be able to attain and develop at a much later time in the future.

At the same time, however, other—potentially dangerous—capabilities were awakened as well; for the Atlantean people also began to work with life ether forces in nature. They learned to control the etheric forces that are active in the forming of the plant seeds and in the fertility of the animals. These new abilities were, for the most part, applied toward the betterment of human life on Earth. The cultivation of new edible plant species, for example, as well as the breeding of livestock and other animal species reached hitherto unknown heights.[192] But, along with these new abilities, came new dangers. It was no longer just the fertility and reproduction of plants and animals that people were interested in and gained power over; the whole realm of human sexuality could now also be used for selfish reasons. This is a more specialized aspect of the general misuse of etheric forces we have called *the transgression of the Atlantean forefathers* in the chapter about the second commandment. In the circumstances we are presently examining, related to the seventh commandment, this transgression had to do with the misuse of *life ether* forces in particular. The dangers of such practices were well known in the mysteries. Hence it was important, even well into post-Atlantean times, to provide guidance for that special realm of human life that incorporates sexuality and reproduction, in other words, the realm of the life ether forces.

In the time of Moses all this found a more permanent expression in the seventh commandment. It aimed to strengthen the human "I" by supporting the life ether forces—for these are intimately connected—thus enabling people to gradually learn how to handle their passions, desires, and sexual instincts in the face of the coincidences of life. This also would make it possible for human beings to gradually find their way from sensual love to true spiritual love; for this, ultimately, is the deeper meaning of the commandment "You shall not commit adultery."

Christ and the Seventh Commandment

How did Christ transform the seventh commandment? We can find various accounts in the Gospels relating to the issue of infidelity. On one such occasion Jesus stated that breaking the marital bond should be avoided, even if it were to take place for reasons that had still been considered acceptable within the framework of the Mosaic laws, "Whosoever puts away his wife, and marries another, commits adultery: and whosoever marries her that is put away from her husband commits adultery" (Luke 16:18). To get a sense of the difference, compare this statement to the original Mosaic law as it appears in the Old Testament (Deuteronomy 24:1), "When a man has taken a wife, and married her, and it come to pass that she find no favor in his eyes, because he has found some uncleanness in her: then let him write her a bill of divorcement, and give it in her hand, and send her out of his house." Jesus now encouraged people to use their own faculty of judgment in evaluating the Mosaic laws that dealt with the topic of marital fidelity. But then Jesus expanded even further on this new concept with the statement that *thoughts* of infidelity should already be considered detrimental in this regard, "All of you have heard that it was said by them of old time, You shall not commit adultery: But I say unto you, that whosoever looks on a woman to lust after her has committed adultery with her already in his heart" (Matthew 5:27–28). Now the *inner* human being was addressed. The outer law had to make room for an inner law, a law grounded in the conscience of each human being. With these words Jesus lifted the notion of marital fidelity to an entirely new level.

The Gospel of St. John shows a profound understanding of this theme. A scene is presented in which a woman, who "was taken in adultery, in the very act," was brought before Jesus with the question, "Now Moses in the law commanded us,[193] that such should be stoned: but what say you?" (John 8:2–11). Much can be learned from contemplating this scene, because it reveals how Christ invariably appeals to the "I" in human beings. The act of stoning, as it was executed in those days, was the collective deed of a group, in which no one could be held responsible for the death of the accused. But by introducing the concept of one person "throwing the first stone," which would transform a collective deed into an individual one, a change in consciousness ensued.[194] By appealing to the power of the "I," the group's collective consciousness could be superseded by the individual consciousness—and hence by the personal sense of responsibility—of those present.

This is exactly what we encounter in this scene. Challenged by the voice of their conscience, the accusers withdrew, leaving only Jesus and the woman, alone in the great temple.[195] She was, one could say, standing at the edge of her grave. The threat of a horrible death through stoning had temporarily been lifted; human authority had been replaced by a higher judge. It may have only taken a few minutes for the accusers to leave the temple, but for her it must have seemed an eternity. Finally Jesus addressed her with a curious question, "Woman, where are those your accusers? Has no man condemned you?" to which she answered: "No man, Lord" (John 8:10–11).

In the description of this scene in the Gospel of St. John we actually encounter a unique account of Christ's karmic evaluation of a human life. The reader will recall from our examination of the sixth commandment that, gradually, more and more people will meet the figure of Christ as their *Lord of Karma* shortly after death. This is what occurred in the case of this woman, only with one significant difference: it happened *while she was alive*, albeit at the brink of death. At that moment she experienced what other human souls, many centuries later, will experience only after death. She perceived how the moral value of her life was being weighed not only against her own karmic circumstances, but also *against humanity's level of moral development* at that time—for this is what happens when we meet Christ as our karmic judge. The woman responded to this challenge by calling Christ "Lord," thus acknowledging him as her judge, as the Lord of her Karma. And Jesus, in turn, affirmed this recognition with the words, "Neither do I condemn you: go, and sin no more" (John 8:11).

It would not have been difficult for her to follow this advice; not on account of the urge to obey commandments, nor out of fear, but because of the profound soul experience this event had awakened in her. It had made her aware that human beings are spiritual beings, connected to the divine world, and therefore capable of developing a higher form of love than she had hitherto been exposed to. Her astral body had been healed and her "I" awakened, instantaneously giving her life a whole new direction that would stand the test of time. This is the experience of someone who had approached the portal of death with anxiety and in mortal fear, and subsequently was given an entirely new life through Christ's guidance.

In this episode the seventh commandment was fulfilled for one individual human being. But Christ went through death and resurrection *for all humankind.* And it is especially in contemplating the crucifixion itself that we can begin to see a link to the life ether forces, that is to say, to those forces that were meant to be supported through the seventh commandment. The cross was made from wood, the hardest material in the plant kingdom—the realm of the life ether. The body of Jesus was pierced by nails through the hands and feet, by a spear into the rib cage and by a crown of thorns placed on the head. One could say that it was an all-out attack on the body's life ether forces. But Christ, as the divine bringer of the "I," was able to renew these forces by guiding them *through death to resurrection*. Whereas the substance of his physical body submitted to death and was taken up by the Earth, a whole new form arose, uniting with his own life ether forces: the *resurrection body* of Christ.

What is the resurrection body? The main difficulty people have encountered over the centuries while trying to find answers to this question stems from the fact that the resurrection body of Christ appears to exhibit both physical and suprasensory qualities. It can really only be understood with an entirely new way of thinking.[196]

We know that the crucified physical body of Christ was taken up into the earth and would not reappear as such ever again.[197] The resurrection body is not a material body. It is a bodily form that is fully penetrated by purified life ether forces. Life ether forces are forces that, we recall, always lead through death to resurrection. The resurrection body can only be perceived through a special kind of clairvoyance, a clairvoyance that Christ had awakened in his disciples beforehand. In that sense it is a suprasensory body. But this resurrection body was so fully permeated with everything Christ had experienced during his life on Earth, that its form had become qualitatively different from all other suprasensory manifestations. Having been infused with the fruits of Christ's earthly experiences, this resurrection body appeared, at first, to be a physical material body—and was perceived as such, until people suddenly recognized its true essence. Mary Magdalene initially saw a gardener (Johannes 20:15) and, likewise, some apostles believed at first that a fellow traveler had joined them on their way to Emmaus (Lucas 24:13–31).

The resurrection body represents an entirely new form of existence that in a far distant future, namely in the Jupiter phase, will become the norm for all humanity. In that future time the human body will, according to Rudolf Steiner, no longer consist of physical substance. One could say that, with the resurrection body, Christ inaugurated a new form of existence, which for humanity as a whole will still take eons to develop.

Contemplations such as these can also shed new light on the closing words of the Gospel of St. Matthew. These words, spoken by the risen Christ, sound like a promise, "And, lo, I am with you always, even unto the end of the world" (Matt. 28:20). It is as though we hear the life ether forces resonating in these words; for these are forces of *loyalty* that not only conquer death, but also embrace the Earth's entire cycle of development. *Christ remains loyal to humanity.*

THE SEVENTH COMMANDMENT IN OUR TIME

Is there a place in today's world for the basic premise of the seventh commandment? Until recently, people still had a sense of the intrinsic value of fidelity within the sanctity of marriage—a last remnant, one could say, of the impulse inaugurated by the Atlantean mysteries. But this sense has now, for the most part, been displaced by widespread uncertainty. Today, a true lifelong bond between two people is more the exception than the norm. Flexible relationships, infidelity, and divorce have become part of everyday life. And it would be unreasonable to suppose that a compelling commandment, or, for that matter, any other form of legislation would carry enough weight to alter this situation. People dislike being governed by a commandment whose original impulse is not understood, especially if its message interferes with deeply rooted desires. Many people today experience life as a continual tug-of-war between contradictory passions and desires, resulting in a sense of powerlessness, of not being able to resist such feelings. Consequently, life often seems meaningless, accidental, and chaotic, especially also with respect to people's most intimate personal relationships. These conflicting emotions, incidentally, also affect the health of the etheric body and particularly of the life ether forces that are at work not only in the enfolding of our intimate relationships, but in all enduring social interactions between people. But, in our time, it is almost impossible to work on the etheric body directly. These forces can only be supported and kept healthy *indirectly*, that is to say, by consciously cultivating suitable spiritual ideals in our souls.

To be able to do this, however, we must first try to understand why the aforementioned kind of feelings are so prevalent today and to identify the underlying causes, which, if not recognized, may well bring about a social crisis in this regard. Rudolf Steiner spoke about these matters on several occasions, particularly in the lecture, *How can the Psychological Stress of Today be Overcome?*[198] Our time stands in the sign of the development of the consciousness soul and consequently has a different quality than the previous epoch of the intellectual soul.[199] This qualitative difference is revealed in the way we as human beings stand in the world and interact with our fellow human beings.

In the intellectual soul era people were able to get to know one another quickly and thoroughly. In our fifth post-Atlantean epoch it has become much more difficult to build a bridge from one human soul to another, resulting in widespread feelings of inner and outer isolation. It therefore takes longer to get to know and understand another person, and even longer before we can learn to trust that person. This is a peculiarity of our time—the age of the consciousness soul—we simply must accept as given, but one that has a bearing on all our human relationships, not just our intimate ones. But we *can*, with the help of Anthroposophy, develop a deeper understanding of what it means to be a human being, in other words, acquire a *practical knowledge of the human being*. With this knowledge as our starting point we can then try to cultivate our social life with others in such a way that we learn to take into account the individual needs and impulses of our fellow human beings. The quality of our human relationships should not be determined primarily by our feelings of sympathy and antipathy that oftentimes arise subconsciously from karmic situations in earlier incarnations. Instead we should try to develop a *loving interest in the other person*, a consciously acquired warm and loving interest in the true being of the other person. This can create a basis for enduring relationships in the age of the consciousness soul.

Another aspect of human life that has changed over time has to do with belief in authority. In the intellectual soul age authority had its proper place; it was established through dogmas and principles upon groups of people as common to them all. In that age people's intellectual abilities developed as a natural faculty, whereas in the consciousness soul era—our time—we need to cultivate our faculty of understanding and increase our knowledge *through our own efforts*, so as to develop our own sense of judgment in matters of religion, science, and other human pursuits.

And thirdly—this is something that was not yet possible in the age of the intellectual soul—we need to develop a concrete knowledge of the spiritual worlds through Anthroposophy today, especially knowledge about the spiritual beings, and how they interact with us. Then the world can become for us a place filled with spiritual content, inhabited by spiritual beings. This will make it possible for us to rediscover the spiritual as the basis of everything, both in the outer world and in ourselves, but especially also in our human relationships.

These three aspects—social understanding, liberty of thought, and knowledge of the spirit—are taken up once more by Rudolf Steiner from a more esoteric point of view in the noteworthy lecture "What Does the Angel Do in our Astral Body?"[200] There he describes how the Angels continually form imaginations in the astral bodies of human beings, to prepare them for the next era of soul development, the sixth post-Atlantean epoch. These imaginations are intended to bring about 1) the impulse of fellowship in social life, 2) the ability to see the hidden divinity in other people, and 3) the possibility to reach the reality of the spirit through the faculty of thinking. For the Angels to be able to fulfill this task we human beings need to learn to be aware of what the Angels are doing in our astral bodies. This can only be done through the consciousness soul, through our faculty of thinking. We need to gradually deepen our spiritual-scientific understanding; we need to come to a living acknowledgment and recognition of the existence of the spiritual world. When this knowing then becomes a certainty, a living reality in our souls, the Angels can continue to have a beneficial influence on us human beings. Without our ongoing efforts to comprehend the spiritual world in this way, the Angels would be forced to form these imaginative pictures in the physical and etheric bodies of human beings while they are asleep, instead of in their astral bodies while they are awake. But in that case these impulses will arise as instinctive faculties that will have a negative impact on the intended evolution. In this lecture Rudolf Steiner also mentions that this turn of events would have an especially harmful impact on the whole realm of human sexuality.

In summary we can state that the modern configuration of the seventh commandment stands in sharp contrast to its original form in the time of Moses. Trust, faithfulness, and loyalty are qualities that can no longer be imposed on people in the form of a commandment. Moreover, these qualities generally cannot be trained through a direct approach; only in a more indirect way can trust and loyalty become strong inner forces in us, namely by gradually deepening our knowledge of Spiritual Science, and by cultivating social understanding and liberty of thought. But for us to be able to take up these qualities as true objective impulses out of the spiritual world, we need to become aware how the Angels are working in our astral body to bring this about in the best possible way. The more we can strengthen these qualities out of this insight, the more we will be able to cultivate a loving interest in others and thus create a healthy basis for all our human relationships. Then, and only then, can *trust, fidelity*, and *loyalty* gradually become strong inner forces in our souls again, forces that do not belie the freedom of human beings. This is essential for the further development of humankind in the age of the consciousness soul; otherwise the human soul will wither.

It has become clear, we trust, that these contemplations about the modern form of the seventh commandment are not intended as a new set of standards to be followed, but rather as a tool toward developing a deeper understanding of the true significance of soul qualities like faithfulness and loyalty; of the way these forces work in our soul; how they can be re-enlivened; why this is so difficult in our time; and what the inevitable consequences will be if this does not happen.

We need to approach this whole subject matter with the help of spiritual-scientific insights today; for it will indeed become ever more difficult to understand the moral value of the aforementioned special soul qualities—and of fidelity in marriage in particular—by relying on past traditions. We will increasingly have to rely on our own judgment in assessing the importance of these values, both in our own lives and in society at large. In pondering these questions it is also important to know that, seen from a spiritual-scientific perspective, our value judgments and conduct in these matters are not inconsequential. We need to know, for instance, that *infidelity* will gradually paralyze our spiritual wings. There is, however, an even more profound reason to value faithfulness and loyalty; for *the spiritual stature of the "I" depends on the degree of inner loyalty we are able to summon*, or, one could say, the spiritual development of our own "I" depends on our striving toward harmony with the other "I." This insight can become today's metamorphosis of the seventh commandment.

8

The Eighth Commandment

The eighth commandment: *"You shall not steal."* According to the basic premise of this book, both the eighth and the ninth commandment have a special connection to the astral body. The astral body had been given to our human ancestors on old Moon by the *Spirits of Movement* (the *Dynamis*), and has been further transformed and refined ever since. But this refinement could not embrace all of the astral body. Part of it remained (and is even today) more like it was on old Moon. Put another way, the older part of the astral body remained coarser, whereas the younger part—the part that emerged under the influence of the subsequent Earth phase—became more refined. It was essential that part of the astral body be transformed in this way, for it was precisely this refined astral component that was able to receive the "I" during the Lemurian phase of the Earth evolution. As a result, the refined astral body became intimately linked to the "I"-forces. Even today, the impulses of the higher astral body are aimed at serving the "I," while the desires of the lower astral body are mostly directed at fulfilling the needs of the etheric and physical body. We will turn our attention to this newer, more refined part of the astral body in connection with the ninth commandment, but in this chapter we will focus on the older, "unpolished" part of the astral body. Its connection to the eighth commandment will then become apparent in due course.

Back on old Sun, where human beings did not yet have an astral body, everything had been permeated by peaceful, harmonious forces, emanating from high spiritual beings. Although some spiritual beings had remained behind in their development, already at that stage of evolution, there was as yet no interaction between those laggard beings and our human ancestors. Old Sun existence was imbued with the harmonizing influences of spiritual beings that had evolved as intended. In such a world order, permeated by cosmic harmony and wisdom, the notion *theft* did not yet exist.

On old Moon we encounter very different circumstances. At a particular point in time during the Moon evolution the single planetary body had split into two; one part became the Sun and the other part became what we have earlier called the Moon–Earth (because at this stage the Moon and the Earth still formed one body). The Sun was to be the abode of high spiritual beings whose development depended upon a faster pace than that of human beings. The Moon–Earth, or *old Moon*, became the dwelling place of our human ancestors and other beings in various stages of their respective development, including certain spiritual beings who had not reached their intended level of development on old Sun. Accordingly, human beings on old Moon were now exposed to two kinds of external influences. At specific times they experienced the influence of the Sun and the lofty Sun-beings; at other times that of laggard Moon-beings. These beings, we recall, rebelled against the Sun-beings, thus causing the cosmic *struggle in Heaven*. They wanted to isolate the Moon–Earth from the influence of the Sun-beings and take everything under their own leadership. One could say that these Moon-beings tried to divert the Moon–Earth from the intentions of the Sun-beings. With this notion we are led to the origin of the eighth commandment. In these cosmic events we can recognize *the archetype of all later forms of theft.*

The consciousness of our human ancestors on old Moon underwent a gradual change because of these events. While living under the influence of the Sun, their consciousness remained in a dreamy state. With that level of consciousness they experienced the enlivening qualities of the cosmic harmonies. In the intermittent Moon periods their level of consciousness became somewhat more awakened and defined. This latter state of being, however, tended to harden the physical body, causing our ancestors again and again to seek out the enlivening power of the Sun.

This alternating exposure to contrasting states of consciousness had specific consequences. While it allowed our human ancestors to maintain a certain inner balance, their fellow creatures were not able to escape the hardening impact of the Moon in the same way—these are the beings that now live on our Earth as the higher animals. Our human Moon ancestors were shielded from this premature solidification; for, whenever the danger of excessive hardening became tangible, the beneficial influence of the Sun and the Sun-beings would cause these early human beings to become slightly detached from their physical bodies, thereby allowing their bodies to absorb refreshing, re-enlivening impulses.

Even so, because of the turbulent times on old Moon, our human ancestors were no longer the harmonious, well-balanced beings they had once been. A seed had been planted that would eventually, in a later stage of evolution, give rise to deficiencies, illness, and death. And, ever since that time, the possibility has existed that this seed of dissonance—which, in itself, is actually an important ingredient of the ongoing development of human beings—would grow beyond its intended limits and cause harm.

Because our human ancestors received an astral body against the backdrop of the *cosmic rebellion,* the human astral body has absorbed, and still carries, traces of this rebellion—to this very day. Human consciousness, dependent as it is on the state of the astral body, had been affected as well. Ever since these events on old Moon, human beings have increasingly experienced a sense of independence, of separation from the cosmos. This, in turn, caused them to become more susceptible to certain luciferic influences. What did this mean, particularly for people living in the time of Moses? It meant that people now had a tendency to want to assert their autonomy, to impose their particular way of being onto the world around them. If taken to excess, this tendency could potentially lead to specific transgressions. It could, as we have discussed in the chapters about the third and the sixth commandments, lead to a particular misuse of speech; or, under different circumstances, to a desire to kill; or—and this is what concerns us presently in connection with the eighth commandment—it could lead to *stealing*.

Achieving a certain level of autonomy and independence is a necessary stage of human development. Even the ensuing desire to claim a part of the world just for oneself is, by and of itself, not a problematic soul gesture in developing human beings. Only if this tendency is taken to selfish extremes, can it potentially lead to problems, such as stealing.

If people regularly succumb to such temptations, which are essentially luciferic in nature, their bodily constitution gradually weakens. To some extent, this will already be the case in their present life on Earth, but to a greater extent in a subsequent incarnation. People will then, according to Rudolf Steiner's insights into the working of karma, become more susceptible to certain illnesses—illnesses that are accompanied by pain, infections, and fever.[201] (In the chapter about the ninth commandment we will look into the corresponding ahrimanic temptations, and their impact on the health of human beings.) Although these resulting illnesses will help people overcome karmic shortcomings from a former life, the overall state of their bodily constitution nevertheless will be weakened as time goes on. The Israelite people, in particular, had to learn to withstand such temptations; for they had the task of preparing, through many generations, a suitable human body for the future incarnation of Christ— not just a physical, but also a suitable etheric and astral body. And so, along with the instructions provided by some of the other Mosaic commandments, which were directed at the healthy development of the physical and the etheric body, people also needed specific guidelines to help them resist those luciferic influences that could potentially harm the *astral body*. Such guidelines were provided by the commandment "You shall not steal."

The human astral body is home to all manner of instincts and desires, some of which are triggered without our conscious participation, and need, therefore, not be subjected to any kind of value judgments. After all, just as is the case with the animals, the whole realm of these instincts is guided by a higher wisdom. We can think, for example, of the various instincts needed to sustain life. But, unlike the animals, human beings often long to exceed these elementary needs. To mention just one example of many, people often succumb to the desire to eat more than is needed for physical sustenance, simply to prolong the joy of eating, or for a variety of other reasons. Sooner or later this will damage both the natural instincts and the astral body, a course of events that, in turn, has an effect on the physical and etheric bodies as well. By going beyond our inborn, healthy boundaries in this way, it is as though we were taking something into ourselves that in a deeper sense does not belong to our real being. The eighth commandment was intended to protect human beings from corrupting their astral bodies in this way. It meant to convey the message: *Do not allow entry into your astral body to desires that do not conform to its original impulse of creation.*

Following this line of thought, we may say that *stealing* in its broadest meaning can be defined as *an attempt to own something that does not belong to our innermost being.* What we usually call stealing can certainly fit this description; after all, by violating the boundaries and rights of our fellow human beings we take hold of a domain that does not belong to us, and, in doing so, we end up harming ourselves as well. It may have become clear from the whole context thus far, that the eighth commandment is not aimed just at everyday stealing, but also at theft in the broader sense we have just described with the words "You shall not steal."

Aspects of Stealing

In a cosmic universe where harmony was the prevailing element, theft did not yet exist. Only when specific circumstances began to develop in the evolution of humanity, could the potential for stealing arise in human beings. These specific circumstances can be characterized as:

1. independence and separation
2. ownership
3. conflict

Only when the human "I" begins to develop a sense of *independence*, of a *separation* between it and everything else, can such a thing as stealing arise in the world. This can take place even if the "I"-consciousness is not yet fully individualized. In olden times one's own personality was felt to be present in all the members of the family, tribe, folk, or other group one belonged to. An insult, for example, directed at one member of such a group, would have been experienced as a personal insult by all. A group of people, therefore, could also collectively come to experience the previously mentioned sense of independence. As human beings gradually—be it individually or collectively—began to experience themselves as independent beings, they also became aware of a separating border between their own group and anyone outside that group or, on a more personal level, between *me* and *you*. And, with this awareness, the possibility of stealing emerged.

An individual, or a group, developing this kind of self-awareness will then attempt to occupy its own place in the world by taking *possession* of things. As a result, the awareness of *I* and *you* changes into the broader recognition of *mine* and *yours*. There are many forms and levels of ownership. Insofar as one can own something exclusively and absolutely, we can speak of ownership. But there are things one cannot possess. The stars cannot become our personal possession; nobody can own the stars. Wisdom cannot become our exclusive possession; after all, the fact that one person has made a specific idea his or her own, does not exclude the possibility that someone else, independently, can obtain that same wisdom, that same idea. Hence we cannot exclusively possess wisdom or knowledge.[202] But we *can*, as an individual, own the food we eat. Put another way: what one person knows, another can also know; but what one person eats, another cannot eat.[203] As soon as we are able to *own* a part of the world exclusively, it can also be taken from us, in other words, it can be *stolen*.

The third factor related to stealing was characterized as *conflict*. In economies all over the world goods are exchanged. Raw materials and foodstuffs are produced and/or processed in order to be utilized and consumed in human society. Any exchange of goods—also between individual people—can take place in the form of selling and buying, or by means of lending and borrowing, or even of bartering. This, essentially, is the basis of all economic life. In all these cases we are dealing with reciprocal actions of comparable value. This is why such transactions (usually!) don't lead to conflict between the parties. There are, however, two additional ways of exchanging possessions, namely *stealing* and *giving*, both of which, obviously, have a different quality from the aforementioned types of transactions. *Giving* occupies a very special place among the various types of exchange—we will come back to this. *Stealing*, on the other hand, can be characterized (among other things) by the fact that it leads to *conflict* between the people or groups involved. With this characterization we have arrived at the third factor that comes into play wherever and whenever we are confronted with the activity called stealing.

And yet, we have not entirely outlined the concept of stealing with the words *separation, ownership,* and *conflict*; for stealing primarily applies to the human realm. Beyond that realm one could think of various borderline cases where stealing can, at most, be used as a figure of speech. Could one say, for example, that the Moon steals the sunlight from the Earth during a solar eclipse? Or that a parasitic vine steals the light and nutrients from its host plant, causing it to die? Here we are crossing a borderline beyond which the concept of stealing no longer applies. But in the animal kingdom—animals, after all, have astral bodies(!)—we can observe incidents that may well remind us of stealing as it applies to human society. Take a squirrel, for example, who has stashed away a stockpile of nuts for the winter; it now possesses this stockpile in the literal sense of the word. In such cases another animal cannot get at this supply without an ensuing struggle. In most cases, however, animals simply live in and with nature; in that world the concept of stealing is neither suitable nor applicable.

It is really only in human society that stealing exists and potentially becomes a problem. In the time of Moses the human constitution was such that the Hebrew people needed a special commandment to help strengthen the astral body, particularly the coarser part of the astral body that had remained more closely affiliated with its Moon existence, and was therefore more susceptible to the impact of the unsettling cosmic conditions on old Moon. The aim of the eighth commandment was to help free this part of the astral body from the tribulations in which it had become entangled in that far-distant past, by pointing out the importance of "You shall not steal."

Christ and the Eighth Commandment

In contemplating how the core message of the eighth commandment might be transformed into a Christian ideal, one could well assume that this should take the form of renouncing all of one's personal possessions. But such an assumption would fail to take into account the fact that similar attempts had already been made *before* the beginning of the Christian era. Communities already existed whose members aspired to purify the astral body of excessive desires, both by disposing of personal possessions and by adopting a frugal lifestyle in which all extravagance was avoided. This was the case, for example, in the Essene communities that flourished from approximately the second century BC to the first century AD.[204]

True, the earliest Christian communities initially encouraged similar ideals,[205] and the later medieval cloisters adopted some of the principles that had governed these earlier societies, but one cannot maintain that the ideal of forsaking all forms of personal ownership was an entirely new principle that originated in the Christian era. It is also true that in much more recent times (including our own), various groups have opted for communal ownership in one form or another. These endeavors tend to meet with varying degrees of success and personal satisfaction, depending on individual needs and expectations. In any case, we must conclude that this principle cannot represent a broad, universal ideal, Christian or otherwise, at least not in our present time.

What, then, did Christ do with the eighth commandment? He transformed this commandment during his life on Earth in such a way that it can inspire people with new impulses for the future. The "I," having been born in human beings through the coming of Christ, can now gradually permeate the astral body, enabling it to take up the healing Sun-forces of Christ into itself. This can bring a new harmony to the whole realm of human instincts and passions, which had been adversely affected by the events on old Moon. Through the Sun-forces of Christ, working in the human "I," the astral body can now gradually be transformed. This process will unquestionably take a long time for humanity as a whole, but the important thing is that the human "I" is now *able* to develop inner strength to bring balance to the passions and desires originating from the astral body.

What does this mean with respect to the focus of the eighth commandment in particular, that is to say, to the problem of stealing? Jesus did not dwell overmuch on the evils of stealing as such, but rather pointed out how we can learn to transform our innate desire *to own* things—or, if taken to excess, the desire *to steal*—into the soul quality of learning *to give*. This is the lofty metamorphosis of the eighth commandment through the impulse of Christ! The soul gesture of *taking* can now be transformed into one of *giving* through the strength of the "I" and the new forces of love, radiating out from it into the astral body. This kind of transformation will, of course, be a long, gradual process, but one that can eventually free the soul of the basic urge to accumulate and possess things.

However, Jesus did not only instruct people about the "right way of giving," but also taught them how to change the potentially problematic soul gesture of *taking* into the "right way of *receiving*."

In the Gospel of St. Matthew, for example, we can find the following statements regarding this new principle, "And if any man will sue you at the law, and take away your coat, let him have your cloak also" (5:40) and, "Give to him that asks you, and from him that would borrow of you turn not you away" (5:42). Both are part of a discourse in which Jesus gives various examples of how he intended to fulfill (not destroy) the Mosaic Law. Each section begins with Jesus first calling to mind one of these laws, and then continues with the transformation—the fulfillment—of that particular law. In the passage we are considering here, the old notion of "an eye for an eye, and a tooth for a tooth" is transformed into several new Christian principles. One is the often-quoted idea of "turning the other cheek," and another one is given in the form of the two statements we mentioned at the beginning of this paragraph about the value of giving.

In the parallel passage in the Gospel of St. Luke, Jesus does not take the Mosaic laws as a starting point, but emphasizes how to develop new human soul capacities through these transformed principles, "Give to every man that asks of you; and of him that takes away your goods ask them not again" (6:30); and "Give, and it shall be given unto you" (6:38). Special mention is made in this Gospel of the fact that, before Jesus spoke these words, he had spent "all night in prayer to God" (6:12).

One of the few indications we find in the Gospel of St. Mark refers to a particular, and rather unexpected, interplay between giving and taking. These words, however, are not only found in the Gospel of Mark, but also in Matthew (13:12 and 25:29) and Luke (8:18 and 19:26), "For he that has, to him shall be given: and he that has not, from him shall be taken even what he has."

This particular saying has given rise to many discussions. Clearly, it is not meant as an axiom pertaining to the field of economics! Its meaning will be less of an enigma if we consider an analogy given by Rudolf Steiner on several occasions: when pouring water out of a cup, the cup will soon be empty; in the spiritual world the opposite holds true, that is to say, the cup will be filled. Transcribed onto the human realm this means that, for example, the more we love, the more love will be generated; or, with reference to the statement under discussion, the more we give of ourselves, the more we will grow. If, for example, we strive for wisdom and knowledge not just for our own benefit, but for the greater good, the fruit of this striving will actually lead to inner growth, that is, more will indeed be *given* to us. But if we try to acquire wisdom and knowledge solely to enrich ourselves, this spiritual possession soon will become dead weight in our souls, leading us away from our true path of inner development, that is, something will actually be *taken* from us. In other words, the spiritual world continuously bestows its riches unto those who are willing to let others benefit from the knowledge they have acquired. But if people believe they can keep it all to themselves, this spiritual possession soon will become less fruitful and wither.

That this is, in fact, the meaning of "For he that has, to him shall be given: and he that has not, from him shall be taken even what he has," can be inferred from the context in which these words appear in the various Gospels. Immediately preceding this statement we find various parables pointing out that human beings who have been given a special talent or capacity should use this in service to the world and other human beings. In Matthew, for instance, we find the parable about the sower and the seed. There Jesus says to the disciples that "it is given unto you" to know the mysteries of the kingdom of heaven (13:11). These words imply that this knowledge is an inexhaustible treasure that will keep growing as long as we do something with it in the world. From Mark and Luke we learn, at that very point in the narrative, that a candle ought to be allowed to shine its light unhindered, so as to bring out what was hitherto hidden (Mark 4:21-24 and Luke 8:16). Elsewhere in Luke and Matthew we find, again as introduction to the statement under discussion, the parable of the servant who was not able to make constructive use of the talent that his Lord had given him. Consequently the talent was taken from him. Following all these introductory parables we then hear the aforementioned statement, "For he that has, to him shall be given: and he that has not, from him shall be taken even what he has" (Matt. 25:24-30, Mark 4:25, Luke 19:20-27). Thus the Synoptic Gospels[206] provide three nuanced perspectives into the spiritual effects of the act of giving. All three illustrate through various examples that everything we undertake should benefit others; for only then will our "I" develop properly and receive strength from these endeavors.

The Gospel of St. John takes it one step further. It focuses on the gifts we can receive from Christ and from the spiritual world, if we prepare ourselves. Speaking about his own gift to humanity Jesus said, "Peace I leave with you, my peace I give unto you: not as the world gives, give I unto you" (John 14:27). From this Gospel we also learn how Christ, after his death, will take on the role of intercessor to the universal cosmos—the Father God—so that human beings may be able to receive the gifts from the spiritual world. Speaking about that time Jesus said, "Whatsoever all of you shall ask the Father in my name, he will give it you. Until now have all of you asked nothing in my name: ask, and all of you shall receive, that your joy may be full" (John 16:23–24).

Combining the various messages in the four Gospels about the soul gestures of giving and receiving, we can say that Jesus encouraged human beings to *receive* the gifts from the spiritual world in the right way by learning, in turn, how to *give* of themselves to others and to the world, so that they may eventually be able to live in harmony with the spiritual cosmos again.

The Transformation of the Eighth Commandment in our Time

We have described how Christ transformed the eighth commandment by encouraging people to develop the soul quality of *giving*. This is the kind of transformation that can only be accomplished when human beings learn to strengthen their "I," because the impulse of giving can only arise from the "I." Learning to overcome the inherent selfish desires of the astral body is of far-reaching importance, both with respect to personal growth and the potential impact of it on society. We will, therefore, continue this line of thought about the importance of giving in our contemplations about the modern form of the eighth commandment, rather than focus on the problem of stealing as such. After all, the prohibition against stealing still holds a valid position in today's society and does not need to be further examined.

Up to this point we have mainly focused on the value of giving (and receiving) from the point of view of inner personal growth, as supported by the examples from the New Testament. But *giving* also plays an important role in the functioning of modern society. To be able to understand this particular aspect of giving, however, we must first develop some insight in the way human society functions, or rather, *should* function. This requires new concepts and a new way of thinking. Rudolf Steiner's ideas, developed during and after World War I, about what he called the *threefold social order*, are based on such innovative, new concepts. We will here, very briefly, review the basic principles of this threefold social order, in as much as these are relevant to our theme.[207]

Everything that happens in human society ultimately has its origin in the *threefold* human being. This is why society is made up of *three* realms as well: the *cultural* sphere, which includes all forms of education, arts, religion, and sciences; the *human rights* sphere, which is the domain of politics and law; and the *economic* sphere, which governs the production and distribution of goods and services. These spheres operate according to very different laws and principles. For society to function properly, each of these realms should, ideally, conduct its activities without unduly imposing its own sets of rules and ways of functioning onto the two other realms. Although these three spheres naturally interact with each other, they *must* be allowed to have their own organizational structure.

The cultural sphere, for instance, can only come into its own—and thus benefit society—if it is allowed to create space for the unfolding of *free* initiatives. The essence of the judiciary must be that it is based on the premise of *equality* for all people. The economic realm requires interaction between people, an interaction that should be rooted in social *cooperation* and based on the insight that we all depend on each other with respect to our material needs. It would take us too far afield to explore Rudolf Steiner's truly innovative approach to society's problems at length; furthermore, it has proved exceedingly difficult to implement the principles of the threefold social order in today's social environment. But the creative thinking that gave birth to these concepts holds the kind of strength that will be increasingly needed in times to come.

Especially with respect to the cultural realm it is extremely important that people have the freedom to apply the creative power of the "I" in the pursuit of art, education, scientific research, and other creative activities in a responsible way. Such deeds will be spiritually productive; for they benefit everyone. In order to guarantee this kind of freedom within the *cultural* sphere, the influence of the state and the judiciary (the *rights* sphere), should be such that it does not impose excessive legal (and/or other) limitations on the unfolding of spiritual and cultural initiatives and activities in society. The *economic* sphere also has an obligation in this respect, for it needs to make money available if cultural and spiritual life is to flourish in our society. Those who are dedicating themselves to work in the cultural sphere must be able to do so without being unduly hampered by financial hardships. We must, both collectively and individually, come to the recognition that cultural and spiritual endeavors can only be pursued in society if they are financially supported by the economic sphere through donations from organizations and individuals.

This, then, is where the contemporary metamorphosis of the eighth commandment in our time begins to take shape; the outwardly proscribed edict against *stealing* can now, for each individual person, be transformed into a deliberate, insightful *gifting*. But for this metamorphosis to actually take root in wider society, it is important that we develop innovative, and at the same time highly practical, viewpoints about the essential role of donated money, because such thoughts have a direct impact on society as a whole. Donated money forms an essential ingredient of a well-functioning society, because it creates the financial basis for cultural and spiritual activities to develop in freedom and in accordance with their own innate laws. Fortunately, there are already a number of initiatives that operate according to these principles, as well as a growing number of individuals who understand the real function of donated money within the fabric of society. What is most needed, however, is a profound and widespread understanding of the aforementioned three spheres of life—the cultural, rights, and economic sphere—and of the specific ways each of these spheres ought to function in society.

With this theme we have arrived right in the midst of modern life, and it is here that we can find the present-day transformation of the impulse of the eighth commandment, which we can express approximately in the following way: *It is essential that we, individually and cooperatively, provide adequate financial support to those who work in the cultural sphere for the benefit of society as a whole.*

It would be wrong to think that it would indeed be nice and desirable to provide this kind of financial support, but that society would function just as well without it. The truth is that, without freely gifted donations in one form or another, there simply would be no physical basis for any kind of spiritual work to unfold. *Financial support is essential for the pursuit of spiritual work*. If this insight were lacking completely, society would rapidly become unproductive, not only culturally and spiritually, but also technologically, and stagnation would set in.

The modern-day form of the eighth commandment, which we have here proposed, should not be accepted merely as a new commandment. Meaningful and fruitful results can only be expected when new impulses such as these are first fully taken up with our faculty of thinking, and gradually be allowed to become part of our being in the form of a real insight. Only then can it radiate out as a free impulse through the "I"; act as a motivator for the astral body; be guided through the sustaining forces of the etheric body; and, finally, be transformed by the forces of the physical body into actual deeds on Earth.

9

The Ninth Commandment

The ninth commandment: "*You shall not bear false witness against your neighbor.*" This formulation actually points to two concepts—one an extension of the other. The main directive is that people shall not speak untruths; the second one, that this shall especially not be done about another person. The usual reading of this commandment tends to concentrate primarily on the second part of this edict. But the central message of the ninth commandment confronts the uttering of untruths of any kind, in other words, *the speaking of a deliberate lie*. This will be our main focus in this chapter—all the while keeping in mind, however, that "bearing false witness" about or against another person only increases the impact of speaking untruths exponentially. We will also examine the significance of human speaking in general as well as the relationship between the ninth commandment and the refined part of the astral body.

The functioning of human society depends to a large extent on the fact that we have communication among ourselves through the spoken and written word. We can also observe various forms of communication in the world of the animals. We know, for example, that certain species of prairie dogs rely on scouts for their safety. At the slightest sign of danger, their shrill chirps signal a warning to all the members of the group. Birds flying in formation stay in contact with each other through body movements or in other ways that are not yet completely understood. Dolphins and whales communicate by means of intricate whistles and songs. We also know that bees use a series of complex dance movements to communicate the exact location of a source of nectar to each other.

Communication in human society, in contrast, is infinitely more varied and complex because we use language. Not only that. Human communication is of a very different nature and quality as well. We don't just convey messages to each other. We can speak abstract truths, as for example in the interpretation of mathematical axioms. We can ask questions. *And we can lie.*

Human speaking essentially is a bridge from one human being to another, to *communicate truth*. It is the instrument through which the speaker conveys something truthful to the listener, or else hopes to find truth by asking questions. The uttering of a "false witness" account, on the other hand, is undertaken with the intent of presenting to the listener an *untrue* picture of a particular situation, even as the speaker is aware of the true state of things. It is, of course, up to the listener to decide whether to accept a particular statement as true or false. But a well-ordered society cannot really function, or even exist at all, if communication between people were mostly based on lies. This is why our society is intrinsically based on "truth speaking."

Being truthful in one's speaking, however, is not only important for the benefit of society as a whole. It is essential for the all-important development of the human "I"—one's own, as well as the other "I." By being truthful in our speaking we can get to know the "I" of the other human being. The speaking of truths creates a connection between human beings, whereas speaking untruths and bearing false witness destroys that connection. Accordingly, at a crucial point in history a commandment was needed to support the health of this social bridge between human beings with the words, "You shall not bear false witness against your neighbor."

The faculty of human speaking emerged at a relatively late stage of evolution.[208] It was during the actual Earth phase—to be more precise, in the later stages of the Lemurian epoch—that our ancestors first began to produce sounds, which can best be described as a ceremonial singing.[209] No words were used, at least not in the present-day sense. Outer words were not yet needed; people were able to touch each other inwardly with an astral language through forces of the will. These will forces were very powerful; they had magical strength. It goes without saying, then, that human society in those days was very different from our present-day society.

It was only in the next stage of the Earth phase, namely in the Atlantean time, that we encounter the onset of the development of human memory, and therefore also of language. This was an important milestone in human evolution during which both the speech organs and the speech center in the brain became more refined. Simultaneously, part of the astral body also underwent a further refinement,[210] giving it for the first time a truly human character, and thus preparing it to receive the germinal "I." Because of these developments, the refined part of the astral body is intimately connected not only with the "I," but also with human speech.

The quintessential impulse of this finer part of the astral body is *the desire for truth*. This is why any normal conversation between people is based on a fundamental expectation of truthfulness both on the part of the speaker and of the listener. Deep down most people hate lies. But, at the same time, this innate longing for truth frequently gets derailed by impulses originating from the coarser part of the astral body. This has consequences for both the speaker and the listener. It can, in the case of the speaker, make it easier to resort to a lie, or, in the case of the listener, make it more difficult to distinguish between *true* or *untrue* statements. In both cases people's sound judgment can be affected by the feelings of sympathy and antipathy such statements evoke in them. One's inherent desire for truth can be clouded by these astral impulses.

All human beings nevertheless possess a basic feeling for truth.[211] This archetypal desire for truth is supported by and rooted in the refined part of the astral body. But, because the astral body was given to our ancestors on old Moon, it also carries traces of the cosmic *struggle in Heaven*. These traces have remained active not only in the *coarser part* of the astral body, as we have described in the chapter about the eighth commandment, but also in the *refined part* of the astral body. It is because of this influence that we are capable of *speaking untruths*, of *lying*. This is why, in the time of Moses, when the "I" was not yet strong enough, a commandment was needed to support this refined part of the astral body with the edict "You shall not bear false witness against your neighbor."

The Impact of Speaking Untruths

We outlined earlier how the listener is deceived when confronted with untruths. But what happens to the person who is uttering lies? When we try to observe ourselves carefully while speaking untruths, we may actually be able to sense that, in so doing, we harm our own inner being. Most people do not realize the full extent of such harm.

When we speak a lie we know that our words are untrue. One could say that, in order to be able to articulate a lie, we have to connect ourselves inwardly with it, to absorb it into our inner being. In that sense the lie fuses with our "I"—for the act of speaking requires the deployment of the "I"—to be more precise, with that part of the "I" that is closest related to our will forces. This creates an inner conflict situation that becomes increasingly difficult to correct, because our "I" is weakened somewhat every time we consciously utter a lie. And, even though there may be legitimate reasons for speaking a (white) lie—we may even be able to justify doing so from a moral standpoint—we cannot get away from the objective fact that lying affects the "I," which, in turn, affects the whole human being. This can even be verified by modern instruments, such as lie detectors. A person who is speaking a lie undergoes physical changes, especially in the blood and skin, changes that can actually be measured by such instruments. These changes can be picked up regardless of one's reasoning or motivation for lying.

As mentioned, it is not only the "I" that is affected by speaking untruths; nor is it only one's present life that is affected. Lying plants a seed in the astral body, a germ that can become a connecting point for certain ahrimanic influences after death; for *Ahriman is the Spirit of the Lie*. Once someone has gone through the portal of death and is in the process of preparing for a next life, there will be a moment when a new etheric body needs to be acquired. That is the moment when this latent germ becomes active, causing a particular weakness in the new etheric body. This weakness can then manifest in that next life as a disposition for illnesses that exhibit hardening and sclerotic symptoms. (The reader will recall from our explorations into the eighth commandment that a person succumbing to certain luciferic influences, may in a next life be born with a disposition for illnesses that are accompanied by pain, fever, and infections.)[212]

We may conclude, then, that lying affects the whole human being in a negative way. But it has the strongest impact on the *refined portion of the astral body*—the part in which the "I" takes root and develops. In the time of Moses the "I" was only just beginning to awaken. Hence it was important at that pivotal point in time, to help maintain the health of this refined part of the astral body with the commandment, "You shall not bear false witness against your neighbor."

The Search for Truth versus the First Human Lie

In the course of the Atlantic age, and well into post-Atlantean times, people used language in the first place to carefully describe what they observed, and what therefore was true. This required a steady memory, to be sure, but not necessarily a rational, logical way of thinking as yet. Only when human beings began to develop the faculty of logical thinking did humankind enter a stage in which the meaning of *truth* was no longer something that was self-evident. A well-developed faculty of thinking undeniably enabled people to recognize broader aspects of the truth than was possible in earlier times, but, along with this capacity, they could now also come to incorrect or untrue conclusions. The possibility of speaking untruths, then, is intimately connected to the fact that human beings can make use of their intellect. It is for this reason that we will not be able to discover a cosmic archetype for the human vice called *lying*, in the same way we were able to find one for *stealing*. Lying is a through-and-through human singularity, a capacity that emerged for the first time during the actual Earth phase of evolution. It is striking to find, in this connection, that the old Jewish Midrash wisdom also singled out the human pursuit of speaking untruths from among all other human vices. "Everything in the world was created by God," it states in one of these Midrashim, "except the art of lying."[213]

In the Old Testament we encounter what may well be the archetype of this new human capacity in the account of a particular incident in the life of the patriarch Abraham. The focal point of this story is the clever use of a lie. Abraham was the first human being to develop the faculty of logical thinking; for this reason he is sometimes referred to as the Father of Mathematics.[214] In the episode in question we find Abram[215] thinking up a clever plan to save his life. He had taken his wife Sarai to Egypt because of widespread famine in his homeland. But because Sarai was "very fair to look upon," Abram anticipated that Pharaoh would claim her for himself (for such was the custom in those days) and consequently would have no tolerance for a husband. And so, fearing he would be killed, Abram contrived a plan to pass his wife off as his sister. As anticipated, Pharaoh claimed Sarai for himself and accepted Abram as her brother. So the plan succeeded; Abram's life was spared, and he became "a man of standing." Before long, however, the plot unraveled, and Pharaoh deported Sarai and Abram from Egypt (Gen. 12:10–20).

The remarkable thing about this story is that, within the framework of the Old Testament, this episode is told without the slightest condemnation of the fact that Abraham had resorted to a lie. On the contrary, it is the conduct of Pharaoh that is condemned; we hear that God "plagued Pharaoh and his house with great plagues because of Sarai, Abram's wife." Abraham's lie is presented as an ingenious device, or at any rate not as something that God disapproved of. Being able to lie was experienced as something new at that time; not as something that necessarily needed to be condemned.

It was a stage human beings had to go through in their collective development. As if to underscore the importance of this stage, we learn that Abraham's son Isaac, not long thereafter, used the very same lie in his encounter with Abimelech, king of the Philistines (Gen. 26:7). The implication is that, from that time onward, *every human being was capable of lying.*

Long before the time of Abraham, people still had an instinctive feeling for truth and its sustaining power. But in the course of time this inner certainty dwindled. And, as we saw from the above episodes, in the time of Abraham it had reached the point where a deliberate lie was used for the first time. As people gradually became less reluctant to use lies, the inherent natural sense of truth of earlier days began to make way for feelings of uncertainty and ambiguity instead. This is why the old mysteries inaugurated the art of philosophy around the sixth century BC. These earliest philosophers were initiates of the Greek and, to some extent, the Egyptian mysteries; their initiations gave them the required insight to be able to work in this new direction. They attempted to approach with their faculty of thinking what no longer could be embraced with purely instinctive capacities.

Nevertheless, the inner ambiguity about the meaning of truth gradually grew over time, despite the attempts of philosophical thinkers to clarify its meaning. These feelings of uncertainty reached a climax at the beginning of our era in the scene of Jesus standing before Pilate. When Jesus, in response to Pilate's questioning, stated that he had come to "bear witness unto the truth" Pilate could but counter with the words, "What is truth?" (John 18:38). Present-day academic philosophy has, at least with regard to this question, not yet reached a point of agreement. One can find various theories in philosophical discourses regarding the meaning of truth, some even claiming to be fully autonomous, in other words, dissociated from any existing theories about truth. Considering the innate human need for truth, this state of affairs presents a thoroughly unsatisfying situation. When the contrast between truth and untruth becomes more and more obscured, what are we to do with a commandment that implores us to "not bear false witness against your neighbor"?

Christ and the Ninth Commandment

How did Jesus transform the ninth commandment? How did he give new life to the ever-diminishing sense of truth in human beings? To begin with, Jesus pointed to the importance of the truthfulness of the spoken word, of accepting responsibility for that truthfulness—a responsibility that is rooted in the "I." Whenever Jesus wanted to awaken this awareness in people, he spoke the words, "Verily, I say unto you..." These words are found at the beginning of a speech, or whenever a conclusion to a particular statement is formulated.[216] Special weight should be given to this expression. It is not meant rhetorically. These words summon human beings to activate their innate sense of truth, to recognize and experience the truthfulness of what is spoken.

What truth really is can today only be grasped through the spiritual activity of the "I," which has now been born in all human beings because of the Mystery of Golgotha. This means that, ever since this pivotal event, the innate sense of truth, which had gradually dried up, can now be re-enlivened again through the strength of the "I." But, whereas the earlier feeling for truth had welled up out of the depths of the soul as a compelling instinctive force, this new sense of truth must be developed *consciously*, out of the free spiritual activity of the "I." Once we have recognized this, we can find our way to the second aspect, contained in Jesus' words about our relationship to truth. Jesus answered Thomas' question about the path to the spiritual world with the words, "I am the Way, the Truth and the Life" (John 14:6). Profound words, which have given rise to many commentaries over the centuries! And, within the framework of our present line of thought, it is important to note that, in this passage, *Truth* is linked to the "I"-Being of Christ, along with two other essential principles, namely, *Way* and *Life*. What does this mean?

It is indeed important to consider these three concepts as a totality, as belonging together; for, as long as one attempts to look at the question of truth as an isolated issue, it will become more and more difficult (and maybe even impossible) with the passing of time, to distinguish *truth* from *untruth*. One should really only try to approach the question of truth by acknowledging that it is intimately connected to the individual human path (the *way*) of development, as well as to human *life* in its entirety, because, in the words of one of the characters in Rudolf Steiner's first mystery play, "Our judgment (our knowledge) is different at each stage of life."[217]

Hence, if we want to develop a sense or awareness of truth in our time, we should try to take an unprejudiced and comprehensive look at each new situation we encounter. We should then try to immerse ourselves fully into that situation—in other words, try to identify with it through the strength of our "I"—in order to come to a value judgment about the truth of what we observe. Now, we all know that it is easier to identify with some truths than with others. Some truths are self-evident, or one could say, "close at hand," whereas others are far from obvious, or far-fetched. So, even if it is only in a figurative sense, one can indeed experience something like shorter or longer distances to be traversed in the world of truths, in the realm of the spirit. That is why, in this connection, one can indeed speak of a *way*. In order to come to an understanding of truth (especially in those cases where it is not exactly "close at hand"), we have to follow an inner path of free creative activity, a path of self-development. This is the path, the *Way*, Jesus referred to.

Accordingly, the compelling nature of the earlier instinctive perception of truth can, since the coming of Christ, be transformed into a free, *creative awareness* of truth. Jesus taught this to his disciples with the words, "And all of you shall know the truth, and the truth shall make you free" (John 8:32).

In our increasingly complex world it will be more and more difficult to distinguish not only truth from untruth, as we described above, but also *truth* from *illusion*. In order to be able to make valid distinctions in such cases, it is important to consider their relationship to life as a whole; because truth and illusion reveal their real character only if they are seen in relation to life in the stream of time. Life in its entirety is the anchor in our search for truth. This is the *Life* of which Jesus spoke in the previously mentioned quote.

Through the Mystery of Golgotha human beings have been given a new possibility to re-enliven their connection to the living impulse of truth. Jesus spoke about this future spiritual development in human beings with the words, "I have yet many things to say unto you, but all of you cannot bear them now. Nevertheless when he, the Spirit of Truth, has come, he will guide you into all truth" (John 16:12–13). With this *coming of the Spirit of Truth* Jesus pointed to the Holy Spirit who, in times to come, will bring a redeeming impulse toward the question of truth. This is the third aspect of Christ's metamorphosis of the ninth commandment. All three aspects reveal how Christ, the World-"I," unites himself with the truth. The first aspect manifests in the formulation "Verily, I say unto you...," the second in the words "I am the Way, the Truth and the Life," and the third in the sending of the Spirit of Truth who points the way to "the whole truth."

The fact that Christ was able to refer to the Holy Spirit in this way is of far-reaching importance. It reveals that people were, for the first time, capable of understanding this concept. As long as people had experienced themselves primarily as part of a family, nation, or other group, they were not yet able to recognize the Holy Spirit. The concept of the Holy Spirit can only be understood as the "I" grows stronger, in other words, when people become aware of themselves as individuals, but also of the fact that they are members of humanity as a whole. Put another way: being able to have an experience of the Holy Spirit demands an individual level of consciousness, but one that encompasses all of humanity.

We mentioned in an earlier chapter that the Holy Spirit was revealed for the first time *in public*—in other words, no longer just within the mysteries or to a chosen few—during the Festival of Pentecost (Acts 2:1–12).[218] Rudolf Steiner describes how the apostles had, because of their deep sorrow about the death of Christ, existed in a curious state of semiconsciousness, from which they were aroused only by the events occurring during this Festival of Pentecost.[219] Only then did they become aware of all the things that had taken place since the Last Supper, that is to say, in the time period during which they were living in this semiconscious state. Only then did they understand the full significance of the Mystery of Golgotha. It was the power of the descending Holy Spirit that ignited this insight in the apostles. The "I" was now fully awakened in them, permeating the astral body with the impulses streaming from the Mystery of Golgotha. This is portrayed in the New Testament in the account of the apostles seeing "cloven tongues like of fire, and it sat upon each of them" (Acts 2:3).

This inspiration of the Holy Spirit made the apostles speak an exalted language. They proclaimed the earthly–cosmic meaning of Christ to a multitude of people representing a number of different nations. And "every man heard them speak in his own language" (Acts 2:6). By their speaking, the mystery of the Holy Spirit was made public for the first time. Inspired by the impulse of the Holy Spirit, the apostles were able to break through the old tribal and group ties, embracing all nations and people in a fellowship of humanity. Thus a new mystery was inaugurated on Earth through the impulse of the Holy Spirit. It has the power to overcome the isolating and alienating effects of the different languages, and bring a new unifying force that unites all people. This mystery did not manifest by means of a new, abstract, unitary language, but rather through people's sudden ability to understand the apostles as though they were being addressed in their own language.[220] The true significance of the "gift of tongues," the *Glossolalia*, as this mystery is called, will only become a real factor in the lives of human beings in the sixth and seventh post-Atlantean cultural epochs, when the universal impulse for human fellowship will have been fully developed. What is important for our own time, however, is the fact that it was revealed *publicly* for the first time at this first Christian Pentecost Festival through the mystery of the Glossolalia.

As if to underscore the reality of this new presence of the Holy Spirit, the New Testament describes another example, taking place a short while thereafter. Peter had been speaking about Christ's resurrection, and "while Peter yet spoke these words," we are told, "the Holy Spirit fell on all them who heard the word" (Acts 10:44). Special mention is made of the fact that some were astonished that the gift of the Holy Spirit was "poured out" over the Jews (who were "of the circumcision") and Gentiles alike. Here, again, the old divisions according to group and blood ties were bridged through the power, the gift of the Holy Spirit. It can conquer the old tendencies toward separation and isolation and, *through the power of the spoken word*, bring people together in human fellowship.

A mighty new impulse has been bestowed on human beings, an impulse toward a new kind of speaking. It encourages us not only to avoid the uttering of lies in general, and the bearing of "false witness against one's neighbor" in particular, but also to speak in such a way that our speaking may strengthen the "I"-forces in our fellow human beings, so that they may be filled with the *Spirit of Truth*.

The Spirit of Truth works from an ever-present, central germinating point, toward which the individual light beams of all truths converge. This center of growth was established on Earth through the Mystery of Golgotha. By following the path of these light beams of truth, we may be able to find not only the truth about the Mystery of Golgotha itself and about human existence in the past, but also those life-giving forces that are needed for our continuing development well into the future.

The Ninth Commandment in our Time

We have considered the original impulse of the ninth commandment and its ongoing metamorphosis by examining the ever-changing human perception of *truth*. We saw how, in olden times, people still lived with an instinctive feeling for truth; how, in the time of Abraham, with the development of the intellect, people became capable of speaking a lie; how subsequently the Mosaic commandment against "false witness" was introduced; and how, almost a thousand years later, the philosophical way of thinking became a new tool in forming concepts about truth. Next we observed how, a few centuries later, Christ brought an entirely new impulse with the words "I am the Truth, the Way, and the Life"; and how, at the Festival of Pentecost, the working of the Holy Spirit, *the Spirit of Truth*, became manifest, uniting human beings through the spoken word.

What is the situation in our own time with respect to our understanding of truth? The search for truth continues unabated. But what is needed in our time is more than just an instinctive sense of truth; more than just the rejection of a lie; more than abstract, thought-out philosophical concepts of truth. What our time needs, above all, is a *truth that we can inwardly experience, understand, and identify with.*

In our discussions thus far we have described the development of the search for truth primarily in terms that are linked to religious traditions and concepts. It would be equally valid to present the same concepts and ideas in philosophical terminology. How we dress these ideas is a question of taste; the content remains essentially the same. In *The Philosophy of Freedom* and other philosophical works Rudolf Steiner points to the connection that exists between truth and freedom, and between freedom and the activity of the "I." This means that the free spiritual activity of the "I" must guide our search for truth. In this search we must develop a new form of thinking, a new *art* of thinking, a thinking in which truth can *live*, instead of giving up its life in a vortex of abstract thought patterns. *When the spiritual activity of the "I" can bring forth a thinking that lives in truth, it will have conquered the lie.*

Our time urgently requires that we develop this new *art of thinking*. But this is not something that can be expressed in the form of an external commandment, because this new kind of thinking—one could also say, this new art of living—can only emerge from the "I" of a free human being. This is the realm of freedom in which the metamorphosis of the ninth commandment can take shape in our time. It is difficult to find one word to describe this realm, this dimension. We could use the word "truthfulness," but it does not fully define the all-encompassing concept meant here, a concept that includes more than one way of aspiring toward truth.

To begin with, this concept obviously embraces being truthful in one's speaking. But it also includes a sense of responsibility toward other human beings or, in a wider sense, toward all humankind, a sense of responsibility that can only be sustained through love. Cultivating this kind of awareness, incidentally, also creates a natural transition from the transformed *ninth* commandment to the true impulse of the *tenth* commandment, the impulse namely to develop a loving concern in our souls for the wellbeing of our neighbor, our fellow human being.

From this attitude of soul we can then also summon the courage we need in our striving for truth. For it will indeed take more and more *courage* to clearly distinguish between truth and the sometimes painful abstractions we will encounter along the way. The concept we are here attempting to define also includes what we nowadays call *integrity*, in other words, a quality of trustworthiness and sincerity. But it also encompasses the quality of soul that in earlier times, for example in the Bible, was indicated when a human being was referred to as *just*.[221] And, last but not least, this concept embraces an inner attitude of respect toward *truth* as a *spiritual entity*, and toward the spiritual world in which truth ultimately resides; for only with this kind of inner attitude can we come to know the truth.

But in our present time the "spirit of truth" is frequently attacked by the spirit of tradition, hollow phrases, untruths, and even betrayal. More and more inner strength will be needed to defy such tendencies and to find ways of *living in the spirit of truth*, in other words, to develop forces of truthfulness. To be able to do this we must be willing to take our own inner development in hand. We could, for instance, work on improving the quality of our thinking, our speaking, and our actions. Efforts in any one of these fields will benefit the other ones at the same time. But, as we are presently exploring transformations of the *ninth* commandment, we will here concentrate on our *speaking* in particular.

With the original commandment against the "bearing of false witness," people were encouraged to practice what one might call *truth-speaking*. From the art of rhetoric, which was developed in ancient Greece, emerged in later centuries the impulse for what one might call *beauty-speaking*, which was not only truthful, but also poetic and beautiful. These are all things we should work on today as well. But what our time really needs is what one might call *good-speaking*, a speaking that is truthful, poetically beautiful, and also encompasses a healing quality toward the good in human beings.

By being mindful of our speaking in this way we can, already now, contribute something precious for the future development of humankind. For there are forces slumbering in the spoken word, forces that in future times can potentially be used either for good or for evil purposes. Speaking thus can become a moral deed, a creative moral act of the human "I." A mighty contribution for the future can be made in this way. In future times people will then be able to, as it were, pour good soul forces into another human being through the spoken word.[222] And by doing so, the *good* will be strengthened and safeguarded in people who are no longer able to develop this quality on their own. A truly social impulse of fellowship can thus become active in a practical way through the moral use of the *good word*.[223]

In olden times it sufficed to forbid the giving of false witness to shield the refined part of the astral body from harm—something the immature "I" was not yet capable of doing on its own. But in our time this is no longer sufficient; something else is required of us. We have to realize that the way we use our speech is not inconsequential. We need to treat the forces of human speech with reverence. We should, already now, try to be aware of the forces at work in human speech, forces through which human beings, in times to come, will be able to activate the *good* in the world.

A fitting metamorphosis of the ninth commandment for our time could be formulated thus:

> May your speaking be truthful,
> To serve the Spirit of Truth,
> To ripen the good in human souls
> And give form to human lives
> For future times to come.

10

The Tenth Commandment

The Tenth commandment: *You shall not covet your neighbor's house, you shall not covet your neighbor's wife, nor his manservant, nor his maidservant, nor his ox, nor his ass, nor any thing that is your neighbor's.*

The tenth commandment is unlike any of the other commandments. It has a different character. After all, it deals with a propensity of the soul, something that cannot be evaluated by another person. In contrast, one *can* determine whether someone conducts his or her life in compliance with any of the first nine commandments. One *can* ascertain whether a person worships other gods, makes (or bows down to) idols, uses God's name in vain, works on the Sabbath, doesn't honor his or her parents, murders, commits adultery, steals, or lies. Because such infringements can be evaluated objectively, any or all of the first nine commandments can also form the basis—albeit not necessarily an equally solid basis—for a social, religious, or judicial ordering of society. But in the tenth commandment the *invisible inner human being* is addressed. What goes on inside a person cannot be known or judged by anyone else. Hence the tenth commandment could never, in the same sense, occupy a credible position within a society's legal structure. To be able to comply with the tenth commandment, one's everyday consciousness, which normally tends to be focused on the outside world, must now be directed at the inner self instead. In other words, observing the tenth commandment calls for a certain degree of *self-consciousness*. Self-consciousness is a manifestation of the "I"; its very character, therefore, leads us to conclude that this commandment has a special connection with the human "I," or, to put it more specifically, that the tenth commandment was intended to support the developing human "I."

The "I" is the youngest member of the fourfold human being. It was still slumbering "in the lap of the gods" during Saturn, Sun, and Moon evolution. Only around the middle of the Lemurian time was the germ of the "I" embedded in human beings by the *Spirits of Form* (the *Exusiai*). In the subsequent Atlantean epoch this germ continued to grow; but even in the post-Atlantean time, right up to the time of Moses, the "I" was not yet fully awakened. It was only in the fourth cultural epoch, when the Mystery of Golgotha came to pass, that the "I" was born in human beings. In the time of Moses, however, the young "I" was still surrounded and protected by the astral sheath. This is why the tenth commandment addressed the "I" only indirectly, namely by instructing it to avoid certain desires rooted in the astral body. The sevenfold structure of this commandment's formulation also points to this astral connection, just as we observed earlier with respect to the wording of the fourth commandment. In that case we encountered seven categories of animals and human beings, all of whom were expected to observe the Sabbath rest; here we find seven classes of human beings, animals, and objects that should not be *coveted*. Here the actual desires appear in a sevenfold garb. And, just as we observed with respect to the wording of the fourth commandment, there is no logical reason or need for the sevenfold formulation of the tenth commandment either. It could simply have stated, *You shall not covet anything that is your neighbor's.*

Likewise, one could argue, the seventh and the eighth commandment would actually become redundant if people were to fully observe the tenth commandment. After all, there would be no need for a commandment forbidding adultery or theft if people would refrain from coveting in the first place. But we have already discovered that applying this type of logic to the wording of the Ten Commandments is not very useful. The form in which these commandments appeared was not created for the purpose of avoiding apparent redundancies. Rather, this form was used to reveal the profound relationship that exists between the Ten Commandments and the creative impulses working in the various members of the tenfold human being. By identifying the specific form of the tenth commandment, we have already determined that it, because of its unique message, has a special connection with the "I" of the human being. In the same way, we can tell from its sevenfold structure that the immature "I" in the time of Moses could actually be strengthened by learning to overcome specific desires living in the astral body.

All the same, is it not striking that this commandment confronted *coveting*, in other words, a longing that, one might argue, arises spontaneously in the soul in response to specific circumstances? One could conceivably envisage a commandment ordering people not to give in to whatever they covet, but the longing itself—is that not something one simply undergoes or experiences? What, then, is the practical purpose of prohibiting the actual emotion?

Before the time of Moses it would indeed not have been appropriate or useful to forbid soul passions as such. People did not yet have the ability to respond autonomously to such feelings that instinctively welled up in the soul. But in the time of Moses the human "I" was beginning to stir and was no longer wholly dependent on its protective astral sheath. For the first time human beings were able, through the growing power of the "I," to face and even control their own feelings and longings. The tenth commandment was aimed at supporting this new ability with the words, "You shall not covet...."

The "I" of the Human Being

In all preceding chapters we have referred to the "I" of the human being without, however, defining it precisely. We have assumed that its meaning could be inferred from the immediate context. But the reader will undoubtedly have noticed that this meaning fluctuated somewhat, depending on that context. What then, we must ask at long last, is this "I" of the human being?

It is almost impossible to put this into words because the "I" is not a constant object that can be defined and grasped with a static way of thinking. The "I" is forever moving, changing, renewing, developing, forming, becoming. The "I" is constantly busy creating itself and giving of itself. We can only begin to understand the "I" if we observe it during this activity. And, depending on whatever this activity is directed at, the "I" continuously takes on a different character, reinvents itself. It constantly changes its character through its own activity. As the "I" matures, it becomes more multifaceted and more able to transform itself. In his book *Theosophy* Rudolf Steiner describes this capacity of continual transformation thus: "for the "I" receives its nature and significance from whatever it is united with."[224]

We can recognize the existence of our own individual "I" by means of our self-consciousness or "I"-consciousness. For we know: whatever I may be thinking, I know that *I* am the one who is doing the thinking. Incidentally, this also holds with respect to our feelings and actions, for I know that *I* am the one who is feeling or doing something. So we may justifiably view this "I" as our true being, our real self. Perceiving one's own "I" belongs to the most intimate of all inner experiences a human being can have. It leads to the secure knowledge: I am an independent, individual, unique, indivisible entity. Simultaneously we can perceive that this "I" is always in the process of transforming and renewing itself. This is why the "I" has so many facets, why it is so ever-changing, so difficult to grasp, but, for the same reason, why it is so secure and irrefutable.

Our modern "I"-consciousness needs specific points of contact in daily life to maintain its presence. It is supported by the continuing stream of impressions we take in with our sense organs. Should this stream be completely interrupted—as has been tried in test experiments, for example, by keeping people in totally isolated cubicles—it would be almost impossible, after a certain length of time, to maintain one's "I"-consciousness. Under such conditions most people fall asleep or begin to hallucinate. Put another way, the "I" disappears from human consciousness once it is no longer exposed to sense impressions.[225]

But the "I"-consciousness is linked to memory as well. Through our capacity of remembering we know that a connection exists between the impressions and experiences we had yesterday and those we have today. Our faculty of memory creates continuity in our daily lives. In other words, we know that yesterday's "I" is the same entity as today's "I." Although this may seem obvious, it is not something that can be taken for granted. After all, our memory reaches only those blocks of time during which we are awake, not those in which we are asleep. One could say that our memory provides us with a dotted line of experiences with periodic interruptions for sleep; and yet, (under normal circumstances) we experience both our memory and our "I"-consciousness as an uninterrupted whole. Memory and "I"-consciousness, then, are intimately linked in present-day human beings.

There is, in addition to these recurring periods of sleep, a particular time in human life that cannot be penetrated with our memory either; and, again, it involves both our faculty of remembering and our "I"-consciousness. We are referring to the earliest phase of childhood. Most people cannot remember further back than approximately their third year of life; this is also the time a child begins to use the word "I." One could well assume, then, that the "I" plays no role before that particular time in a person's life. This would be incorrect. It is true that our "I"-consciousness, in as much as it is based on memory, cannot cross the border into the earliest years of life. But the "I" itself is actively engaged in other processes in those early years of life, processes that are not connected to memory.[226] We will come back to this.

The Development of the "I"

Rudolf Steiner has frequently pointed out that each child, as it is developing, is retracing the developmental phases of humankind. It will therefore be helpful, in this context, to compare the development of the "I" in the individual human being with that of humanity as a whole.

Today, small children become aware of their own "I" between the ages of two and three, when they begin to use the word "I" for the first time.[227] Simultaneously, our permanent memory begins to develop, by means of which, later on in life, we can remember back to this particular point in time. This first-time recognition of oneself as an "I" represents an important milestone in the development of self-consciousness on the path of becoming a human being! A comparable milestone for humanity as a whole was reached in the time of Moses with the introduction of the Ten Commandments to support the development of this awakening "I."

Before the child has its first "I"-experience around age three, however, the "I" had already been active—albeit more from the outside—in preparing for this stage. Immediately after its birth the baby cries. For every baby this is a unique sound that reveals something of the individuality of the child, because it is an expression of the "I." After the first few months of life the body begins to establish its own stable temperature through the blood flow. This is how the "I" puts its own, individual stamp on the body. During the whole first year of life the cranial bones in the head, still pliable at birth, gradually harden, resulting, around the end of that first year, in the closing of the fontanel. This is how the "I" prepares the child's body for the later development of "I"-consciousness.

After this preparatory phase one can clearly distinguish three developmental stages in which the "I" is actively involved. These are the stages of learning to *walk, speak, and think*. We have discussed these three uniquely human capacities in connection with the life ether; presently we will consider this topic from the perspective of the activity of the "I."

During the first of these three phases, which partially overlaps with the preparatory stage we just described, the skeletal system continues to grow stronger. Especially the back and legs have to become strong enough to carry the weight of the body. These growth processes come to an initial culmination when the child learns to *stand* and *walk* in an upright position, while the hardening of the bones will continue for many years thereafter.

During the second phase the "I" works on the etheric body of the child, resulting in the development of the faculties of memory and imagination. It is because of these abilities that the child is able to imitate whatever it encounters in its surroundings. One of the things it imitates is the spoken word and the use of language. This second phase finds an initial culmination when the child learns to *speak*.

In a third phase the faculty of remembering already begins to weaken somewhat. The "I" now becomes active in the development of *thinking*. This is a long process that only comes to full fruition in the adult. But it reaches an initial juncture around the thirteenth year when the child is able to follow an abstract line of thought as, say, in an algebraic formula. Human thinking is the foremost activity of the self-conscious "I." One could also say that the development of a person's self-consciousness culminates in the ability to form free, independent, active thoughts.

And, again, we can find corresponding phases in the developing "I" of humanity as a whole. With respect to the development of the child we found that the first stage of standing and walking partially overlaps with the preparatory stage. We can distinguish a comparable phase in the middle of the *Lemurian* epoch when the two human sexes had already emerged. This was the time when our human ancestors began to produce primitive sounds, when their body temperature began to stabilize, and when the whole physical body had solidified sufficiently for people to assume the upright position.

In a next phase of humanity's evolution, namely during the *Atlantean* time, people began to develop the faculties of memory and speech, just as the child does during the comparable phase of its development. The memory of the Atlantean people, however, was infinitely more powerful; indeed, it formed the basis for the whole Atlantean civilization. Our present faculty of memory is but a weak echo of this once powerful capacity.

In the *post-Atlantean* time, notably during the Greek cultural epoch, people began to think independently, just as the growing child does in its comparable phase of development. In the Greek time it was especially the birth of philosophy that further stimulated this new capacity in human beings; it became another important stepping stone on humanity's path of development.[228]

The human capacities of walking, speaking, and thinking—the fruits of the Lemurian, Atlantean, and post-Atlantean eras respectively—thus form the basis for the development of the "I," both in the individual human being and in humanity as a whole. The "I" is actively involved in developing these three capacities, through which human beings increasingly become aware of themselves as individuals. In our own time this "I"-consciousness usually comes fully into its own around the twenty-first year of life. One could also say that at that age the "I" is born in the human being (just as the etheric body and the astral body are born around the ages of seven and fourteen respectively).[229] This awakening of the individual "I," again, has an archetype in the history of humanity as a whole, namely in the deed of Christ on Golgotha. With this pivotal event on Golgotha something took place that we initially might be inclined to view just as an analogy, but that, upon further examination, must be understood in a real sense as the birth of the World-"I."[230]

The Sense of "I" and the "I"

We human beings have not only an *"I,"* but also a *sense of "I."* This special sense organ is the highest of the twelve human senses as they are recognized in Anthroposophy.[231] The sense of "I" gives us the ability to perceive the "I" in someone else.

We become aware of our own "I" by means of our "I"-consciousness. With our *"I"-sense* we can recognize the "I" of another human being—our neighbor. This recognition is a very special process through which one identifies temporarily with the other's "I." In *The Philosophy of Freedom* Rudolf Steiner describes, from an epistemological viewpoint, how this identifying with another human being can take place. The separation between one's own and another person's consciousness is lifted when we learn to perceive that person's thinking. During this process we may be able to observe how our consciousness periodically unites with that of the other person, as it were, and then retreats back to itself again.[232]

Nonetheless, it would be incorrect to assume that, by identifying with another "I" in the way we just described, one would be able to fully penetrate into all the sacred depths of that other person. The above indications actually present us with what seem to be contradictory truths. On the one hand we hear that, through our sense of "I," we can observe the "I" of someone else; but on the other hand Rudolf Steiner also mentions that, in reality, we can perceive only our own "I" "directly."[233] Consequently, whatever we can perceive of the other "I" by means of our sense of "I" is, at best, only an indirect and veiled impression. Even a person who is clairvoyant cannot perceive the "I" of another person in its real essence. This "I" is hidden in the sacred innermost human being, always veiled. What one can perceive is the working of the "I" on that person's aura.[234] This is where *the other "I"* is revealed in its activities and where one may get to know it.

As a matter of fact, being aware of one's *own "I"* also occurs with varying levels of consciousness. To begin with, we are aware of our own "I" as we live our daily lives as "I"-beings. One could say that with this level of "I"-consciousness we perceive that our "I" is at work in our physical and etheric bodies. Inasmuch as the "I"-consciousness is based on our thinking, our feeling, and our being active, it arises from our perceiving that the "I" is at work in the astral body. With this level of "I"-consciousness we can also be aware of how our "I" works on balancing the desires and passions living in this astral body (such as, for example, the "coveting" mentioned in the tenth commandment). All these activities of the "I" in the physical, etheric, and astral bodies are manifestations of what we might call the *lower "I."* We also have a *higher "I."* It is much more difficult to be aware of this higher "I." The old mysteries encouraged their pupils to develop a connection to their higher "I" with the injunction, "Human being, know yourself!" This advice, still applicable today, points to a long and difficult path. Only at the end of this path of development will we be able to know our higher being, our higher "I."[235]

Something of this higher "I" is revealed in a person's biography, which really is the key to the "I." The study of a person's biography can give insight into the importance of inner and outer influences on that person's life. One can, for instance, note how certain talents or limitations already existed right from the start; how well the person in question uses these talents and limitations; how life bestows fortunes and misfortunes, and how these help shape that person's life. Our higher "I" works not only in what we bring to the world, but also in whatever the world brings to us, and in the way we incorporate these outer circumstances into our life. The inner aspect of the "I," which stimulates our inner impulses, is sometimes referred to as our *genius* or *daimon* (in the sense of Socrates); the outer aspect of the "I," which instigates the outer circumstances determining the course of our life, is said to be *the complementary "I."* Both are manifestations of the higher "I." This higher "I" thus reveals itself both as the inspiring genius and as the complementary "I" in the life of every human being. It shapes the individual's biography from the flowing together of these two aspects. Every "I" forms its own life; this is what gives each human biography its individual expression. A person's biography reveals this unique character in the sum of all the inner and outer events occurring in that person's life.

When we study someone's biography with all this in mind, allowing the living totality of this particular life in all its diversity to work on us, we may get to know the essence of that life. We may possibly even find an answer to the deeper question, "Why did this person incarnate on Earth?"

This is a question we can ask about our own life as well, "Why have I come to the Earth in this life and at this time?" It is particularly helpful to ask this question from the standpoint of the aforementioned double aspect of the higher "I": "To which extent is my life guided by the inspiration of my genius, my daimon, and to which extent by my complementary 'I'?"

By truly getting to know oneself through the path of esoteric schooling—in the sense of "human being, know yourself"—one can eventually penetrate the ground of all being in the spiritual world. A person who is thus far advanced on the esoteric path will then be able to recognize not only his or her former incarnations but also essential aspects of the earlier planetary incarnations of the Earth and of the cosmos. The "I" will then know itself as an "I"-being amid a multitude of other "I"-beings. What this means can hardly be expressed in words. Even so, we will here make an attempt to portray this spiritual state of being in pictorial images.

This multitude of "I"-beings appears before our spiritual eye as a twelvefold host of beings. Together, they form a spiritual, zodiac-like circle, allowing each group's essential forces to interact and collectively radiate out. When we observe these ever-changing interactive streams radiating from the circle of beings, which appear in a manifold pallet of colors, we may become aware that the circle is held together by spiritual beings. And in the center of the circle we find the Spirit of the Earth. This is where the divine Christ-being lives as World-"I." His being radiates out to all parts of the circle; these are rays of cosmic love, carried by his being. And from the circle of "I"-beings something like an answer radiates back to this middle point, like an offering through a song of gratitude. This song, radiating from each of the "I"-beings, proclaims the intent to keep incarnating on Earth and thus to keep growing and maturing. And from the middle point a promise radiates back from the Being of the Earth, distributing itself like a blessing onto the whole circle, a promise that he will unite his own growth process with that of each human "I"-being, in love. In this way all human "I"-beings are eternally connected to the Christ-being, the Being of the Earth, in an enduring, mutual, spiritual relationship.

Commandments that Are Related to the "I"

We have indicated in previous chapters that several of the commandments have a connection to the "I" of the human being. How can we identify and characterize this connection in each of these commandments?

The *fourth commandment,* by urging people to remember the Sabbath, was intended to help prepare the *physical body* to create a space for the "I." Here people's faculty of memory—the precursor of independent thinking—was specifically addressed, a faculty without which people would not have been able to commit to the required periodic cessation of all physical work.

The *seventh commandment,* by forbidding adultery, was intended to help prepare the *etheric body* to assimilate the "I." Here people were urged to remember their promise of marital fidelity, so that loyalty and trust would become strong, formative components in the unfolding of their lives.

The *ninth commandment,* by prohibiting "false witness," was intended to help prepare the *astral body* to take in the "I." Here people had to learn to resist certain desires so that the "I" could develop truthfulness and attain truth.

And finally, the *tenth commandment,* by encouraging people not to covet other people's possessions, was intended to help keep the *"I" itself* strong and healthy. To be able to do this, people needed to learn how the intensity of their inner longings and desires should be weighed against the overwhelming allure of the sensory world. The tenth commandment was introduced to help people maintain a healthy balance between the forces of the inner and the outer worlds.

Four related qualities were to be fostered in these four commandments. The fourth commandment (Sabbath) obliged people to periodically spend some time in *devotion* to the spiritual world. The seventh and the ninth commandment (adultery and false witness) introduced the ideals of *trust* and *truthfulness* respectively. Devotion, trust, and truthfulness together form a trinity we may well call *the servants of* the "I." But the highest ideal was revealed in the tenth commandment, where the "I" itself was addressed. By activating their sense of "I" people could become aware of the "I" of another person in relation to their own "I," and thus learn to respect the uniqueness of this other person.

It may be helpful to compare the fourth to the tenth commandment to illustrate the subtle difference between perceiving one's own "I" through "I"-consciousness and perceiving the "I" of another person through the sense of "I." The *fourth* commandment aimed to make people aware of the power of their own "I," which in the time of Moses was just beginning to awaken. The Sabbath rest was to be observed by seven categories of beings, both human and animal, all of whom were subject to the will of the master—the "I." Thus the "I" could become aware of itself through the subservience of these people and animals. The *tenth* commandment, in contrast, awakened the sense of "I" by making people aware of the rights of other human beings. Again we meet a sevenfold set of beings and objects, but now in connection to "your neighbor"—in other words, to the "I" of the other human being. The tenth commandment aimed to make people aware of the fact that the other human being also is an "I"-being whose rights should be respected. The tenth commandment encouraged people to find their own place in the world and, at the same time, to respect the place that others have found for themselves in that same world. In other words, the human "I" had to learn to "live and let live."

Striving for Balance

We observed that both the "I" and the sense of "I," with which we perceive the "I"-being of another person, began to awaken in the time of Moses. And, ever since, the adversary powers have attempted to fetter the human "I" to the outer world and to undermine the sense of "I." It is a spiritual necessity that we incarnate on Earth and learn to deal with earthly matter. We all need physical things to be able to live on Earth, but, inspired by ahrimanic influences, we often tend to acquire an ever increasing quantity of material objects (and/or money), hoping to find our spiritual footing in it, while disregarding the needs and rights of other human beings. This tendency leads to outer selfishness.

The luciferic forces are working in an entirely different direction. They strive to convince us of our own importance and of our own spiritual existence to such a degree that we tend to undervalue the "I" of the other human being. Our inner world of impressions, feelings, and desires then becomes the determining factor in our lives, while the external world, including the other people living in it, becomes inconsequential to our existence. This tendency leads to inner selfishness.

The "I" must become strong enough to keep both kinds of coveting in balance. This can only be achieved through insight. By learning to distinguish between the objective merit of the other human being and the relative (in)significance of our own existence in the scheme of things, we can develop the necessary balance with respect to our desires, be they ahrimanic or luciferic in nature. In the time of Moses the developing "I" still needed outer guidance to achieve this goal. This was the aim of the tenth commandment that united all of the above into a most concise form, "You shall not covet...what...is your neighbor's."

Christ and the Tenth Commandment

Finding and maintaining a healthy balance between the luciferic and ahrimanic longings to which the "I" is exposed: this is, as we have pointed out above, ultimately the aim of the tenth commandment. How did Christ further transform this guiding principle of the tenth commandment?

At the baptism in the Jordan, Christ had entered into a human body, that is to say, into human existence. With this deed he willed to take upon himself the weaknesses of human nature and destiny, including being exposed to Lucifer and Ahriman.[236] As a result, he met these beings right after the baptism in the Jordan. We read in the Bible that Christ had to undergo three specific temptations. These temptations appear to human beings as the result of the human "fall into sin," of the inherited sinful nature we all share. In the lecture cycle referred to as *The Fifth Gospel,* Rudolf Steiner describes these three temptations not only in more detail than the accounts we find in the New Testament, but also as having unfolded in a different sequence.[237] This is because Matthew and Luke describe the temptations from the human perspective, while Rudolf Steiner depicts them through the perspective of the divine being of Christ descending from the spiritual *sin-free* world into the accumulated sin afflicted physical world of human beings.[238]

Seen from this divine perspective, Christ was first tempted by Lucifer alone, then by the combined efforts of Lucifer and Ahriman, and finally by Ahriman alone. In the first temptation, by Lucifer alone, "the devil, taking him up into a high mountain, showed unto him all the kingdoms of the world in a moment of time. And the devil said unto him, all this power will I give you...." Christ endured against this temptation and answered, "It is written, you shall worship the LORD your God, and him only shall you serve" (Luke 4:5–8, Matt. 4:8–10). In the second temptation, by the combined forces of Lucifer and Ahriman, the tempter "brought him to Jerusalem, and set him on a pinnacle of the temple, and said unto him, if you be the Son of God, cast yourself down from behind...." Christ endured against this temptation and answered, "It is said, you shall not tempt the Lord your God" (Luke 4:9–12, Matt. 4:5–7). In the third temptation, by Ahriman alone, "the devil said unto him, if you be the Son of God, command this stone that it be made bread." Christ answered, "It is written, that man shall not live by bread alone, but by every word of God" (Luke 4:3–4, Matt. 4:2–4).

With these temptations in the desert, Christ confronted the same luciferic and ahrimanic longings of the soul as had been addressed in the tenth commandment for all human beings. By overcoming these temptations, Christ has opened a point of entry to the spiritual world where the human "I" can follow, and find the strength, out of the Christ-forces, to deal with the impact of the luciferic or ahrimanic influences. Thus the foundation has been laid upon which all human beings can follow in the footsteps of Christ. By his example the human being can now act as a free "I"-being, learning to withstand the forces of Lucifer and Ahriman that would otherwise fetter the "I."

We can find another situation described in the New Testament during which Jesus had to respond to a temptation-like question. This time his answer took on a different form. Having first affirmed and substantiated the authenticity of the Mosaic laws by replying to the temptations with quotations from the Old Testament, ("It is written..." and "It is said..."), Jesus could now respond with new forces from the heart. One of the Pharisees, a "lawyer," had asked Jesus which of the commandments "is the great commandment in the law." He receives a twofold answer. The first part aims to awaken the love of God—we have examined this aspect in connection with the first commandment. The second part has a particular connection to the tenth commandment, "You shall love your neighbor as yourself" (Matt. 22:39, Mark 12:31, Luke 10:27). This passage then ends with the words, "On these two commandments hang all the law."

The concept of loving one's neighbor already existed within the Mosaic laws as well. And, again, we must read these texts very carefully to be able to recognize the qualitative difference between the original form and Christ's approach to it. In the original formulation we read, "You shall not avenge, nor bear any grudge against the children of your people, but you shall love your neighbor as yourself: I am the LORD" (Lev. 19:18). Here the love of the neighbor barely extended beyond one's own people, one's own nation. As Jesus quoted only the *second* part of this commandment, namely to love one's neighbor, it is understandable that the Pharisaic scribe, the lawyer, was interested in knowing whether Jesus' concept of neighbor was different from the one used in the Old Testament. That is why he asked, "And who is my neighbor?" (Luke 10:29). To this question Jesus responds with the story of the Good Samaritan who offered help to a severely injured man for whom two earlier passersby had done nothing. In almost Socratic manner Jesus then poses the question, "Which now of these three, think you, was neighbor unto him that fell among the thieves?" (Luke 10:36).

Let us picture the situation of this scribe. He had listened. He now had to activate his own will forces to respond. This raised the discourse from the level of an abstract theory to that of an inspired knowing. The answer, of course, was obvious: "The one who showed mercy." This kind of mercy, however, was no longer intended only for a restricted group. It now could become a universal mercy for all human beings. This also means that the focus of the tenth commandment—the relationship to one's neighbor—underwent a transformation as well: *everyone can now be that neighbor.* For the scribe who asked the original question this insight must have been particularly enlightening and life altering. It must have been as though he had received a new direction to understand his own karma, inspiring him to rise above the immediate folk connections and to recognize the *humanity in every single human being.* Because of the ripening process that had taken place in him, Jesus was then able, at the end of the story, to address the scribe's forces of will directly, "Go, and do you likewise" (Luke 10:37).

This is how Christ intensified the tenth commandment for humanity. We are called upon to make the step from the more passive state of *not desiring what belongs to someone else* to actively learning to *recognize the "I" of the other human being in love*, and act accordingly.

The Tenth Commandment in our Time

Does the tenth commandment still have any significance in our time? If so, in what form? As we have seen, the goal of this commandment was to support the developing "I" by instructing human beings to resist certain unhealthy desires rising up from the astral body. Obviously, envy and jealousy were not only a problem for people in the time of Moses. These were, and still are, sentiments that, by rights, do not belong in the astral body, and therefore have a negative impact on the developing human "I." But, because of the decisive impact of the Christ impulse on the ongoing development of the "I," today's human beings are far more capable of holding such impulses and desires at bay.

Where can we find evidence of this ongoing development of the human "I"? To begin with, we could point to an interesting remark made by the German philosopher Max Scheler. He once defined with a few succinct words what distinguishes us from the animals: "The human being is a being who can say No."[239] He meant that, in contrast to the animals that *must* follow their instinctive desires, human beings possess an inner higher power through which they can balance such desires. In our discussions we have called this power *the "I."* A definition like this one could only have been formulated by a modern human being; it could neither have been uttered nor understood in olden times.

One could also think of today's international war crime tribunals. In such cases the person on trial is expected to have acted *according to his own judgment*, and consequently can be found guilty of crimes against humanity, despite the inevitable attempts to justify such crimes with the "orders-from-superiors" excuse. This also is a modern phenomenon, one that could not have occurred in antiquity. After all, the crucial point in such cases is that today, in circumstances endangering humanity as a whole, one is expected to be able to say "no" to the whisperings of the astral body, out of the strength of one's "I."

On the other hand, one could also think of situations in which the present-day condition of the human "I" is *not* taken into consideration, as, for instance, when certain esoteric societies aim to keep their knowledge secret. This kind of secrecy was necessary in the time of the old mysteries, because it was known that people would not be able to tolerate such revelations lest they had been prepared first. Secrecy was maintained in those days, not to exert power over people, but to protect those who did not belong to the mysteries. The situation is different today. The stability of the "I" is much more dependable; consequently, human beings are now capable of receiving esoteric knowledge without being thrown off balance inwardly. Keeping esoteric knowledge secret, therefore, is neither required nor suitable in our time.

The Mystery of Golgotha (in which, one could say, all old mystery impulses flowed together) has brought a profound change to this whole situation. Christ, the bearer of the World-"I," went through death and resurrection. Because of this divine–human deed every human "I" can now surpass the group-"I" stage and become an individual "I." In earlier times this could only have occurred—albeit only to some degree—by *secret* initiation in the old mysteries. What happened at Golgotha truly was a mystery deed, but one that was undertaken *publicly* and therefore was very different in nature from the secret mystery customs of former times. Had the Mystery of Golgotha not taken place, human beings would not have developed into independent "I"-beings, for whom any kind of secrecy regarding mystery wisdom is no longer appropriate.

It was truly an act of great historical significance when Rudolf Steiner, at the occasion of the founding of the General Anthroposophical Society in 1923, declared that there is no longer any place, or indeed any need, for secrecy with respect to knowledge—including esoteric knowledge—in our time. This required a great degree of courage, responsibility, and insight! Such knowledge, then, must no longer be the exclusive possession of one person or a closed society. Knowledge belongs to all humanity. This is why it can be published in books and why it must be placed outside those realms where envy and possessiveness prevail. This, one could say, is a *modern nuance of the tenth commandment.*

There is another realm we should mention in this regard; it has to do with our understanding of and relation to other people. We should try to develop a feeling for the uniqueness of the other person, a refined sensitivity for the unique, personal elements in the life of the other individual. "Loving your neighbor as you love yourself" in our present-day setting means that we should try to recognize and understand the unique, individual elements in the other person's biography, especially those elements in which the "I" is active. Only if we understand the other human being in this way, can we try to establish a valuable relationship between our own "I" and the unique impulses of the other "I." We must learn to ask: *Can I get to know my "neighbor" in such a way that, by initiating the appropriate, creative response in myself, I may be able to contribute something of value toward this person's tasks on Earth?* Living with a question such as this may well constitute the metamorphosis of the tenth commandment for modern people today.

To be able to find the right tone for this kind of question, we should try to keep alive in our minds the image of the *first* and the *last* commandment, as expressed in the Gospel of St. Matthew (22:37–40), "You shall love the Lord your God with all your heart..." and, "You shall love your neighbor as yourself." These words are like two strong pillars that, on the one hand, support the whole moral law of the Old Testament ("on these two commandments hang all the law..."), but at the same time stand as the Alpha and Omega with respect to today's questions of morality in the lives of human beings. The Mystery of Golgotha itself gives us the assurance that the spiritual cosmos has been structured in such a way that our "I" can indeed be strengthened morally through the personal contributions we are able to give one another according to our mutual and individual needs.

All this undoubtedly sounds far too idealistic and impractical for some. But the question contained in the modern form of the tenth commandment is a question we must not ignore. It has, we trust, become clear from our explorations into this topic that we cannot permit ourselves to avoid questions like these. It is of the utmost importance in our time that we work on strengthening our "I" lest we be negatively impacted by the desires of the astral body. Even today, the whole question of human morality ultimately depends on our "I" being strong enough to respond to the needs of the world from out of the transformed *first* and *last* commandment.

11

Concluding Thoughts

Having walked this long path of discovery we now will try to bring together the various elements. We took for our starting point the fact that the evolution of the Earth is closely tied to the evolution of human beings. The Earth has gone through four planetary stages; so has the human being. This means that our physical body today reveals a fourfold structure; our etheric body a threefold structure; our astral body a twofold structure; while our "I" is a single entity. Seen from this vantage point the human being is a *tenfold being*.

At a crucial moment in the history of humanity *ten* commandments were given—out of the spiritual world and through the mediation of Moses—to help strengthen, guide, and cultivate the spiritual hygiene of human beings: one specific commandment for each one of the members of the tenfold human being respectively. The Ten Commandments contained, in the most concise form possible, the qualitative essence of the various spiritual impulses that collectively gave rise to the tenfold human being. Therefore, with the help of the instructions given in these Ten Commandments, human life in the time of Moses could be structured in such a way that it would unfold in harmony with these original creative impulses.

The first four commandments concentrated on the human relationship to the divine and the way this manifests in our *physical body*. The *first* commandment pointed to the all-encompassing *unity* of the divine cosmos, a unity that is reflected in the physical body as a whole. The *second* commandment pointed to the need to keep the etheric forces pure and healthy to help maintain the whole physical body as the living *image* of the macrocosm. The *third* commandment pointed to the cosmic astral impulses at work in human *speech* and the importance of using these forces responsibly. The *fourth* commandment prepared a *space* in the physical human being, dedicated to receive the spiritual power of the "I" into itself.

Because the first four commandments have a connection to the physical body—and thus to the physical brain as well—the human faculty of logical thinking was addressed by means of an explanation, by a further clarification of that particular commandment. In the texts of the second, third, and fourth commandments this clarification begins with the word "for." In the formulation of the first commandment, which has a connection to the warmth on old Saturn, this explanation can only be inferred, because Saturn's warmth forms a transitional stage between a purely physical and an etheric condition. Yet, even here we can discover an implied clarification by changing the sequence of the wording somewhat: "You shall have no other gods before me, *for* I am the LORD your God." From the fifth commandment onward no logical explanation was given in the formulation of the respective texts because these commandments have their origin in cosmic impulses that are not related to the kind of thinking that is bound to the physical brain.

The next three commandments have a connection to *the etheric body* that, along with the entire etheric realm, has gone through three planetary stages. The *fifth* commandment is connected to the Sun-like light ether forces. It pointed to the *path of reverence* as "sustenance" for the light ether forces that are working through the hereditary stream in subsequent generations. The *sixth* commandment is connected to the Moon-like sound ether forces, which, among other things, carry the seed of *death*. This commandment aimed to restrict the influence of these death forces. The *seventh* commandment is connected to the life ether that evolved during the Earth phase; these forces enable the

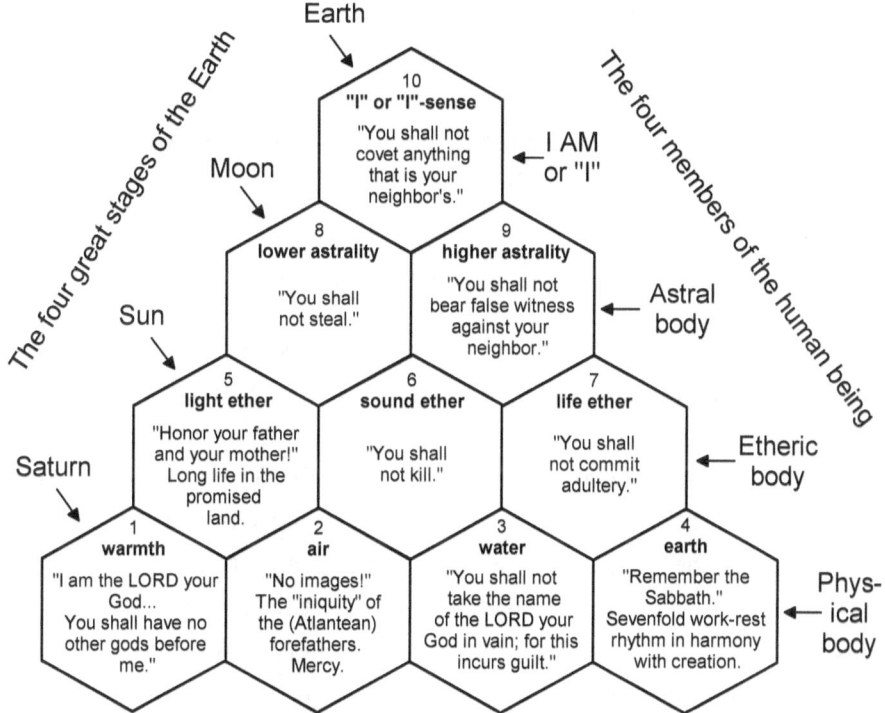

**THE TEN PARTS OF THE HUMAN BEING
AND THE TEN COMMANDMENTS OF MOSES**

human being to attain to a higher spiritual unity. This commandment specified that people must be *faithful* to their higher "I," as it lives in the marriage bond between two people.

The eighth and ninth commandments are connected to *the astral body*, which today has a twofold structure. One part still has ties to its former Moon existence and the other part has been further developed and refined during the Earth phase. The less refined part of the astral body is focused more on the outer world; the refined part on the inner life. One could also say that these two commandments refer to the astral body as such, and to the astral body as "I"-bearer respectively. The *eighth* commandment regulated certain lower passions by forbidding *theft*; the *ninth* commandment pointed out that human beings harm their own inner being (and that of others) by *speaking untruths*.

The *tenth* commandment is the actual "*I*"-commandment." It encouraged the human "I" to know itself in its relation to the other human being, to the neighbor; to recognize that this neighbor also is an "I" whose wellbeing must be considered; and hence not to *covet* what belongs to that neighbor.

From Moses to the Birth of the "I"

The more we learn about the old mystery wisdom concerning Earth and humanity, newly brought to light again by Rudolf Steiner in the twentieth century, the more respect and admiration we can feel for Moses and for the beautiful structure of the Ten Commandments! This structure appears like a ten-faceted diamond, reflecting the whole essence of the *old* mystery wisdom. At the same time, if we learn to approach it meditatively in the right way, this ten-faceted diamond can, in turn, shed new light on the *new* mystery wisdom, that is to say, on the anthroposophic knowledge regarding the evolution of Earth and humankind. This structure stands in its tenfold radiance as a guidepost on the pathway of humanity into the future!

Just as the harbor pilot climbs aboard and helps guide large ocean ships safely into the harbor, so humanity was in need of a navigator to help it reach a crucial point on its journey. Moses, one could say, took on the role of harbor pilot on the ship of humanity. After a long evolutionary voyage on the "ocean of time," the goal of the whole undertaking was in sight. And the successful culmination of this eon-long voyage—not only for the Israelite people, but ultimately for all humanity—depended at that crucial moment on the capabilities of the pilot. Guided by the spiritual world, Moses was able to mediate the unveiling of new, far-reaching ordinances, in a way that was unparalleled in his time. These ordinances brought humanity through a critical phase in its development that would lead to its ultimate destination: the physical manifestation of the divine power of love in all human beings, through Christ's deed on Golgotha.

We all know how difficult it is—despite the manifold tools we have been given by Rudolf Steiner in Anthroposophy—to develop even just a basic understanding of the Mystery of Golgotha! And yet, this pivotal event is now a historical fact, almost tangible in its reality. How exponentially more difficult would it have been for Moses, who lived more than a thousand years before this mystery came to pass, to be aware of the importance of this (for him) future event! Not only did he have to live his own life accordingly, he also had to help guide the Israelite people in their task of preparing for Christ's incarnation on Earth. Although the spiritual world, and particularly the Christ-being himself, inspired and assisted Moses throughout his mission, one cannot but have the greatest respect for the individual human contribution he was able to bring toward this lofty goal. The fact that Moses was able to withstand the weight of such cosmic powers is an indication of his immense inner strength—truly the strength of a great initiate![240]

In the light of both the old and the new mystery knowledge, the whole evolution of Earth and humanity can be seen as the work of high spiritual beings, under the continual guidance of the Christ-being himself. Everything that led to the formation of the various planetary stages and of the human physical, etheric, and astral bodies was aimed at the birth of the human being as an independent, free "I"-being.

In the time of Moses this long, gradual development had reached a decisive point. Human beings now had an autonomous "I," an individual "I." But it was not yet mature enough to function on its own. It was wholly dependent on the enveloping protection of the other human sheaths, that is to say, the physical, etheric, and astral bodies. Hence it was extremely important to secure the health of these sheaths. This had to be done by means of very specific ordinances concerning people's social and individual life. The precise formulation of each of these ordinances, as they appear in the Ten Commandments, was exquisitely aimed at one specific aspect of each of these human sheaths respectively.

But, as we have seen, these commandments—in their original form, that is—were not meant for all eternity. They were intended to address the needs of a people, living at a particular time in history, a time period that unfolded right in between two eras. The old mystery wisdom, which up to that point in time had guided and inspired the development of humanity, was increasingly headed toward "a Twilight of the Gods," while the dawning of a new mystery wisdom was still far off in the future. During that crucial phase the Ten Commandments rendered an outer supportive structure for the young human "I" until it would be strong enough to provide that support itself. When that time came, Christ transformed the Ten Commandments in such a way that, collectively, they could become one single, unitary commandment. This one commandment, which obviously is no longer a commandment in the literal sense, encouraged people to learn to use the new strength of the "I" in the right way: "A new commandment I give unto you, that all of you love one another; as I have loved you, that all of you also love one another" (John 13:34). This kind of love, inspired by the divine example of Christ, can then become the new source of health, justice, and morality in the lives of human beings.

The birth of the "I": we have frequently used this expression. But what does it really mean? And how is it related to the life of Christ on Earth? It is very difficult for us, present-day human beings, to fully understand its true significance. We learn from Anthroposophy that "the 'I' was born" in human beings because of Christ's coming to the Earth. We also hear that, not long after the crucifixion and resurrection, an esoteric reality has been established "for all human souls on Earth," a reality that is expressed in the words "the 'I' is born." How are we to understand this?

To be able to assess this esoteric reality properly, we have to take our starting point from the old mysteries in pre-Christian times and the role they played in the history of humankind. We have described how the initiates, who were trained in these mystery schools, supported and guided every social and cultural aspect of human life at that time.[241] To be able to take on this task, they had to undergo an initiation. But no initiation could take place in those days without the help and guidance of those who had already been initiated themselves. Every pre-Christian initiate was dependent on such mentors, and this dependency continued after the initiation itself. Only after Christ's coming to the Earth would it gradually become possible to bring about an initiation through the power of the "I."

During the baptism in the Jordan a new force, a new quality descended from the spiritual world on Jesus—the "I AM" principle in its purest, most esoteric, and at the same time most public form. This new quality worked ever more deeply and intimately into the body and soul of Jesus Christ during the subsequent three years, at the culmination of which he then was able to go through his crucifixion and resurrection, and thus fulfill the *Mystery of Golgotha*. Through this deed Christ accomplished a new form of initiation.

It bears underscoring that this was not just an expanded form of a pre-Christian initiation. What happened at Golgotha, rather, was the direct result of—and could only occur because of—a *new spiritual quality*, a power that radiated from the cosmos to the Earth and fully united with a human being. This new force—one could also call it *divine love*—thenceforth works in and through the "I" of human beings. Not long after the resurrection had taken place, this force, this new inner principle became available to all human beings, regardless of religious affiliations. This is what is expressed in the words, "the 'I' has been born in all human beings." Consequently, it is now *possible*, in principle, for anyone to undergo a new form of initiation, through the power of the "I," provided the correct tools are used and the correct paths are followed. Christ has become the new initiator of the whole of humanity for all future times.[242] We can hear this promise resounding in Christ's words, "I am with you always, even unto the end of the world." And, because Christ lived on the Earth as the spiritual I-AM, as the divine love, the human "I" is now potentially capable of learning how to infuse everything it undertakes with love, in other words, how *to act out of love for the deed*.

To act out of love for the deed! How this can be achieved is described, in philosophical concepts, in *The Philosophy of Freedom*, especially in the ninth chapter. There Rudolf Steiner analyzes a variety of factors that motivate, determine, or stimulate us into action. But in the end one factor remains, one factor that leaves us completely free with respect to our actions; Steiner calls this factor *pure intuition*. This intuition wells up out of our own inner being in the form of free initiatives; it can bring us closer to our higher self as well as to the spiritual cosmos. Actions arising out of this intuitive source are *free* deeds. They are no longer the causal result of any other factors. As human beings we can undertake such free deeds for the sake of the deed itself, out of love and enthusiasm, but also with a certain degree of insight as to the impact such actions may have both in human society and within the larger spiritual context. This force, this ability, which in earlier times could only be achieved through initiation, now is—albeit only potentially—present in every human being.[243]

In *Theosophy* Rudolf Steiner presents a descriptive imagination in relation to this intuitive force that can be developed through inner schooling. There it is stated that this force can lead the human being to communion with the "All-Spirit." This involves a growth process that can be compared to an ever-widening colored circle, eventually uniting with other similarly expanding circles. However, "if we wish to have a simile for this union of the individual spirit with the 'All-Spirit,' we cannot choose that of different circles that, coinciding, are lost in the one," we read in *Theosophy*, "but we must choose the picture of many circles of which each has a distinct shade of color. These differently colored circles coincide, but each separate shade preserves its existence within the whole. Not one loses the fullness of its individual power."[244] Each person's unique color, as conferred in this picture, then, represents the aforementioned new qualitative force Christ has bestowed on us, a force through which human beings can eventually unite toward a higher common goal.

Ten Moral Impulses through Christ

We have described how Christ has fulfilled each of the Ten Commandments and united them into one commandment. But to come to a true understanding of the all-encompassing meaning of this one commandment, it was necessary to evaluate how this transformation occurred for each one of the Ten Commandments. Here is a brief summary of what we found:

1. Jesus said, "The Lord our God is one Lord: And you shall love the Lord your God with all your heart, and with all your soul, and with all your mind, and with all your strength." Here Jesus points out that it is the *unifying* soul force of *love* that must be developed in human beings to be able to form a sustainable relationship to the divine.
2. The second commandment was meant primarily for the time period from Moses to Christ. Images were forbidden because people had to learn to value the outer sense-perceptible world as such, without being exposed to the still prevalent impact of graven images on one's inner state of being. In Jesus Christ a suprasensory *image* and a sense-perceptible *reality* became one. Henceforth, spiritual images can be experienced inwardly, independent of the presence of outer images. Christ himself was the fulfillment of the second commandment.
3. Jesus put a stop to the potentially harmful residues of the earlier speech magic, still lingering in his time, with the words, "Swear not at all..." Along with this he encouraged a new, higher responsibility toward the *spoken word*, "For by your words you shall be justified, and by your words you shall be condemned." In the future this will specifically hold true for words spoken against the Holy Spirit—a sin that cannot be forgiven.
4. Jesus answered those who aimed to promote an excessively rigid interpretation of the Sabbath regulations with, "The Sabbath was made for man, and not man for the Sabbath," and with, "Wherefore it is lawful to do well on the Sabbath days." He performed healings on the Sabbath; for that day was specifically intended to restore the *healthy balance* between the human "I" and the physical body, and, in a wider sense, the whole physical world.

5. Jesus uncoupled feelings of *reverence* from the blood ties (the parents) and directed them at the divine world instead, "He that loves father or mother more than me is not worthy of me" or, put differently, "Free yourself from the blood ties; follow the "I AM" principle. Now people can experience that the divine, the spiritual, is the true source of life.

6. By voluntarily accepting death on the cross, Christ added something of his own spiritual substance to the sixth commandment. He has become the Lord of Karma, which, in this context, means that he can bring a new balance to the karma of those people who become victims of what may be called the Cain-destiny. Because of Christ's deed, human death has undergone a transformation—human beings can now experience what it means to *die in Christ*.

7. Jesus expected a stricter observance of faithfulness: even *thoughts* of infidelity must be considered detrimental. But when someone had transgressed, his response did not come in the form of punishment and retribution. Instead Jesus offered encouragement that brought healing and forgiveness. On a higher level *Christ remains loyal to humanity;* "I am with you always, even unto the end of the world."

8. Jesus countered the vice of stealing by pointing to the merit of giving. *Stealing* always brings personal guilt, both on account of other people and with respect to the spiritual world; *giving* and *receiving*, if handled in the right way, facilitate spiritual growth and productivity. This is why Jesus said, "Give, and it shall be given unto you."

9. Christ requires a higher kind of truthfulness from people than merely the avoidance of lies (false witness). This truthfulness is not rigid; it constitutes a step forward in human development, connecting the "I" with life in the cosmos, "I am the Way, the *Truth*, and the Life." By connecting ourselves with this all-encompassing truth, we can find wisdom and freedom, "And all of you shall know the truth, and *the truth shall make you free.*"

10. Jesus lifted the meaning of "You shall not covet what belongs to your neighbor" to the level of "Love your neighbor as yourself." The initially more restricted meaning of *neighbor* now is expanded to *all of humanity*. By trying to follow this direction, the "I" and the sense of "I" will be strengthened, making it

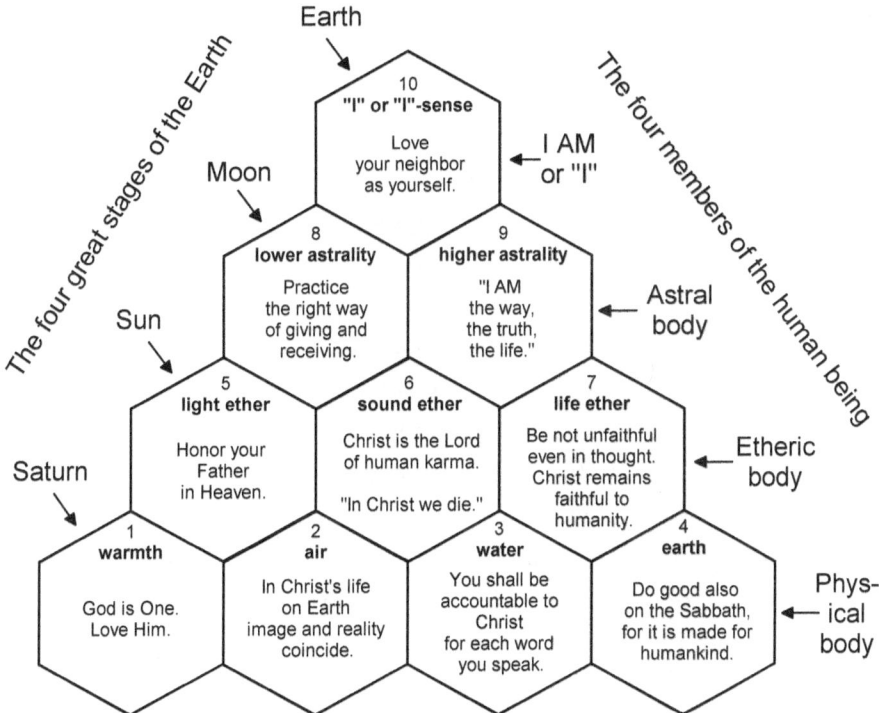

**THE TEN PARTS OF THE HUMAN BEING
ADDRESSED BY TEN MORAL IMPULSES OF CHRIST**

possible to keep the combined luciferic and ahrimanic longing for self-importance and material possessions in balance. Jesus himself had to confront Lucifer and Ahriman right after his baptism in the Jordan and, in overcoming their temptations, made it possible for human beings to learn to withstand those longings that would fetter the "I."

By fulfilling the commandments, Christ brought their original impulses in harmony with the all-encompassing love he bestowed on humanity. One could also say, he filled them with their true potential.

Ten new Ideals in our Time

What is the situation today as far as the Ten Commandments are concerned? Most people nowadays likely do not look at a body of commandments as the ultimate source for moral consultation. Many of us are searching for a new moral source, a new moral understanding, which would allow us, in inner freedom, to form our own ideals and insights about moral issues in life. Our quest for a true moral paradigm may well lead us to accept Christ's comprehensive commandment as the embodiment of all moral renewal. And indeed, this very special commandment represents a most sublime ideal. But this highest moral archetype can, in reality, only be the endpoint of a long and difficult path; for, who among us can claim to be capable of loving others with the all-encompassing, heartwarming, all-forgiving, divine love, which Christ had for his disciples? After all, this commandment not only invited them to "love one another," but added to this "as I have loved you." If we, nonetheless, are prepared to accept this notion as the most sublime ideal human beings can strive for today, the question may well arise: How can we find our way to this all-inclusive ideal in our time? And how is it related to the original commandments?

In keeping with the *Law of Historical Symmetry*, we expected to find that the impulse of the Ten Commandments would reappear in our time, but in a completely new form: the externally imposed commandment can now be transformed into a freely accepted inner striving. Accordingly we found that there are indeed *ten* different ways our moral ideals can take shape today—each new ideal a metamorphosis of one of the original Ten Commandments:

1. Our time has developed the modern, scientific–philosophical way of thinking. With our faculty of thinking we are able to conceptualize the spiritual world—to which all thought concepts ultimately belong—as a *unitary* world that exists beyond the separation of subject and object. In this world we can come to true knowledge by means of the intuitive capacities of the "I." This capacity of intuition can be strengthened by our love for the world around us—the divine ground of all being.

2. Through the forces of the heart we can enliven the *good* in ourselves, by striving to maintain a dynamic balance between the *twofold evil*, between the luciferic and the ahrimanic forces. The good forces of the heart can be strengthened by the beauty of artistic images, but especially also through a meditative life that leads us to inwardly create, perceive, and evolve true ideal images.
3. Avoiding the *vain use* of the spoken word will bring us closer to *the truth*. Truth can unite and connect all humanity. In contrast to this stands the unforgivable sin against the Holy Spirit, a sin that aims to isolate and divide. The inspiration of the Holy Spirit works in Anthroposophy in such a way that, through it, we can learn anew to permeate our *words* with spiritual content. Only then will it be possible for us to receive the restorative forces that the Archangels bestow on us during sleep—forces we need to stay healthy.
4. The path to the spiritual world is a path of self-development through inner schooling. At the beginning of this path we aim to create daily moments of inner quiet for ourselves. In such moments—during which the basic mood should be one of devotion to truth and wisdom—we think intently about a subject of our own choosing, thus gradually learning to distinguish the essential from the nonessential. This *inner Sabbath* can then take the form of meditation and eventually lead us to a clearly defined awareness of the suprasensory world, by developing imagination, inspiration, and intuition as new suprasensory capacities. Thus we can awaken the eternal in ourselves and create a living connection to the eternal in the cosmos.
5. Reverence and veneration are soul gestures that need no longer be chained to the blood ties. Family members of different generations should not feel bound to each other in this way, but try to understand each other as developing human beings. We should instead cultivate feelings of *reverence* for those things that are truly worthy of esteem, foremost *truth* and *wisdom*. Out of this inner mood, the soul may find the connection to its true spiritual homeland.
6. With respect to all our endeavors—and this includes any decisions or thoughts concerning the death of a human being—we will increasingly feel a sense of responsibility toward Christ as *the Lord of our Karma*. Souls, who could not find a connection to Christ while living on Earth, remain in a state of crisis after death, a state that cannot be softened by any means available to them in the

spiritual world. Such souls can be helped by special meditations, thereby making it possible for them to be comforted and re-enlivened through the forces radiating from Christ. Such *meditative help*, offered to the dead as a free deed and out of spiritual love, can then become a profound reality for both parties, with far-reaching consequences.

7. Life ether forces are forces of loyalty, trust, commitment, and perseverance. The *spiritual stature of the "I"* depends on the degree of *inner loyalty* and *trust* we can summon, in other words, the spiritual development of our own "I" depends on our striving toward harmony with the other "I." To be able to do this we should try to develop a loving interest in the other human being; allow for liberty of thought in ourselves as well as others; and, by continually deepening our anthroposophic understanding, acknowledge the living reality of the spiritual world and the Mystery of Golgotha.

8. It is necessary that we develop fundamental concepts not only about ourselves, but also about the three realms that give structure to human society: the cultural realm, the human rights sphere, and the economic domain. The latter one functions mostly by means of reciprocal transactions such as buying and selling; but there are two additional ways of exchanging goods—namely *stealing* and *giving*. Stealing obviously has a negative impact, but *gifting* is absolutely essential for the advancement of a free cultural life in our society. It is important to realize that those who pursue cultural and spiritual endeavors for the benefit of society *must* be financially supported *through donations from individuals and organizations*.

9. Our time demands that we develop *truthfulness*. This can only happen if we take our own inner development in hand. Especially with regard to our *speaking* we should try—guided by the Holy Spirit, the *Spirit of Truth*—to develop a new moral quality, a quality of inner integrity and truthfulness. This new moral quality in our speaking will help awaken *the good* in human souls; it will increasingly be needed to give structure to human life, now and in the future.

10. The human "I" is continually busy creating. A modern-day metamorphosis of the tenth commandment, therefore, calls for an imaginative, constructive, creative relationship between one's

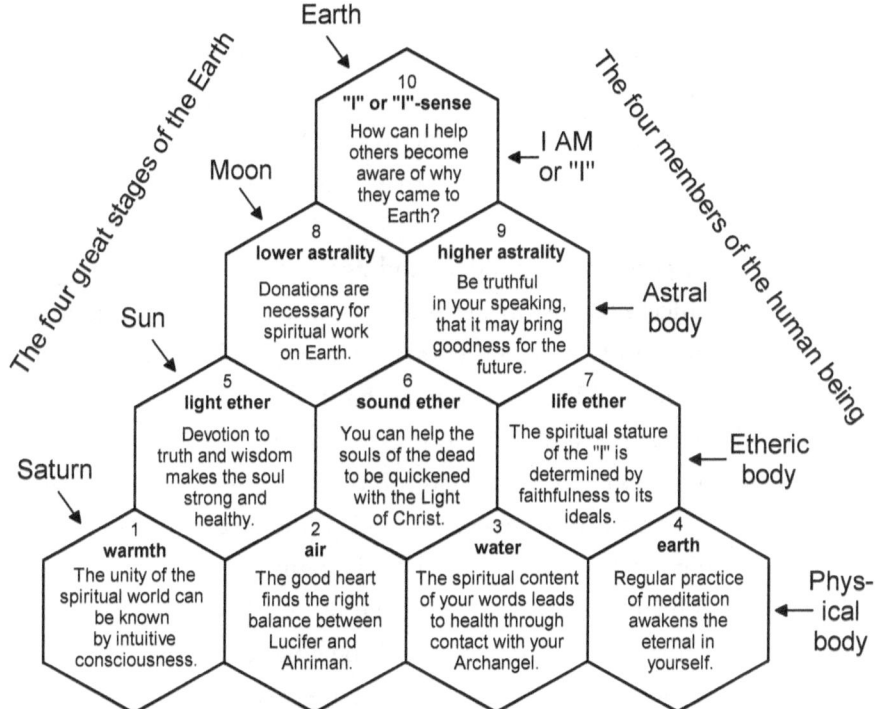

THE TEN PARTS OF THE HUMAN BEING

TEN IDEALS THAT CAN LEAD TO HEALTHY, FREE MORALITY

own "I" and the "I" of the other human being, the neighbor. This ideal cannot be formulated as a one-time conclusion, but only as an ongoing question: Can I get to know the "I" of my fellow human being in such a way that I can develop creative initiatives that may contribute something of value toward that person's unique tasks on Earth?

The Spiritual Constellation of our Time

The fact that we are capable of striving toward moral ideals such as the ones we have outlined, or for that matter, that we can inwardly conceptualize these ideals at all, has to do with the spiritual constellation of our time. Our physical, etheric, and astral constitution is gradually undergoing a subtle change. This means that human beings will increasingly become aware, already now, and more so in the near future, of very specific impressions coming from the spiritual world. More and more people will start to have very delicate experiences of the etheric world; they will be able to *see Christ in the etheric world*. In the Bible this experience is referred to as *the Son of Man returning in the clouds*.[245]

To avoid potential misunderstandings, it bears underscoring that the appearance of Christ in the etheric should not be confused with a second coming of Christ to the Earth in a physical body. The central importance of the Mystery of Golgotha within evolution as a whole can only be properly understood if we recognize that Christ could only incarnate *once* as a physical human being. Perceiving Christ in the etheric is an entirely new experience in the history of humankind. Rudolf Steiner has pointed out that, beginning in the 1930s, some people will begin to have such an experience and that, over the next centuries, more and more people will be able to perceive the etheric Christ as a matter of course.[246] It is an experience that will manifest in different ways for different people. Although it can happen to those who are on an esoteric path of schooling, it can also come about spontaneously. Moreover, this perceiving of Christ in the etheric will occur in varying shades of clarity and intensity. It may well occur with such intensity as to touch the deepest core of one's being. St. Paul was the first human being who—as an advanced initiate, and, in his own words, "through grace"—was able to see the etheric Christ at the gates of Damascus, at a time when this was not yet possible for other people. The experience was so overwhelming that it made him "fall to the Earth" and that he "was three days without sight, and neither did eat nor drink" (Acts 9:3–9). At the other end of the scale, Rudolf Steiner points out, there will be people in our own time for whom this experience may only leave a fleeting impression that would hardly be noticed; and there will be many gradations of intensity in between these extremes.

All this is connected to the fact that, by the end of the 20th century, certain changes were beginning to unfold—in the consciousness of human beings, in the etheric realm, and in relation to the Christ-being himself.[247] We have, in connection with the sixth commandment, described how Christ will gradually be taking on the role of the *Lord of Karma* in our time; that Christ will increasingly take on the task of evaluating the life and karma of individual human beings. This will essentially be a suprasensory event, but an event that will be of the utmost importance for human beings living on the Earth. More and more people will, in the words of Rudolf Steiner, "develop the feeling that by all their actions they will be causing something for which they will be accountable to the judgment of Christ." This feeling—we have earlier referred to it as "a higher conscience"—which is now emerging quite naturally in the course of human development, "will be transformed so that it permeates the soul with a light that little by little will shine out from the individual human being." This light "will illuminate the form of Christ in the etheric world," and "the more this feeling is developed—a feeling that will have stronger significance than the abstract conscience—the more will the etheric form of Christ be visible in the coming centuries."[248]

It will be of the utmost importance, then, that people increasingly learn to strengthen this inner light in their own inner being, because it is this light, radiating from human souls, which will make visible the form of Christ in the etheric.[249] But this inner light power can only be developed *on Earth*, by becoming increasingly aware, namely, of one's responsibility toward Christ. This realization can then work as the new forming force in our life.

This aspect can also shed light on a related topic we brought up in connection with the sixth commandment and that may well seem enigmatic. We described there that human beings will not be able to find Christ in the spiritual world after death, unless they had established a relationship to him during their life on Earth (or unless they receive meditative help from people who are willing to help the dead in this way).[250] Why is this so? It is because Christ, who has united his being with the Spirit of the Earth, can, since the Mystery of Golgotha, only be found *from the Earth*. And what is puzzling for many people in this regard is the fact that, apparently, one *can* relate to other spiritual beings in the spiritual world after death, but one *cannot* find Christ by one's spiritual strength alone, regardless of the level of development one might otherwise bring to the spiritual realm.

In the physical world one can move directly from one point to another point. In the spiritual world this, apparently, is not the case. In that realm everything depends on *the degree of inner affinity* one has developed for particular spheres and beings; only the quality and strength of this inner relationship determines where one can be and which beings one will be able to perceive in the spiritual world after death. But, as we have seen, since the Mystery of Golgotha we can lay the basis for this kind of relationship to the Christ-being only during our life on Earth, not after death. One way of doing this is by learning to recognize Christ as our Lord of Karma; for, only by being aware of our responsibility toward him can we create a real basis for the inner affinity that opens the path to Christ after death. This, ultimately, is also why human beings repeatedly find their way back to Earth again.

We live in a crucial time period. The whole spiritual character of our time has reached a point of culmination for many spiritual impulses and events. The most important of these events is the reappearance of Christ in the etheric. It would be a grave hindrance to human development if this event were to pass unnoticed. The emerging new capacities, which will make it possible for human beings to perceive the etheric Christ, must be developed in the right way over the next centuries. Anthroposophy, which was established on Earth just when these capacities began to awaken, can provide the necessary understanding regarding these events, and thus help guide this process along for the benefit of humanity.

The Reality in which we Live

As we live inwardly with the concepts developed in Anthroposophy, the more we come to realize that everything ultimately originates from, and will return to, the Christ-being. He stands at the beginning and at the end of the Earth's development.

We have a physical body to be able to live in the physical sense-perceptible world. This world has gradually been formed through the impulses of the Christ-being. This means that these impulses are incorporated in our *physical body* as well, and can thus guide its ongoing development. These processes, however, can only take place because we also have an etheric body, which gives us life. But the life forces can become weakened by illness. Health is a manifestation of the power of Christ in the *etheric body*. But, in order to maintain a viable state of health, it is important that we be righteous and just. Justice and injustice are rooted in the astral body. Righteousness is a manifestation of the power of Christ in the *astral body*. But true righteousness can only arise on the basis of moral freedom and free morality. Morality is a manifestation of the power of Christ working in the "I." The power of Christ permeates the whole human being!

The process by which an individual human being forms his or her moral ideas is revealed in four distinct steps. To begin with, it is an *intuitive process* during which the "I" forms a moral idea arising from a particular life situation. Once intuition becomes part of a person's own initiative, then his or her conceptualization of this idea can become a *moral inspiration*. Any further development of such an idea into concrete forms is done through *moral fantasy*, that is, through *moral imagination*. As a last step, the effective implementation of this idea then requires a *moral ability*, a moral skill.[251]

The same essential force that works from the "I" through the human sheaths out into the world also works through these four steps by which the moral process takes shape in human beings; for the forces working in the "I" were bestowed on us by the Christ-being.

Everything that supports us in our efforts to implement consciously what arises from our moral initiative we owe to the Christ-force working in our "I."

Everything that supports us in our efforts to act as just and righteous human beings we owe to the Christ-force regulating our astral body.

Everything that supports our health we owe to the Christ-force living in our etheric body.

Everything that supports us as physical human beings we owe to the Christ-force working in our physical body.

We owe our whole existence as human beings to the Christ-being! This is *the reality in which we live*.[252]

Notes

In the following, "CW" refers to volumes in "The Collected Works of Rudolf Steiner," elsewhere often using the German reference, "GA" ("*Gesamtausgabe,*" or complete edition). These instances, of course, assume Rudolf Steiner as the main author or lecturer.

1. *Core Anthroposophy: Teaching Essays of Ernst Katz*, SteinerBooks, Great Barrington, MA, 2011.
2. Compare, for example, F. S. Frick, *A Journey through the Hebrew Scriptures*, Harcourt Brace College, Fort Worth, 1995.
3. These (almost) identical listings of the Ten Commandments can be found in Exodus 20:1–17 and in Deuteronomy 5:6–21. The Bible book *Exodus* describes the experiences of the Israelite people as these originally unfolded, including the Exodus from Egypt and the receiving of the Ten Commandments at Mount Sinai; in *Deuteronomy* Moses recalls all these events that happened during the past forty years once more to the Israelite people, shortly before he dies at age 120.
4. See also Exodus 25:16 and 21; and 40:20.
5. For further study compare Emil Bock, *Moses: From the Mysteries of Egypt to the Judges of Israel*, Floris Books, Edinburgh, 2011.
6. Compare, for example, *Turning Points in Spiritual History* (CW 60), lecture of March 9, 1911.
7. *Inner Experiences of Evolution* (CW 132), lecture of October 31, 1911.
8. For a more elaborate description compare *An Outline of Esoteric Science* (CW 13); *Cosmic Memory* (CW 11); *Inner Experiences of Evolution* (CW 132).
9. For this particular aspect regarding the research into cosmic developments, compare *Inner Experiences of Evolution* (CW 132), especially the first lecture.
10. Dionysius the Areopagite, a disciple of St. Paul, describes in his book, *Celestial Hierarchies*, nine hierarchies of Angels, in descending order: the Seraphim (Spirits of Love), Cherubim (Spirits of Harmony), Thrones (Spirits of Will), Kyriotetes (Spirits of Wisdom), Dynamis (Spirits of Movement), Exusiai (Spirits of Form), Archai (Spirits of Personality), Archangeloi (Archangels), and Angeloi (Angels). Rudolf Steiner sometimes uses these Greek and Hebrew names and at other times the designations here given in brackets.
11. Rudolf Steiner describes the fourfold development of the Earth and of human beings in terms of the four elements, known since antiquity as "fire," "air," "water," and "earth." (Today these are referred to as warmth, gases, liquids, and solids.) In this study we use quotation marks to denote the elements.
12. It is difficult to imagine a being whose physical body consisted only of gases and warmth. Perhaps it is easier to grasp the notion of a space filled

with living gas structures by comparing it to the localized fragrances wafting over an herbal garden on a warm summer day.

13   All living organisms are maintained by etheric forces. When these forces form an enclosed system, sustaining a particular living being, we may speak of an etheric body, rather than just of etheric forces. But it is important to realize that this designation does not point to a rarefied material body, but to a *system* of life forces. We will take a closer look at the characteristics of the etheric body in "Introduction to the Fifth, Sixth, and Seventh Commandments"; compare also *Theosophy* (CW 9).

14   The designation *astral* body is used because the astral forces have a specific connection to the world of the stars. And again, just as we observed with regards to the etheric body, the concept "astral body" denotes a *system* of forces.

15   For more on the Elohim and the Exusiai compare, for example, Emil Bock, *Genesis: Creation and the Patriarchs*, Floris Books, Edinburgh, 2011.

16   For a clarification as to why we focus on *three* kinds of ether in this study and on *four* in other contexts, see our "Introduction to the Fifth, Sixth, and Seventh Commandments."

17   It is important to note that, only because of further differentiations, new phases could arise during the course of evolution. On old Sun the etheric body could be assimilated into the human physical body only because a further differentiation of gases and warmth occurred. On old Moon the astral body could be taken up only because of a further differentiation of fluids, gases, and warmth in the physical body; and of light ether and sound ether in the etheric body. Finally, during the Earth phase the "I" could become part of the human being only because a further differentiation of solids, fluids, gases, and warmth occurred in the physical body; of light, sound, and life ether in the etheric body; and of two distinct soul configurations in the astral body.

18   Pythagoras of Samos (c. 570–495 BC), Greek philosopher and mathematician; founded his famous philosophical school around 530 BC in Croton, in the south of Italy.

19   Compare, for example, *According to Matthew* (CW 123).

20   Compare, for example, *Approaching the Mystery of Golgotha* (CW 152).

21   A long-standing theological tradition views the following words spoken by God to Moses (Deut. 18:18) as a proclamation of the coming of the Messiah: "I will raise them up a Prophet from among their brethren, like unto you, and will put my words in his mouth; and he shall speak unto them all that I shall command him." Christ himself points to this prediction at a later time, "For had all of you believed Moses, all of you would have believed me; for he wrote of me" (John 5:46).

22   Rudolf Steiner, *The Festivals and Their Meaning*, Rudolf Steiner Press, London, 1981, lecture of April 11, 1909.

23   *Christ and the Spiritual World and the Search for the Holy Grail* (CW 149), lecture of December 31, 1913.

24   In the Bible book *Leviticus*—particularly in chapters 17 to 26, referred to as the *Holiness Code*, where the Mosaic laws governing secular, ritualistic, moral, and festival regulations are listed—we encounter the "I AM" words again (starting at 19:18). Here, nearly each subsequent law gets authenticated with the powerful words, "I am the LORD."

25 Compare, for example, *Egyptian Myths and Mysteries* (CW 106); *Christian Initiation and the Mysteries of Antiquity* (CW 8); *From Jesus to Christ* (CW 131), especially the lecture of October 4, 1911.
26 A beautiful description of some characteristic features of the old Egyptian initiations can be found in Rudolf Steiner's fourth mystery play, *The Souls' Awakening* (CW 14) in scenes 7 and 8; compare also *The Gospel of St. John* (CW 103), lecture on the raising of Lazarus, for a description of the "death-like sleep" the neophyte had to go through during initiation.
27 Compare, for example, *The Christ-Impulse and the Development of Ego-Consciousness* (CW 116). Also Virginia Sease and Manfred Schmidt-Brabant, *The New Mysteries and the Wisdom of Christ*, Temple Lodge, London, 2005, lecture 1.
28 "Think not that I am come to destroy the law, or the prophets: I am not come to destroy, but to fulfill" (Matt. 5:17).
29 After the coming of Christ, a new impulse was given to the culture of the Mysteries; these so-called New Mysteries are connected to esoteric Christianity. For further study compare Virginia Sease and Manfred Schmidt-Brabant, *The New Mysteries and the Wisdom of Christ*, Temple Lodge, London, 2005; also Bastiaan Baan, *Old and New Mysteries: From Trials to Initiation*, Floris Books, Edinburgh, 2014.
30 To complicate matters further, this third version (Deut. 34:1–26) is actually quite different from the original. Scholars refer to this version as the *Ritual Decalogue* because these instructions—ten, we are told, although it is not easy to subdivide them in the text—relate mostly to religious sacrifices and obligations. It would, however, lead us too far afield to explore how this version relates to the original set of commandments.
31 In the few indications Rudolf Steiner has given about the Ten Commandments, he generally referred to the Lutheran numbering—the one more commonly used in Germany—which is different from the traditional way of counting the commandments. Furthermore, he sometimes interchanged the eighth and the ninth commandment. But what he said about the commandments holds, regardless of what number was mentioned.
32 Rudolf Steiner gave a fascinating description of this growing uncertainty in Abraham's soul, for example, in *The Gospel of St. Matthew* (CW 123), especially the lecture of September 4, 1910; also in *The Deeper Secrets of the Development of Humanity in Light of the Gospels* (CW 117), lecture of November 9, 1909. *The Gospel of St Matthew* appears elsewhere in the notes as *According to Matthew* (for example note 19).
33 Compare also Emil Bock, *Genesis: Creation and the Patriarchs*, Floris Books, Edinburgh, 2011.
34 As an interesting sideline we note that in modern-day physics we can still find remnants from ancient Saturn. The science of physics works with various classes of quantities. Some of those, the so-called tensor and vector quantities, deal with spatial directions. Others, the so-called scalar quantities, are essentially non-spatial. Examples of such scalar quantities are: time, temperature, and energy—in other words, exactly those characteristic qualities mentioned in connection with the Saturn phase. When we consider the laws that are used in physics from this point of view, we can observe that one of the most fundamental laws, the so-called *Second Law of Thermodynamics*, reveals a deep connection between warmth and time. It is almost as though this law shows an affinity to the

Saturn existence where warmth and time came into being. Likewise, in *Heisenberg's Uncertainty Principle* we may, even today, see an expression of the fact that time and energy are in reality complementary quantities—products of ancient Saturn.

35   We cannot ask what existed *before* the Saturn phase. That was a world of divine timelessness that human cognition cannot penetrate or comprehend presently. We simply cannot develop such concepts as long as our thinking is bound to our brain, because the nerve–sense system itself only emerged in embryonic form on Saturn. With our brain as cognitive instrument we can only go as far back as Saturn.

36   See footnote 10 about the nine Hierarchies.

37   According to Rudolf Steiner we have twelve senses: the sense of touch, life, movement, and balance; the sense of smell, taste, sight, and warmth; and the sense of hearing, of speech, of thinking, and of the other "I." See *The Foundations of Human Experience* (CW 293), especially the eighth lecture. Compare also Albert Soesman, *Our Twelve Senses: Wellsprings of the Soul*, Hawthorn Press, Stroud, UK, 1990.

38   For example in, *The Inner Nature of Man and the Life between Death and a new Birth* (CW 153), lecture of April 10, 1914.

39   These words also form the most important part of the central prayer of Judaism. The *Shema* is an affirmation of Judaism and a declaration of faith in the one God. It is the oldest prayer in the Siddur (prayer book). The whole prayer consists of three biblical passages strung together (Deut. 6:4–9, 11:13–21 and Num. 15:37–41). But it is especially the first line of the Shema, "Hear O Israel, the LORD is our God, the LORD is One" (Deut. 6:4) that is repeated throughout the prayer services. It is said in the morning blessings as well, as a bedtime prayer, as part of the deathbed confessional, and at various other times. Compare George Robinson, *Essential Judaism: A Complete Guide to Beliefs, Customs, and Rituals*, Pocket Books, New York, 2000.

40   In the introductory section "Moses and the Proclamation at Mount Sinai"; see also footnote 7.

41   There are, according to Rudolf Steiner, seven post-Atlantean cultural epochs that, together, make up the fifth stage of the Earth phase (compare also footnote 46). The first of these cultural epochs is the Ancient Indian (c. 7200–5050 BC), followed by the Ancient Persian (c. 5050–2900 BC), the Chaldean-Egyptian (c. 2900–750 BC), the Greco-Roman (c. 750 BC–AD 1400), and our own fifth cultural era, which will continue until approximately AD 3500. In the future there will be two more cultural epochs, each one also lasting about 2,160 years.

42   Anthroposophy speaks of three kinds of soul configurations in the human being: the sentient soul, the intellectual soul (or mind soul), and the consciousness soul, which are meant to come to full development during the third, fourth, and fifth post-Atlantean cultural epochs respectively. Compare *Theosophy* (CW 9).

43   Michael is one of seven Archangels, who successively act as guiding spirits of humanity, each one for approximately 300 years. Michael, whose reign commenced in 1879, is considered the most important amid the seven Archangels. His current emphasis is first and foremost on the development of human freedom.

44   See *The Philosophy of Freedom* (CW 4), chapter 7.

45 *Truth and Knowledge* (CW 3); see also *Philosophy and Anthroposophy* (CW 35).
46 Anthroposophy recognizes seven planetary stages of the Earth: Saturn, Sun, Moon, Earth, and, in a far future, Jupiter, Venus, and Vulcan. Each of these phases, in turn, can be divided into seven subdivisions. For the *Earth* these are: the Polarian, Hyperborean, Lemurian, and Atlantean eras, followed by our own fifth post-Atlantean, and, in the future, a sixth and seventh era. The Atlantean time period, therefore, is the *fourth* phase of the Earth's incarnation.
47 Compare footnote 10 about the nine hierarchies.
48 *An Outline of Esoteric Science* (CW 13), chapter 4, subsection "Sun."
49 Ibid.
50 Plato, *Timaios* and *Kritias*. Plato (c. 427–347 BC) was an ancient Greek philosopher, a student of Socrates, and a teacher of Aristotle. He also founded the Academy in Athens.
51 Compare *An Outline of Esoteric Science* (CW 13), chapter 4; and *Cosmic Memory* (CW 11).
52 Manu is also referred to as the "leader of the Christ-initiates," or the "leader of the Christ-Oracle," *An Outline of Esoteric Science* (CW 13), chapter 4, subsection "The End of Atlantis."
53 *The Principle of Spiritual Economy* (CW 109), lecture 6.
54 *Cosmic Memory* (CW 11), chapter on "Transition of the Fourth into the Fifth Root Race."
55 Compare footnote 41 about the post-Atlantean cultural epochs.
56 To determine possible dates for the Exodus out of Egypt, some scholars take their starting point from 1 Kings 6:1, which states that Solomon began building the Temple "480 years after the Exodus." The beginning of the building of the Temple is usually dated around the year 968 BC. This would then fix the date for the Exodus around the year 1448 BC. Others base their calculations mainly on the time span of the 440 years mentioned in the *Septuagint* (the earliest translation of the Hebrew Bible into Greek). One more uncertainty in determining these dates arises from the conflicting accounts of the number of years the Israelite people would have spent in Egypt before the Exodus (Genesis 15:13 mentions 400 years, but Exodus 12:40 refers to 430 years). Despite all these discrepancies most biblical scholars are inclined to conclude that the Exodus took place in the thirteenth century BC.
57 Compare Emil Bock, *Moses: From the Mysteries of Egypt to the Judges of Israel*, Floris Books, Edinburgh, 2011.
58 Rudolf Steiner describes how the various lotus flowers can be developed by means of esoteric training in *How to Know Higher Worlds* (CW 10), Chapter 6.
59 For more on this subject, compare also Florin Lowndes, *Enlivening the Chakra of the Heart*, Sophia Books, London, 1998.
60 Strictly speaking, the expression "hardening of the heart" is used more than twelve times in *Exodus* during the discussions with Pharaoh; but there are clearly *twelve* such occasions, twelve groupings. One grouping can be found in the depiction of the prelude to the plagues; one grouping (or single occurrence) in the description of each of the ten plagues; and one grouping in the portrayal of the events that took place after the last plague. The hardening of the heart thus occurs within the following twelve conditions:

I	Prelude to the plagues: rod becomes serpent—7:13, 7:14
II	The first plague: river turns to blood—7:22
III	The second plague: frogs—8:15
IV	The third plague: lice—8:19
V	The fourth plague: swarms of flies—8:32
VI	The fifth plague: cattle murrain—9:7
VII	The sixth plague: boils—9:12
VIII	The seventh plague: hail—9:34, 9:35, 10:1
IX	The eighth plague: locust—10:20
X	The ninth plague: darkness—10:27
XI	The tenth plague: death of the firstborn—11:10
XII	Postlude: Egyptians pursue Israelites—14:4, 14:8, 14:17

61   The traditional English translation of this part of the Hebrew text as "Red Sea" is no longer considered to be correct. The Hebrew "Yam Suf" should be translated as "Sea of Reeds." The actual location of this Sea has not yet been unequivocally ascertained by biblical scholars. Compare Nahum M. Sarna, *Exploring Exodus: The Origins of Biblical Israel*, Schocken Books, New York, 1996. Also note that the name "Sea of Reeds," by its very nature, would imply a *shallow* body of water that, in turn, would validate Rudolf Steiner's indications about these events as well; compare *Turning Points in Spiritual History* (CW 60), lecture of 9 March, 1911.

62   In these contemplations about the second commandment we have explored the idea that the concept "the children of the third and fourth" generation refers to people who lived in the third and fourth cultural epochs. Naturally, this does not invalidate other interpretations. These words could simply mean that God would punish three or four successive generations of the perpetrator. This type of punishment, which in our own time would seem both radical and flawed, was not unusual in that time. People experienced that the blood, the stream that flowed through the generations, was of more importance than one single member of any one generation. It would not have seemed unreasonable, then, that God would punish someone for an offense that another member of the same generation stream had committed. Consequently, these words about "the third and fourth" generations could have this literal meaning as well. All the same, it is interesting to note that the original Hebrew text does not include a word for "generation." It literally says "the third and fourth of them that hate me." So we have reason to ask which "third and fourth" are meant. Also compare how Rudolf Steiner explains the feeding of the four- and five thousand in relation to the people of the fourth and fifth post-Atlantean cultural epochs respectively, for example, in *The Gospel of St. Matthew* (CW 123), lecture 10.

63   *Disease, Karma and Healing* (CW 107), lecture of November 16, 1908. Note that, in this particular lecture, Rudolf Steiner refers to the Lutheran numbering of the Ten Commandments, which is different from the traditional one used in this book (see our introductory section "The Structure and Numbering of the Ten Commandments").

64   The number forty indicates renewal in the Bible. It takes forty days (or years) for older forces to yield to newer forces and to create fertile ground for these new forces to take root in human beings and in the Earth. It took "forty days and nights" for the old world to be washed away by the rains of the biblical flood (Gen. 7:12); it took forty days without food or drink for Christ to unite his cosmic being with the body of Jesus (Matt 4:1–11,

Mark 1:12–13, Luke 4:1–13). Elijah walked for forty days and nights to the same mountain (1 Kings 19:8) where, several centuries earlier, Moses had received the divine revelation out of the external forces of nature. Thus Elijah prepared himself for the new experience of hearing the voice of God *within his own inner being* instead.

65 Joshua 5:6, Deuteronomy 2:14, Numbers 14:33.

66 *The Sorcerer's Apprentice* is a ballad written by Goethe during his stay in Weimar in 1797. In it the apprentice uses his newly acquired magical powers to teach a broomstick to fetch water. But, not having full command yet over these powers, the floor soon is awash in water. He then manages to have the broom split in two pieces; but when both brooms continue to fetch water, all seems lost until the old sorcerer returns and breaks the spell.

67 Matthew 22:39–40, "And the second is like unto it [the first commandment], you shall love your neighbor as yourself. On these two commandments hang all the law and the prophets" (compare also Mark 12:31).

68 *The Fifth Gospel* (CW 148), especially the lectures of October 5, 1913 in Oslo; 4 November in Berlin; 22 November in Stuttgart; and December 8 in Munich. The last two lectures are not included in the English edition.

69 The Essenes were members of a Jewish religious order, related to the Therapeutae. They lived from the 2nd century BC to the first century AD in communal life, dedicated to asceticism. Early accounts of the Essenes can be found in the writings of Josephus, Philo, and Plinius the Elder.

70 Rudolf Steiner describes this "secret law" for example in *Egyptian Myths and Mysteries* (CW 106), lectures I and II; and in *Christ and the Spiritual World and the Search for the Holy Grail* (CW 149), lecture 5.

71 Compare footnote 41.

72 There is a third kind of evil, caused by spiritual beings (the so-called Asuras) that remained behind at an even earlier stage of evolution. Their influence will increasingly become a factor both now and in times yet to come, but within the context of our present contemplations we must focus on the dual aspect of evil.

73 As quoted in *The Spiritual Foundation of Morality* (CW 155), lecture of May 30, 1912.

74 It is interesting that, even back then, the Israelites were encouraged to take *the path in the middle*; compare for example Joshua 23:6, "Be all of you therefore very courageous to keep and to do all that is written in the book of the law of Moses, that all of you turn not aside from it *to the right hand or to the left*" (italics added). See also Joshua 1:7, Deuteronomy 5:32 and 28:14.

75 Rudolf Steiner frequently referred to these two adversarial forces in lectures and books. Additionally, in collaboration with the artist Edith Maryon, he devoted considerable time to the creation of a large wooden sculpture, called the *Representative of Man*, showing the Christ figure in between a winged Lucifer and a sclerotic Ahriman. Christ as the central figure radiates all-encompassing love. The presence of this Being of Love causes a second sculpted image of Lucifer, located on the upper right, to tumble into the abyss while a second sculpted image of Ahriman, located underneath, finds himself caught in metal-like strands. This is how Rudolf Steiner saw the Christ-being, holding the adversarial forces in balance. This Statue is located at the Goetheanum in Dornach, Switzerland.

76 *Karma* is a Sanskrit word that refers to the laws of human destiny as it unfolds over many incarnations. Karma and reincarnation are two fundamental concepts in Anthroposophy.
77 Compare footnote 46.
78 Compare *The Spiritual Hierarchies and the Physical World* (CW 110), lecture of April 17, 1909.
79 *An Outline of Esoteric Science* (CW 13), chapter 4, subsection "Moon."
80 It is almost impossible to describe the situation on ancient Moon in modern language. Rudolf Steiner tried to overcome this difficulty by making use of rather unconventional "double concepts." He did not use these double concepts as a result of inexact observations, but because these actually reveal an essential characteristic of the old Moon existence. (Also compare our description of these double concepts in the chapter about the sixth commandment.)
81 One can still observe remnants of this process within the animal kingdom; think, for instance, of reptiles that periodically shed their skins.
82 Within the context of our contemplations about the third commandment—and the origins of speech and sound in particular—we should note that Rudolf Steiner used musical metaphors to describe the situation on ancient Moon. This is especially evident in his description of the two states of human Moon-consciousness. In those periods where human beings were exposed to the influence of the Sun, they experienced the "cosmic harmonies." Human beings then lived within their astral and (part of) their etheric bodies, which were temporarily freed from their physical bodies, and had become "like a marvelous, delicate musical instrument, and the mysteries of the universe resounded from its strings." The other part, meanwhile, was "shaped according to the harmonies of the universe, because the Sun-beings were at work in these harmonies"; it was "shaped by the spiritual tones of the cosmos." In those periods when the Sun was not shining on human beings, they experienced how "cosmic harmonies resounded within the stillness of their being." *An Outline of Esoteric Science* (CW 13), chapter 4, subsection "Moon."
83 In *An Outline of Esoteric Science* (CW 13), chapter 4, section "Moon," Rudolf Steiner refers to these rebellious beings as "Moon-beings," but in *The Spiritual Hierarchies and the Physical World* (CW 110), lecture 5, it is made clear that these beings were of the rank of the Spirits of Movement. There we find the following description: "At a certain point of the Moon evolution, the Dynamis were at different stages of maturity. Some longed to rise spiritually as high as possible; others lagged behind, or had at least progressed at a normal stage of development. Thus, on old Moon, there were Dynamis who had progressed far beyond their companions. As a result, the two classes of Dynamis separated from one another. The more advanced drew out with the Sun and the ones who stayed back formed the Moon that revolved around it. This gives a sketchy description of the *war in Heaven*...."
84 For example in *Knowledge of Higher Worlds* (CW 10) and *Anthroposophy in Three Steps* (CW 25).
85 The German philosopher Immanuel Kant (1724–1804) once said, "Two things fill the mind with ever new and increasing admiration and awe, the more often and steadily reflection is occupied with them: the starry heaven above me and the moral law within me. Neither of them need I seek and merely suspect as if shrouded in obscurity or rapture beyond my own

horizon; I see them before me and connect them immediately with my existence."
86 Compare footnote 18.
87 Such numerical relationships in music can be demonstrated, for example, by dividing a string in half, resulting in a second tone sounding one octave higher than—and in harmony with—the original tone. The harmonic interval of the octave thus displays a numerical relation of 1:2 (the fifth shows a relation of 2:3 and the fourth of 3:4, etc.).
88 *An Outline of Esoteric Science* (CW 13), chapter 4, section "Earth."
89 This phase also is reflected in Genesis (1:27), "So God created man in his own image, in the image of God created he him; male and female created he them," in other words, each human being initially was both male and female.
90 Even today the unborn fetus responds with movements and by developing organs for hearing and speaking when it receives its own astral body, a few months before birth; and right after birth the baby brings forth its very own sound.
91 Compare also Emil Bock, *Genesis: Creation and the Patriarchs*, Floris Books, Edinburgh, 2011.
92 Compare Emil Bock, *Moses: From the Mysteries of Egypt to the Judges of Israel*, Floris Books, Edinburgh, 2011.
93 Leviticus 24:14–16.
94 Even today in some religious traditions people avoid writing "God," instead using just the designation "G-d."
95 Compare for example Ex. 23:13, "And in all things that I have said unto you be circumspect: and make no mention of the name of other gods, neither let it be heard out of your mouth!"
96 For more on this topic, compare, for example, Carol Meyers, *Exodus*, Cambridge University, New York, 2005.
97 *Christ and the Spiritual World and the Search for the Holy Grail* (CW 149), fourth lecture, December 31, 1913.
98 Compare, for example, Jay Williams, *Ten Words of Freedom: An Introduction to the Faith of Israel*, Philadelphia: Fortress, 1971.
99 Mark 4:39, "And he arose, and rebuked the wind, and said unto the sea, Peace, be still. And the wind ceased, and there was a great calm."
100 Mark 3:16–17, "And Simon he surnamed Peter; And James the son of Zebedee, and John the brother of James; and he surnamed them Boanerges, which is, the sons of thunder" (compare also Matt. 16:17–18).
101 Mark 5:8–13, "For he said unto him, Come out of the man, you unclean spirit. And he asked him, what is your name? And he answered, saying, my name is Legion: for we are many... And the unclean spirits went out, and entered into the swine: and the herd ran violently down a steep place into the sea... and were choked in the sea."
102 John 12:28–29, "Father, glorify your name. Then came there a voice from Heaven, saying, I have both glorified it, and will glorify it again. The people therefore, that stood by, and heard it, said that it thundered: others said, an Angel spoke to him."
103 *Christ and the Human Soul* (CW 155), July 12–16, 1914, especially the last two lectures.
104 *From Jesus to Christ* (CW 131), especially the lecture of October 14, 1911.
105 Matthew 25:40, "Verily I say unto you, Inasmuch as all of you have done it unto one of the least of these my brethren, all of you have done it unto me";

Matthew 25:45, "Verily I say unto you, Inasmuch as all of you did it not to one of the least of these, all of you did it not to me..."

106 Matthew 25:46, "And these shall go away into everlasting punishment: but the righteous into life eternal."

107 The Eighth Council of Constantinople took place from AD 869 to 870. Here it was decided that the notion of the so-called Trichotomy—the image of the human being as consisting of body, soul, and spirit—was to be retracted in favor of a twofold image, consisting of body and soul, with the soul possessing "some spiritual properties."

108 Rudolf Steiner frequently used this expression when speaking about the Council of Constantinople, for example, in *Death as Metamorphosis of Life* (CW 182), lecture of Oct. 16, 1918.

109 Rudolf Steiner speaks of this distinction in his lecture in Hamburg, May 15, 1910 (CW 118); an English translation of the lecture is in *The Festivals and Their Meaning*, Rudolf Steiner Press, London, 1981.

110 Hebrews 9:6-8, "Now when these things were thus ordained, the priests went always into the first tabernacle, accomplishing the service of God. But into the second went the high priest alone once every year, not without blood, which he offered for himself, and for the errors of the people: *The Holy Spirit this signifying, that the way into the holiest of all was not yet made manifest*, while the first tabernacle was yet standing" (italics added).

111 Compare Steiner's lecture of May 15, 1910, in *The Festivals and Their Meaning*, Rudolf Steiner Press, London, 1981.

112 In his letter to the Hebrews (6:4-6) Paul, likewise, pointed out that the sin against the Holy Spirit can only be committed after a person would have achieved a high degree of insight, or even an initiation, "For it is impossible for those who were once enlightened, and have tasted of the heavenly gift, and were made partakers of the Holy Spirit, and have tasted the good word of God, and the powers of the world to come, if they shall fall away, to renew them again unto repentance; seeing they crucify to themselves the Son of God afresh, and put him to an open shame." This passage also confirms that such a deed is irreversible.

113 For a more detailed illustration of this theme compare the essay "Contemplations about the Holy Spirit" in *Core Anthroposophy: Teaching Essays of Ernst Katz*, SteinerBooks, Great Barrington, MA, 2011.

114 In *Original Impulses for the Science of the Spirit* (CW 96), Berlin, lecture of March 25, 1907; compare also *Man's Being, His Destiny, and World Evolution* (CW 226), lecture of May 17, 1923.

115 *Inner Experiences of Evolution* (CW 132), lect. 1.

116 According to Eastern tradition there are twelve Bodhisattvas; they are the great teachers of humanity. One after another they descend into earthly incarnation. Once a Bodhisattva has fulfilled his earthly mission he becomes the next Buddha and is no longer obliged to return to the earth in physical form. Rudolf Steiner refers to the Maitreya, who will become a Buddha in three thousand years' time, as "a bringer of Good through the Word."

117 Compare *Esoteric Christianity and the Mission of Christian Rosenkreutz* (CW 130).

118 Compare *The Human Soul and its Connection with Divine–Spiritual Individualities* (CW 224). Not all eleven lectures are available in English; but the lectures of 6 and 13 April appeared in *The Golden Blade*, 1973,

Rudolf Steiner Press, London, printed for the Anthroposophical Society in Great Britain.

119 Quoted from the lecture of May 23, 1923, in the aforementioned cycle, (not available in English, freely translated).

120 *Verses and Meditations* (CW 40), combining several translations of this verse, including Ernst Katz's own.

121 Note that in the Bible book *Deuteronomy*, where the Ten Commandments are reiterated once more by Moses at the end of his long life, an alternate explanation is given for the Sabbath: "And remember that you were a servant in the land of Egypt, and that the LORD your God brought you out thence through a mighty hand and by a stretched out arm: therefore the LORD your God commanded you to keep the Sabbath day" (5:15). Now the Israelites are called upon to remember their subservient status in Egypt, rather than the seven days of creation, as the reason for the Sabbath. It is as though the Sabbath, during the forty years that had passed since its first unveiling at Mount Sinai (described in the Bible book *Exodus*), had taken on a more human dimension, and had arrived on Earth.

122 By postulating a connection between memory and brain function, we do so in full awareness of the fact that Rudolf Steiner often described our memory as being rooted in the etheric body. Our ability to remember, however, has a special connection with *all* members that make up the human being. It has a connection with the "I": memories only go back to approximately the third year of life when the child begins to say "I." It has a connection with the astral body: memories must be recalled through the forces of will. And, as already mentioned, it has a connection with the etheric body: memories are pictorial in character. But, as far as our everyday memory is concerned, we depend on the functioning of our brain, which is essential for bringing memories into our consciousness. This does not mean that memories are *stored* in our brain, but that the brain mediates our becoming *conscious* of the content of our memories.

123 *The Philosophy of Freedom* (CW 4), chapter 8; compare also *Theosophy* (CW 9), chapter 2.

124 Rudolf Steiner often pointed out that the rhythmical processes in the human being are related to cosmic rhythms. Human beings, for instance, breathe roughly 26,000 times every 24 hours. This figure approximately equals the number of years (25,920) in the so-called Platonic Year—the time it takes for the spring Sun to travel through all 12 constellations (also called the precession of the equinoxes). See, for example, *the Karma of Untruthfulness*, vol. 2 (CW 174), lecture of January 28, 1917.

125 Compare *Genesis, Secrets of Creation* (CW 122) and *The Gospel of St. John* (CW 103), especially the third lecture.

126 This is one of the places in the Hebrew Bible where both names (YHWH and Elohim) are used—hence, "the LORD your God" in the English translation.

127 Compare, for example, *Theosophy* (section on "The Soul World"), where Rudolf Steiner describes seven regions of the soul world; and the lecture about Moses in *Turning Points in Spiritual History* (CW 60/61) in which reference is made to seven soul forces (Berlin, 9 March, 1911).

128 The New Testament describes a total of *seven* cases of healing on the Sabbath: (1) cleansing a person of a demon in Capernaum; (2) the healing of Peter's mother-in-law; (3) the healing of a man with a withered hand; (4) the healing of a woman crippled for eighteen years; (5) the healing of a

man with dropsy; (6) the healing of a man paralyzed for thirty-eight years in Bethesda; and (7) the healing of a man born blind. The last two are mentioned only in the Gospel of John; the first five in Luke; the first three in Mark, as well, and two of those also in Matthew.

129 Compare also Mark 3:4 and Luke 13:15, 6:9, and 14:3.
130 It is true that we can find a phrase in the second part of this commandment that contains a "You shall not..." formulation, but it is preceded by a "You shall..." instruction, as if to soften the impact of the "You shall not..."
131 Compare Emil Bock, *Genesis: Creation and the Patriarchs*, Floris Books, Edinburgh, 2011. Compare also footnote 214.
132 Compare our description of imagination, inspiration, intuition in chapter 3, in the section "Three Key Concepts of the Astral World." It is interesting to note, in this context, that the imaginative consciousness brought about through meditation shows certain similarities to human consciousness during the process of remembering. Rudolf Steiner has described this aspect of imaginative consciousness precisely, for example in his book *A Way of Self-Knowledge and the Threshold of the Spiritual World* (CW 16/17), especially in the second aphorism of CW 17.
133 *How to Know Higher Worlds: A Modern Path of Initiation* (CW 10), chapter 1.
134 Ibid.
135 *How to Know Higher Worlds: A Modern Path of Initiation* (CW 10), chapter 2.
136 Ibid.
137 Meditation is, of course, not a discovery of our time. Meditation has been practiced for centuries and has long been recognized as the means toward attaining knowledge of suprasensory realms. But in the past this way of schooling could only be mastered in the mystery centers and was strictly reserved for select groups of people. In those days one could meditate only by retreating from life or isolating oneself inside the walls of a cloister. We would do well to realize that the Rosicrucians made the discovery in the fourteenth century that one could practice a daily, meditative, inner Sabbath—unnoticed by others—and at the same time do one's daily work. But these Rosicrucians still belonged to a secret society that comprised only a relatively small number of people. In our culture meditation should be something that is readily available for everyone. To comply with the spiritual requirements of our time, however, meditation should always take place in the realm of human freedom; the pupil should not become dependent on the teacher. It should be possible for anyone to step onto the meditative path regardless of his or her life situation. Escaping from life is no longer needed, nor required. See also the essays on meditation in *Core Anthroposophy: Teaching Essays of Ernst Katz*, SteinerBooks, Great Barrington, MA, 2011.
138 *How to Know Higher Worlds: A Modern Path of Initiation* (CW 10), chapter 2.
139 The tenth commandment on its own, naturally, does not constitute a group, although some Christian traditions hold the view that there are two categories of things that should not be coveted, resulting in their subdividing this commandment into a ninth and a tenth commandment (see our introductory section on "The Structure and Numbering of the Ten Commandments").

140 For a more elaborate description of the etheric body compare, for example, *Theosophy* (CW 9), chapter on "The bodily nature of the human being."
141 Compare, for example, *The Effects of Spiritual Development* (CW 145) fourth lecture, March 23, 1913.
142 For further study compare the essay "About Rudolf Steiner's Concept of Four Types of Etheric Forces" in *Core Anthroposophy, Teaching Essays of Ernst Katz*, SteinerBooks, Great Barrington, MA, 2011; also Ernst Marti, *The Four Ethers*, Schaumburg Publications, Roselle, IL, 1984.
143 Rudolf Steiner also pointed out that in specific cases we need to take our starting point from *seven* elemental and etheric forms, because warmth and warmth ether are indistinguishable. Compare for example *According to Matthew* (CW 123), third lecture; *Second Scientific Lecture Course: Warmth Course* (CW 321), lectures 13 and 14, which includes a table with these seven forms; *Curative Education* (CW 317), third lecture.
144 Compare, for example, Michael Coogan, *The Ten Commandments: A Short History of an Ancient Text*, Yale University, New Haven, CT, 2014.
145 Compare *The Christ Impulse and the Development of Ego-consciousness* (CW 116), lecture of Dec 22, 1909.
146 For more on the development of the child, compare Eva A. Frommer, *Voyage through Childhood into the Adult World: A Guide to Child Development*, Hawthorn Press, Stroud, England, 1995; also Bernard C. J. Lievegoed, *Phases of Childhood: Growing in Body, Soul and Spirit*, Floris Books, Edinburgh, 2005.
147 The concept of an ever-developing etheric body, as described in Spiritual Science, is not an easy one for people to accept today. We are generally taught that only an accidental mutation, a mistake in the precise gene configuration during cell division, can lead to changes within species. This kind of model does not allow for the notion that a gradual—and intentional—change can take place over many generations. To be sure, the etheric bodies of plants and animals have indeed become less pliable, less capable of further development with the passing of time because of the impact of forces of hardening. The human etheric body, in contrast, remained capable of continued development, a development, moreover, that required ongoing spiritual guidance, such as the kind provided by the second and fifth commandments in the time of Moses.
148 Compare also Matthew 4:22, "And they immediately left the ship and their father, and followed him," and Luke 14:26, "If any man come to me, and hate not his father, and mother, and wife, and children, and brethren, and sisters, yea, and his own life also, he cannot be my disciple."
149 *How to Know Higher Worlds: A Modern Path of Initiation* (CW 10), chapter 1.
150 Compare *Rethinking Economics: Lectures and Seminars on World Economics* (CW 340/341); *Social Issues: Meditative Thinking and the Threefold Social Order* (CW 334).
151 *The Reappearance of Christ in the Etheric* (CW 118), lecture of March 13, 1910 (not included in the English edition).
152 Ibid., lecture of March 15, 1910.
153 *Verses and Meditations* (CW 40).
154 For more on this aspect compare Brevard S. Childs, *The Book of Exodus: A Critical, Theological Commentary*, The Westminster Press, Philadelphia, 1974.

155 "And Cain talked with Abel his brother: and it came to pass, when they were in the field, that Cain rose up against Abel his brother, and slew him" (Genesis 4:8).
156 "And he [Moses] looked this way and that way, and when he saw that there was no man, he slew the Egyptian, and hid him in the sand" (Exodus 2:12).
157 Parenthetically, it is interesting to note that the prohibition against murder is included in the so-called *Noahide laws* as well. These are seven universal laws that, according to the Jewish Talmud, were given by God as a binding set of laws for the "children of Noah"—that is, *for all people*, since all people are considered to be descendants of Noah. These seven laws can thus be seen as the pillars of human civilization, as the minimal moral duties demanded of *all* people, whether Jewish or not. The Noahide laws include five of the Ten Commandments (murder, theft, idolatry, blasphemy, and sexual immorality).
158 For example in *Universe, Earth and Man* (CW 105), fifth lecture, August 8, 1908.
159 *An Outline of Esoteric Science* (CW 13), chapter 4, section "Moon."
160 Ibid.
161 *Genesis, Secrets of Creation* (CW 122), lecture of August 25, 1910.
162 Compare *Cosmic Memory* (CW 11), chapter on "The Lemurian Race."
163 For a more elaborate description compare *Genesis, Secrets of Creation* (CW 122).
164 We can even find references in Genesis (3:16–22) to certain adaptations in the human makeup that accompanied the integration of the sound ether and the astral body. We find reference to a change in consciousness ("Behold, the man is become as one of us, to know good and evil"); to the emergence of new passions and desires ("and your desire shall be to your husband"); and to a change in metabolism ("and you shall eat the herb of the field; In the sweat of your face shall you eat bread").
165 "And Adam had sexual contact with his wife again; and she bare a son, and called his name Seth: For God, said she, has appointed me another seed instead of Abel, whom Cain slew" (Gen. 4:25).
166 "And Seth lived a hundred and five years, and brings forth Enos... And Lamech lived a hundred eighty and two years, and brings forth a son: And he called his name Noah" (Gen. 5:6–29).
167 "And Lamech took unto him two wives: the name of the one was Adah, and the name of the other Zillah... And Zillah, she also bare Tubalcain, an instructor of every artificer in brass and iron" (Gen. 4:19–22).
168 "And Adah bare Jabal: he was the father of such as dwell in tents, and of such as have cattle. And his brother's name was Jubal: he was the father of all such as handle the harp and organ" (Gen. 4:20–21).
169 "Joseph, which was the son of Heli... Which was the son of Enos, which was the son of Seth, which was the son of Adam, which was the son of God" (Luke 3:23–38).
170 Compare *Christian Initiation and the Mysteries of Antiquity* (CW 8); *Building Stones for an Understanding of the Mystery of Golgotha* (CW 175); *From Jesus to Christ* (CW 131).
171 Compare *The Inner Realities of Evolution*, (CW 132), especially the last lecture.
172 This concept of "dying in Christ" also was part of the Rosicrucian expression, *"Ex Deo Nascimur* [from God we are born], *In Christo*

Morimur [in Christ we die], *Per Spiritum Sanctum Reviviscimus* [through the Holy Spirit we will be revived]."

173   Matthew 27:38 and 44; Mark 15:27 and 23; Luke 23:32–33 and 39–44; John makes mention only of "two others" (19:18).

174   *From Jesus to Christ* (CW 131), lectures of October 7 and 14, 1911; also compare *Esoteric Christianity and the Mission of Christian Rosenkreutz* (CW 130), lecture of September 21, 1911.

175   See also the concluding chapter of this book.

176   Compare *Life between Death and Rebirth* (CW 140); *Between Death and Rebirth* (CW 141).

177   One way to establish a relationship with Christ is by studying Anthroposophy. From the lecture of 6 February, 1917 in *Building Stones for an Understanding of the Mystery of Golgotha: Cosmic and Human Metamorphoses* (CW 175), "Anyone who comprehends the deeper purpose of our Spiritual Science, realizes that it not only gives out a theoretical knowledge about different problems of humanity, the principles of human nature, reincarnation and karma, but that it contains a quite special language, that it has a particular way of expressing itself about spiritual things. The fact that through Spiritual Science we learn to hold inner converse with the spiritual world in thought, is much more important than the mere acquiring of theoretical thoughts. For Christ is with us always, even to the end of the Earth epochs. And we must learn His language. By means of the language—no matter how abstract it may seem—in which we hear of Saturn, Sun, Moon and Earth and of the different periods and ages of the Earth, and of many other secrets of evolution—we teach ourselves a language in which we can frame out the questions we put to the spiritual world. When we really learn inwardly to speak the language of this spiritual life, the result will be that Christ will stand by us and give us the answers Himself. This is the attitude that our work in Spiritual Science should bring about in us, as a sentiment, a feeling. Why do we occupy ourselves with Spiritual Science? It is as though we were learning the vocabulary of the language through which we approach the Christ. If we take the trouble to learn to think the thoughts of Spiritual Science, and make the mental effort necessary for an understanding of the Cosmic secrets taught by Spiritual Science, then, out of the dim, dark foundations of the Cosmic mysteries, will come forth the figure of Christ Jesus, which will draw near to us and give us the strength and force in which we shall then live. The Christ will guide us, standing beside us as a brother, so that our hearts and souls may be strong enough to grow up to the necessary level of the tasks awaiting humanity in its further development."

178   Compare *Life between Death and Rebirth* (CW 140), especially the lecture of February 20, 1913. This lecture is not included in the 1968 edition of this cycle, but is part of the selection included in *Staying Connected: How to Continue your Relationships with Those who have Died*, Anthroposophic Press, Great Barrington, MA, 1999.

179   For instance, we could then observe that, comparatively speaking, weather conditions and temperatures tend to change quickly in regions where the mountain ranges follow a north–south alignment, as for example on the American continent.

180   The saying "the tree is known by its fruit" is, interestingly enough, a precise expression of the activity of the life ether. These words stem from the Gospel of St. Matthew (12:33), "Either make the tree good, and his

fruit good; or else make the tree corrupt, and his fruit corrupt: *for the tree is known by his fruit*" (italics added).
181 In "Introduction to the Fifth, Sixth, and Seventh Commandments."
182 Compare Ernst Marti, *Das Aetherische*, Verlag die Pforte, Basel, 1989.
183 Rudolf Steiner mentioned in his lectures to teachers that, despite the almost unlimited variations and differences, we can recognize twelve main groups of animals, each one connected to one of the signs of the zodiac. From out of the cosmos, from the zodiac, different etheric influences are streaming to the Earth. These twelvefold etheric forces of the zodiac manifest in the various characteristic life forms of the animals through the mediation of the life ether.
184 To mention just a couple of examples, we have twelve pairs of ribs; and the human foot is made up of seven tarsal bones and five metatarsals, together forming a twelvefold structure. Further examples could be mentioned, but this is not the place to go into a detailed study of the skeletal system, only to point out that the structure of this system is based on laws in which the activity of the life ether manifests.
185 In this realm we can also discover a twelvefold order. Rudolf Steiner indicated that there are essentially twelve groups of consonants, namely: V(W); R; H; F; T(D); B(P); C(TS); S(Z); G(K); L; M; N. Compare *Eurythmy as Visible Speech* (CW 279), especially the lecture of 8 July, 1924. The life ether forces streaming toward the Earth from the zodiac are reflected in this twelvefold ordering of the consonants.
186 See footnote 37 about the twelve senses.
187 The twelve ways of thinking or worldviews are discussed extensively in Rudolf Steiner's four lectures collected in *Human and Cosmic Thought* (CW 151).
188 In mythological traditions and fairy tales we can find this motif in many variations. The story of Sleeping Beauty may well present the most remarkable account. There, the king's daughter receives heavenly gifts for her life on Earth from eleven of the twelve invited fairies at the time of her birth. Then the voice of the uninvited thirteenth fairy is heard in place of the twelfth. She casts the spell of death of the astral world (compare our discussion about the sixth commandment) over Sleeping Beauty once she will have reached her fifteenth birthday. The true twelfth fairy—the one who closes the circle of the stars—is able to transform this impulse of death into the impulse of new life. When Sleeping Beauty turns fifteen—the time when the astral body is born—all in the castle fall asleep for one hundred years. During this time an impenetrable thorny hedge grows around the castle (thorns, we recall, form a concentration point of life ether forces). These forces protect her from harmful external influences. Many princes come, but end up getting caught in the thorns, and die. When the right time comes, Sleeping Beauty's soul is awakened by the prince (the "I"), who has no problem penetrating the thorny hedge (for the human "I" is master over the life ether forces). The remarkable thing is that all the details in this fairy tale are presented as though seen from the point of view of the life ether, including the ending, "and they lived happily ever after until their end," thus closing the circle.
189 This archetypal image of the uniting of the soul and the "I," too, is reflected in numerous fairy tales where marriage between the princess (the soul) and the prince (the "I") is presented as the ultimate goal, the ideal aim.

190 The expression "Moed, Beleid en Trouw" is also used as the insignia on one of the oldest military decorations in the Netherlands. It is not easy to determine which of the two (the military order or the common phrase) is older, but these three words have been linked ever since in the Dutch language.

191 These three qualities (in reverse order) are also essential for those intending to follow the anthroposophic path of esoteric training. Without *loyalty* toward this path, once it has been recognized and embarked upon, no progress can be made. Loyalty and persistence are needed in practicing the exercises of esoteric training that will then lead to *imaginative consciousness*. But, in order to use this higher consciousness in a fruitful way, a special activity has to be developed which eventually leads to the ability to recognize how such imaginative contents relate to one another. This activity, this ability is *tactfulness*. It leads to *inspirative consciousness*. And finally, *intuitive consciousness* can only be approached through *courage* of soul, especially courage of self-knowledge; for developing self-knowledge requires a great deal of courage indeed!

192 Rudolf Steiner mentions, for instance, that, guided by the Atlantean mystery centers, people were able to breed the honeybee from the fig wasp. *Bees* (CW 351), question and answer period after the lecture of December 10, 1923.

193 Namely in Leviticus 20:10; also Deuteronomy 22:22.

194 ..."and said unto them, he that is without sin among you, let him first cast a stone at her" (John 8:7).

195 "And they which heard it, being convicted by their own conscience, went out one by one, beginning at the eldest, even unto the last: and Jesus was left alone, and the woman standing in the midst" (John 8:9).

196 For further study compare Sergei O. Prokofieff, *Mystery of the Resurrection in the Light of Anthroposophy*, Temple Lodge, London, 2010.

197 Compare also Emil Bock, *The Three Years*, Floris Books, Edinburgh, 1999.

198 In *The Relation between the Living and the Dead* (CW 168), lecture of October 10, 1916.

199 Compare footnote 42.

200 In *Death as Metamorphosis of Life* (CW 182), lecture of October 9, 1918.

201 Compare *Manifestations of Karma* (CW 120), especially the lecture of May 19, 1910; also *Reincarnation and Karma: Their Significance in Modern Culture* (CW 135).

202 For this same reason it is actually wrong to speak of "stealing ideas," because wisdom cannot become the exclusive possession of anyone. The world of ideas is open to all; no one can have exclusive access to ideas. Every human being, in principle, has access to any given idea. What is actually taken in cases of stolen ideas is the possibility of making money from ideas that others have not yet recognized. This argument can be corroborated somewhat by the well-known fact that, throughout history, unaffiliated individuals working in different locations have occasionally come up with comparable inventions *almost simultaneously* when the time was ripe for such discoveries.

203 In Dutch this saying rhymes: "*Wat de een weet kan de ander ook weten, maar wat de een eet kan de ander niet eten.*"

204 See footnote 69.

205 Compare, for example, Acts 4:32–35: "And the congregation of those who believed were of one heart and soul; and not one of them claimed

that anything belonging to him was his own, but all things were common property to them. And with great power the apostles were giving testimony to the resurrection of the Lord Jesus, and abundant grace was upon them all. For there was not a needy person among them, for all who were owners of land or houses would sell them and bring the proceeds of the sales and lay them at the apostles' feet, and they would be distributed to each as any had need" (New American Standard Bible).

206 The word *synopsis* comes from the Greek *syn* (together) and *opsis* (view). The Gospels according to Matthew, Mark, and Luke are referred to as the *Synoptic Gospels* because they frequently give similar descriptions of events. This is why these three texts oftentimes are printed side by side in order to facilitate a comparison or overview (synopsis) for scholars studying the texts. Many theories exist as to the source of the Gospels. One of the prevailing ones (the so-called *Zweiquellentheorie*) proposes that Mark initially wrote his Gospel, which would then have been used by Matthew and Luke respectively for their Gospels. They would then also have made use of an additional source, now lost, unknown to Mark. Rudolf Steiner contrasts these various theories with his spiritual insight that the evangelists received the contents of their Gospels through direct, individually nuanced inspirations from the spiritual world.

207 See footnote 150.

208 For a more elaborate depiction of the development of speech, compare our examination of this subject in the chapter about the third commandment.

209 Compare *Cosmic Memory* (CW 11), chapter on "The Lemurian Race."

210 Compare also our introductory remarks to the eighth commandment.

211 This deep feeling for truth resides in the souls of most people. The ability to recognize whether something is true or not, is a most mysterious soul force indeed! Rudolf Steiner frequently appealed to this feeling for truth, for example in the introduction to his book *Theosophy*, "The feeling for truth and the power of understanding are inherent in everyone...The soul sees nothing, but through this feeling it is seized by the power of truth. The truth then gradually draws nearer to the soul and opens the higher sense in it..."

212 Rudolf Steiner discusses the difference between illnesses that have their origin in luciferic influences on the astral body and those that stem from ahrimanic influences on the etheric body in *Manifestations of Karma* (CW 120), especially in the third and fourth lectures.

213 The Midrash is a copious collection of homiletic stories, Jewish legends, and commentaries on the Hebrew Scriptures, compiled between AD 200 and 1200. The one quoted in our text can be found in Pesitka Rabbati 24.

214 Henry More, for example, referred to Abraham as "the Father of Mathematics," as quoted in Peter Harrison, *"Religion" and the Religions in the English Enlightenment* (Cambridge University Press, 1990). Compare also note 131.

215 In this episode Abraham and Sarah are still referred to as "Abram" and "Sarai." After God's covenant with the patriarch, the names were changed to Abraham and Sarah (Gen. 17:5 and 17:15). For more on the importance of the letter *H* in the Hebrew language, compare Joel M. Hoffman, *In the Beginning: A Short History of the Hebrew Language*, New York University, New York, 2006.

216 As an illustration of how Jesus used the word *verily*, compare for example Matthew 11:11, "Verily, I say unto you, among them that are born of

women there has not risen a greater than John the Baptist: notwithstanding he that is least in the kingdom of heaven is greater than he." In the Gospel of St. John the word "verily" appears *twice* in comparable passages, as for example in, "Verily, verily, I say unto you, he that believes in me has everlasting life" (6:47).

217 These words are spoken by Dr. Strader, a seeker of truth, in the eighth scene of the first mystery drama by Rudolf Steiner, *The Portal of Initiation* (CW 14).

218 In the chapter about the third commandment we described how knowledge of the Holy Spirit initially was kept from the common people, then gradually was disclosed to some, and finally was openly revealed at the Festival of Pentecost.

219 *The Fifth Gospel* (CW 148), especially the lecture of October 2, 1913.

220 Parenthetically, it is interesting to note in this connection that reference is made to sixteen different ethnic groups—namely, 1) Parthians, 2) Medes, 3) Elamites; dwellers in 4) Mesopotamia, 5) Judea, 6) Cappadocia, 7) Pontus, 8) Asia, 9) Phrygia, 10) Pamphylia; in 11) Egypt, 12) Libya; in Rome, 13) Jews and 14) proselytes; and 15) Cretes and 16) Arabians. Traditionally the number 16 was understood to have a connection to the human speech organs. The old knowledge of the chakras (or focal points in the etheric body) associated the sixteen-petalled lotus flower with the throat region, just as the twelve-petalled lotus flower with the heart region (compare our description in the chapter about the second commandment in relation to the hardening of the heart).

221 Compare, for example, Genesis 6:9, "Noah was a just man and perfect in his generations"; and Matthew 1:19, "Then Joseph her husband, being a just man..."

222 Compare also footnote 116.

223 In a future phase of humanity's development the moral strength of *word* and *deed* will also be needed to help form the basis for the next planetary phase of our Earth, the Jupiter phase; we have touched on this in our contemplations about the third commandment, (see also previous footnote).

224 *Theosophy* (CW 9), section on "Body, Soul, and Spirit."

225 It is possible to maintain one's "I"-consciousness, even when all outer sense impressions fall away, by inwardly creating certain images, such as those developed in the field of projective geometry. If the "I" actively unites itself with such inner constructions, it will be less affected by the removal of outer sense impressions because it can fill the resulting emptiness with these inwardly created constructions. Thus we observe that, even in such extreme situations, "the 'I' receives its nature and significance from whatever it is united with," as Rudolf Steiner expressed it in the aforementioned quote from *Theosophy*. (For more on projective geometry, compare for example, Olive Whicher, *Projective Geometry: Creative Polarities in Space and Time*, Rudolf Steiner Press, London, 1985.)

226 It is possible to maintain one's "I"-consciousness without the support of memory in the usual sense, but this requires a more intense kind of training than the one mentioned in the previous footnote, a path of schooling which Rudolf Steiner has described in detail in various lectures and books, notably in *Knowledge of Higher Worlds* (CW 10).

227 For a more elaborate discussion of this process compare *Theosophy* (CW 9), section on "Body, Soul, and Spirit."

228 To be sure, the "I"-consciousness does not *only* manifest in the philosophical way of thinking, but studying the history of philosophy can help illustrate the ever-changing nuances of the development of "I"-consciousness in human beings. Compare, for example, *Riddles of Philosophy* (CW 18).

229 Compare, for example, *Rosicrucian Esotericism* (CW 109/111), lecture of June 7, 1909.

230 We can actually find an echo of this birth of the "I" in human beings in the way the classical languages, around the time of Christ, used the word *I*. In Greek and Latin the first person singular generally was indicated by the appropriate conjugation of the verb. A separate word for "I" existed; but this word *ego*, in both languages, was used infrequently, that is to say, only when it needed to be accentuated. Only much later do we encounter the consistent use of the personal pronoun *I* in the various modern languages to indicate the first person singular. Just compare *"veni, vidi, vici"* with "I came, I saw, I conquered," to get a sense of the immense difference between the two!

231 Compare footnote 37.

232 In *The Philosophy of Freedom* (CW 4), in the Appendix, Rudolf Steiner states (M. Wilson translation), "Through the thinking with which I confront the other person, the percept of him becomes, as it were, transparent to the mind. I am bound to admit that when I grasp the percept with my thinking, it is not at all the same thing as appeared to the outer senses. In what is a direct appearance to the senses, something else is indirectly revealed. The mere sense appearance extinguishes itself at the same time as it confronts me. But what it reveals through this extinguishing compels me as a thinking being to extinguish my own thinking as long as I am under its influence, and to put its thinking in the place of mine. I then grasp its thinking in my thinking as an experience like my own. I have really perceived another person's thinking. The immediate percept, extinguishing itself as sense appearance, is grasped by my thinking, and this is a process lying wholly within my consciousness and consisting in this, that the other person's thinking takes the place of mine. Through the self-extinction of the sense appearance, the separation between the two spheres of consciousness is actually overcome. This expresses itself in my consciousness through the fact that, while experiencing the content of another person's consciousness, I experience my own consciousness as little as I experience it in dreamless sleep. Just as in dreamless sleep my waking consciousness is eliminated, so in my perceiving of the content of another person's consciousness the content of my own is eliminated. The illusion that it is not so only comes about because in perceiving the other person, firstly, the extinction of the content of one's own consciousness gives place not to unconsciousness, as it does in sleep, but to the content of the other person's consciousness, and secondly, the alternations between extinguishing and lighting up again of my own self-consciousness follow too rapidly to be generally noticed."

233 Compare *Wonders of the World, Ordeals of the Soul, Revelations of the Spirit*, (CW 129) lecture of August 23, 1911.

234 Compare *Theosophy* (CW 9), section on "Body, Soul, and Spirit."

235 *A Way of Self-Knowledge: And The Threshold of the Spiritual World* (CW 16/17), aphorism 12 in part 2, "The True 'I' of the Human Being." Also compare Sergei O. Prokofieff's recent research into the *three levels*

of the human "I"—that is, the lower "I," the higher "I," and the true "I"; see, for example, Prokofieff's book, *Rudolf Steiner's Path of Initiation and the Mystery of the Ego: And the Foundations of Anthroposophical Methodology*, London: Temple Lodge, 2013.

236 This is also reflected in Paul's Letter to the Hebrews (4:15), in which we find the following statement about Christ: "For we have not a high priest which cannot be touched with the feeling of our infirmities; but was in all points *tempted like we are*, yet without sin" (italics added).

237 *The Fifth Gospel* (CW 148), lecture of October 6, 1913.

238 For a more detailed description of the differing accounts of the temptations as portrayed by Matthew and Luke, compare *The Gospel of St. Matthew* (CW 123), lecture 5.

239 Max Scheler, German philosopher (1874–1928) said in the passage from which our excerpt was taken, "Compared to the animal, who always must say *Yes* to a given reality—even when it dislikes and escapes from it—the human being is the one who can say *No*, the one who can choose an ascetic lifestyle...the one, therefore, who is capable of lifting the energy that drives his instincts and desires to the level of spiritual activity."

240 In this connection it would be good to remember a particularly moving theme in the life of Moses, the fact namely, that Moses was not allowed to see the fruits of his endeavors himself. Moses died just before the Israelite people reached the Promised Land after having wandered through the desert for forty years. One could look at this motif in the life of Moses as an outer manifestation of a spiritual reality. He was one of the greatest initiates, to be sure, but an initiate of the old mysteries nonetheless. Moses was able to prepare the Israelite people toward the coming of Christ, but would not accompany them on their further journey. He died, at age 120, shortly after God had shown him the Promised Land from Mount Nebo (Deut. 34:1–5).

241 See our introductory section "About the Development of Morality."

242 See also *Christianity as Mystical Fact and the Mysteries of Antiquity* (CW 8), chapter on "The Apocalypse of John."

243 See also "Essays on Rudolf Steiner's Philosophy of Spiritual Activity" in *Core Anthroposophy: Teaching Essays of Ernst Katz*, SteinerBooks, Great Barrington, MA, 2011.

244 *Theosophy* (CW 9), chapter 4.

245 Compare, for example, Daniel 7:13, "I saw in the night visions, and, behold, one like the Son of man came with the clouds of heaven..."; or Matthew 24:30, "And then shall appear the sign of the Son of man in heaven...and they shall see the Son of man coming in the clouds of heaven with power and great glory" ("clouds" here is an image of the etheric world). See also Matthew 26:64; Mark 14:62; Luke 17:24 and 21:27; Revelations 1:7 and 14:14.

246 *From Jesus to Christ* (CW 131), lecture of October 7, 1911. Compare also Sergei O. Prokofieff, *The Appearance of Christ in the Etheric: Spiritual-Scientific Aspects of the Second Coming*, Temple Lodge Publishing, Forest Row, England, 2012.

247 To obtain a more complete picture of these events, compare *The Reappearance of Christ in the Etheric* (CW 118).

248 *From Jesus to Christ* (CW 131), lecture of October 7, 1911.

249 In *How to Know Higher Worlds: A Modern Path of Initiation* (CW 10), chapter 7, we can also find—albeit from a different perspective—a

reference to an inner light shining onto objects and beings, thereby making them visible. We read there how the student of esoteric training can develop a higher level of consciousness by "awakening the spiritual force of perception in the organ formed in the region of the heart." This perceptive force consists of an element of higher materiality "streaming out from this organ near the heart and flowing in shining beauty through the rotating lotus flowers and the other channels of the developed etheric body. Thence it flows outward, into the spiritual world around us—just as the sunlight outside, falling upon objects from without, makes them visible to our physical eyes." And, "not until we are able to direct this organ of perception through the etheric body and into the outer world—so as to shine a light on the objects in it—can we see clearly the objects and beings of the spiritual world. *It follows from this that perfect consciousness of an object in the spiritual world can arise only if we ourselves shed spiritual light upon it*" (italics added).

250   It is important to realize that one does not have to be a Christian to develop a feeling for the working of Christ. Anyone can approach Christ.

251   Compare *The Philosophy of Freedom* (CW 4), chapter 12. See also "Essays on Rudolf Steiner's Philosophy of Spiritual Activity," especially the section on "The Ingredients of Moral Action" in *Core Anthroposophy: Teaching Essays of Ernst Katz*, SteinerBooks, Great Barrington, MA, 2011.

252   *The Reality in Which We Live* is the title of a book by the distinguished Dutch psychiatrist, Dr. W. F. Zeylmans van Emmichoven, who was Ernst Katz's first teacher of Anthroposophy in the Netherlands. If *The Ten Commandments in Evolution* could have been published in Dutch in the late 1960s, Ernst Katz had intended to dedicate it "to the memory of Dr. Zeylmans, who showed me the way to Rudolf Steiner, through words and deeds, through wise advice, and through the manner in which he stood in the world." Dr. Zeylmans van Emmichoven wrote in the introduction to his book, *The Reality in Which We Live,* "In a certain phase of my life I came to the insight that Christ is the reality in which we live."

Bibliography

Authors by Subject

Childs, Brevard S. *The Book of Exodus: A Critical, Theological Commentary.* Philadelphia: Westminster, 1974.

Coogan, Michael. *The Ten Commandments: A Short History of an Ancient Text.* New Haven, CT: Yale University, 2014.

Frick, F. S. *A Journey through the Hebrew Scriptures.* Fort Worth: Harcourt Brace, 1995.

Harrison, Peter. *'Religion' and the Religions in the English Enlightenment.* Cambridge, MA: Cambridge University, 1990.

Hoffman, Joel M. *And God Said: How Translations Conceal the Bible's Original Meaning.* New York: St. Martin's, 2010.

———. *In the Beginning: A Short History of the Hebrew Language.* New York: New York University, 2006.

Meyers, Carol. *Exodus.* New York: Cambridge University, 2005.

Robinson, George. *Essential Judaism: A Complete Guide to Beliefs, Customs, and Rituals.* New York: Pocket Books, 2000.

Sarna, Nahum M. *Exploring Exodus: The Origins of Biblical Israel.* New York: Schocken, 1986.

Williams, Jay G. *Ten Words of Freedom: An Introduction to the Faith of Israel.* Philadelphia: Fortress, 1971.

Authors on Anthroposophy

Baan, Bastiaan. *Old and New Mysteries: From Trials to Initiation.* Edinburgh: Floris Books, 2014.

Bock, Emil. *Genesis: Creation and the Patriarchs.* Edinburgh: Floris Books, 2011.

———. *Moses: from the Mysteries of Egypt to the Judges of Israel.* Edinburgh: Floris Books, 2011.

———. *The Three Years.* Edinburgh: Floris Books, 1999.

Frommer, Eva A. *Voyage through Childhood into the Adult World: A Guide to Child Development.* Stroud, UK: Hawthorn Press, 1995.

The Golden Blade. London: Rudolf Steiner Press, 1973.

Katz, Ernst. *Core Anthroposophy: Teaching Essays of Ernst Katz.* Great Barrington, MA: SteinerBooks, 2011.

Lievegoed, Bernard C. J. *Phases of Childhood: Growing in Body, Soul and Spirit.* Edinburgh: Floris Books, 2005.

Lowndes, Florin. *Enlivening the Chakra of the Heart.* London: Sophia Books, 1998.

Marti, Ernst. *Das Ätherische.* Basel: Die Pforte, 1989.

———. *The Four Ethers.* Roselle, IL: Schaumburg, 1984.

Prokofieff, Sergei O. *The Appearance of Christ in the Etheric: Spiritual-Scientific Aspects of the Second Coming.* London: Temple Lodge, 2012.
———. *Mystery of the Resurrection in the Light of Anthroposophy.* London: Temple Lodge, 2010.
———. *Rudolf Steiner's Path of Initiation and the Mystery of the Ego: And the Foundations of Anthroposophical Methodology.* London: Temple Lodge, 2013.
Sease, Virginia, and Manfred Schmidt-Brabant. *The New Mysteries and the Wisdom of Christ.* London: Temple Lodge, 2005.
Soesman, Albert. *Our Twelve Senses: Wellsprings of the Soul.* Stroud, UK: Hawthorn Press, 1990.
Whicher, Olive. *Projective Geometry: Creative Polarities in Space and Time.* London: Rudolf Steiner Press, 1985.
Zeijlmans van Emmichoven, F. W. *The Reality in Which We Live.* Sussex, UK: New Knowledge Books, 1964.

Rudolf Steiner's Books and Lectures (by CW vol.)

Truth and Knowledge: Introduction to the Philosophy of Spiritual Activity (CW 3). Hudson, NY: Anthroposophic Press, 1981.
Intuitive Thinking as a Spiritual Path: A Philosophy of Freedom (CW 4). Hudson, NY: Anthroposophic Press, 1995.
Christianity as Mystical Fact: And the Mysteries of Antiquity (CW 8). Great Barrington, MA: SteinerBooks, 2006.
Theosophy: An Introduction to the Spiritual Processes in Human Life and in the Cosmos (CW 9). Hudson, NY: Anthroposophic Press, 1994.
How to Know Higher Worlds: A Modern Path of Initiation (CW 10). Hudson, NY: Anthroposophic Press, 1994.
Cosmic Memory: The Story of Atlantis, Lemuria, and the Division of the Sexes (CW 11). Great Barrington, MA: SteinerBooks, 1987.
An Outline of Esoteric Science (CW 13). Hudson, NY: Anthroposophic Press, 1997.
Four Mystery Dramas (CW 14), rev. ed. Great Barrington, MA: SteinerBooks, 2015.
A Way of Self-Knowledge and the Threshold of the Spiritual World (CW 16/17). Great Barrington, MA: SteinerBooks, 1999.
Riddles of Philosophy: Presented in an Outline of Its History (CW 18). Great Barrington, MA: SteinerBooks, 2009.
Verses and Meditations (CW 40). London: Rudolf Steiner Press, 2004.
Turning Points in Spiritual History: Zarathustra, Hermes, Moses, Elijah, Buddha, Christ (CW 60/61). Great Barrington, MA: SteinerBooks, 2007.
Original Impulses for the Science of the Spirit: Christian Esotericism in the Light of New Spiritual Insights (CW 96). Lower Beechmont, AU, 2005.
The Gospel of St. John (CW 103). Hudson, NY: Anthroposophic Press, 1984.
Universe, Earth and Man: In Their Relationship to Egyptian Myths and Modern Civilisation (CW 105). London: Rudolf Steiner Press, 1987.
Egyptian Myths and Mysteries (CW 106). Hudson, NY: Anthroposophic Press, 1971.
Disease, Karma, and Healing: Spiritual-Scientific Enquiries into the Nature of the Human Being (CW 107). London: Rudolf Steiner Press, 2015.

The Principle of Spiritual Economy: In Connection with Questions of Reincarnation: An Aspect of the Spiritual Guidance of Man (CW 109). Hudson, NY: Anthroposophic Press, 1986.
The Spiritual Hierarchies and the Physical World: Zodiac, Planets, and Cosmos (CW 110). Great Barrington, MA: SteinerBooks, 2008.
The Christ-Impulse: And the Development of Ego-Consciousness (CW 116). London: Rudolf Steiner Press, 2014.
Deeper Secrets of Human History in the Light of the Gospel of St. Matthew (CW 117). London: Anthroposophical Publishing Company, 1957.
The Reappearance of Christ in the Etheric (CW 118). Great Barrington, MA: SteinerBooks, 2003.
Manifestations of Karma (CW 120). London: Rudolf Steiner Press, 1996.
Genesis: Secrets of Creation (CW 122). London: Rudolf Steiner Press, 2003.
According to Matthew: The Gospel of Christ's Humanity (CW 123). Great Barrington, MA: SteinerBooks, 2002.
Wonders of the World, Ordeals of the Soul, Revelations of the Spirit (CW 129). London: Rudolf Steiner Press, 1963.
Esoteric Christianity and the Mission of Christian Rosenkreutz (CW 130). London: Rudolf Steiner Press, 2001.
From Jesus to Christ (CW 131). London: Rudolf Steiner Press, 2005.
Inner Experiences of Evolution (CW 132). Great Barrington, MA: SteinerBooks, 2006.
Reincarnation and Karma: Two Fundamental Truths of Human Existence (CW 135). Great Barrington, MA: SteinerBooks, 2001.
Life between Death and Rebirth (CW 140). Hudson, NY: Anthroposophic Press, 1975.
Between Death and Rebirth (CW 141). London: Rudolf Steiner Press, 1975.
The Effects of Spiritual Development (CW 145). Hudson, NY: Anthroposophic Press, 1997.
The Fifth Gospel: From the Akashic Record (CW 148). London: Rudolf Steiner Press, 1985.
Christ and the Spiritual World: And the Search for the Holy Grail (CW 149). London: Rudolf Steiner Press, 2008.
Human and Cosmic Thought (CW 151). London: Rudolf Steiner Press, 2015.
Approaching the Mystery of Golgotha (CW 152). Great Barrington, MA: SteinerBooks, 2006.
The Inner Nature of Man and the Life between Death and a New Birth (CW 153). London: Rudolf Steiner Press, 1994.
The Spiritual Foundation of Morality: Francis of Assisi and the Christ Impulse (CW 155). Hudson, NY: Anthroposophic Press, 1995.
Christ and the Human Soul (CW 155). London: Rudolf Steiner Press, 2008.
The Connection between the Living and the Dead (CW 168). Great Barrington, MA: SteinerBooks, 2017.
The Karma of Untruthfulness, vol. 2 (CW 174).
Building Stones for an Understanding of the Mystery of Golgotha (CW 175).
Death as Metamorphosis of Life: Including "What Does the Angel Do in our Astral Body?" and "How Do I Find Christ?" (CW 182). Great Barrington, MA: SteinerBooks, 2008.
Man's Being, His Destiny, and World-evolution (CW 226). Spring Valley, NY: Anthroposophic Press, 1984.

Eurythmy as Visible Speech (CW 279). Herefordshire, UK: Anastasi, 2015.
The Foundations of Human Experience (CW 293). Hudson, NY: Anthroposophic Press, 1996.
Education for Special Needs: The Curative Education Course (CW 317). London: Rudolf Steiner Press, 2015.
Second Scientific Lecture Course: Warmth Course (CW 321). Chestnut Ridge, NY: Mercury Press, 1980.
Social Issues: Meditative Thinking and the Threefold Social Order (CW 334). Hudson, NY: Anthroposophic Press, 1991.
Rethinking Economics: Lectures and Seminars on World Economics (CW 340/341). Great Barrington, MA: SteinerBooks, 2015.
Bees (CW 351). Hudson, NY: Anthroposophic Press, 1998.
The Festivals and Their Meaning (lecture collection). London: Rudolf Steiner Press, 1981.
Staying Connected: How to Continue your Relationships with Those who have Died (lecture collection). Great Barrington, MA: Anthroposophic Press, 1999.

About the Author

Ernst Katz, PhD (1913–2009), was born in the Silesian region of what today is the Czech Republic. At the end of World War I, Ernst's parents moved with their young family to the Netherlands. This turn of events was to become a decisive factor in the unfolding of the rest of Ernst Katz's life. Dutch became his adopted mother tongue, and he developed a deep connection to Holland and the Dutch people. In The Hague, at age sixteen, he had his first encounter with Anthroposophy in the person of Dr. Zeylmans van Emmichoven; he befriended other important students of Rudolf Steiner; and he met Katherine, his beloved life companion.

Ernst grew up with two younger brothers; his father was a noted painter and his mother a concert violinist. Ernst was grateful for the "rich formative gifts" they bestowed on his life, but his own education soon focused on the sciences. After graduating from high school, he attended the University of Utrecht, where he received his Bachelor of Science. Just twenty years old, he spent two semesters in graduate school in Princeton University, New Jersey—his first encounter with life in the U.S. Back in Utrecht, he obtained his Master of Science in 1937, and in the years leading up to World War II was engaged in research in biophysics at the Rockefeller Institute at the University of Utrecht. He obtained his doctorate in physics on the very last possible day in 1941.

Ernst and Katherine were married in 1939; their son was born during the second year of the war. The small family managed to survive the horrors of war in the Netherlands, and just when life began to return to normal, Ernst Katz received an invitation to join the faculty at the Physics Department of the University of Michigan, Ann Arbor. He specialized in solid-state physics, becoming a full professor after a number of years. He taught, conducted research, and published scientific articles for thirty-three years, until his retirement in 1980. He also taught interdepartmental credit courses in the university on various aspects of Rudolf Steiner's work—likely the only professor in the U.S. at that time to teach courses in both natural science and "spiritual science" at the university level.

Ernst Katz and his wife were instrumental in founding various anthroposophic initiatives in North America, especially in the Great Lakes area. Ernst Katz was deeply interested in every person he met and kept up a lively correspondence with people all over the world, right up to the last weeks of his life. He regularly wrote articles for anthroposophic periodicals, published a number of booklets, and was a frequent lecturer throughout North America and Europe on a wide variety of topics related to Anthroposophy and science.

www.ingramcontent.com/pod-product-compliance
Lightning Source LLC
Chambersburg PA
CBHW022054160426
43198CB00008B/224